George Barnett,
Marine Corps Commandant

George Barnett,
Marine Corps Commandant
A Memoir, 1877–1923

GEORGE BARNETT
Edited by Andy Barnett

McFarland & Company, Inc., Publishers
Jefferson, North Carolina

LIBRARY OF CONGRESS CATALOGUING-IN-PUBLICATION DATA

Barnett, George, 1859–1930.
  George Barnett, Marine Corps Commandant : a memoir, 1877–1923 / George Barnett ; edited by Andy Barnett.
    p.   cm.
  Includes bibliographical references and index.

  ISBN 978-0-7864-9707-2 (softcover : acid free paper) ∞
  ISBN 978-1-4766-1920-0 (ebook)

  1. Barnett, George, 1859–1930. 2. United States. Marine Corps.—Officers—Biography. 3. Marines—United States—Biography. 4. Generals—United States—Biography. 5. United States. Marine Corps.—History—19th century. 6. United States. Marine Corps.—History—20th century. 7. Spanish-American War, 1898—Personal narratives, American. 8. World War, 1914–1918—Personal narratives, American. I. Barnett, Andy, 1954– II. Title.
  VE25.B34 2015
  359.9'6092—dc23
  [B]   2014042249

BRITISH LIBRARY CATALOGUING DATA ARE AVAILABLE

© 2015 Andy Barnett. All rights reserved

No part of this book may be reproduced or transmitted in any form or by any means, electronic or mechanical, including photocopying or recording, or by any information storage and retrieval system, without permission in writing from the publisher.

On the cover: General George Barnett (Library of Congress)

Printed in the United States of America

McFarland & Company, Inc., Publishers
  Box 611, Jefferson, North Carolina 28640
    www.mcfarlandpub.com

Dedicated to
the Mother of Marines
Lelia S. Barnett

and

in recognition of the service of
LT J. Evans Barnett, USMC
LT John Evans Barnett, USN
CPT Jonathan Evans Barnett, Wisconsin ANG
ET2 Daniel Andrew Barnett, USN
SPC Michael Christopher Barnett, Wisconsin ANG

Contents

Preface 1

Chronology 5

I—A Western Boyhood	9
II—A Young Man at Annapolis	16
III—Cadet Cruise—Africa	36
IV—Cadet Cruise—South America	44
V—Graduation and the Marine Corps	51
VI—Sitka	58
VII—Aboard the USS *Iroquois*	72
VIII—Stevenson and Samoa	78
IX—The Columbia Exposition of 1893	88
X—The USS *New Orleans* and the Spanish-American War	92
XI—Seeing the World on the USS *Chicago*	98
XII—The Philippines and the Asiatic Fleet	104
XIII—Marriage and Honeymoon in Peking	110
XIV—The Peking Legation Guard	118
XV—Philadelphia, the Advanced Base Force and Culebra	134
XVI—Appointment as Commandant	140
XVII—The Great War	147
XVIII—Post-War Demobilization	161
XIX—Dismissal of Commandant Barnett	166

XX—The Haitian Affair 178
XXI—Major General Barnett 183
XXII—San Francisco, 1920–1923 and Retirement 188

Epilogue 191

Index 193

Preface

George Barnett may appear to be the last of a series of anonymous Marine Corps commandants preceding John Lejeune and the modern era, but he was the most transformational officer ever to hold that position. Barnett was the indispensable force behind the ascent of the Marines from an antiquated afterthought to a military force with an international reputation.

After a long apprenticeship as a junior officer in a small, endangered and stagnant Corps, Barnett emerged as a pioneer of amphibious warfare. He led the Advanced Base School and commanded the experimental Advanced Base Force Brigade. That brigade's performance at Culebra in 1914 established a new amphibious mission for the Corps and secured its survival. It also resulted in Barnett being named commandant in 1914, where he made the seizure and defense of advanced bases the main focus of Marine training and doctrine. It is on this solid foundation that all later amphibious efforts were built.

With war on the horizon, Barnett organized the Corps for service in Europe despite the official anti-preparedness stance of the Wilson administration and a pacifist secretary of the navy. When the United States entered the Great War, Barnett had to convince the skeptical navy hierarchy that fighting under army command was a suitable mission for a greatly enlarged Corps, when the navy preferred that the Marines focus solely on naval matters. That accomplished, he next had to overcome overt opposition from the army to Marine participation in the American Expeditionary Force (AEF). At the last moment, he even needed to secure transport to France, as the army suddenly could find no room for the Marines. Without Barnett's aggressive moves, the Marines would not have served in France.

These two major accomplishments changed the Corps and its future trajectory in essential ways. No other senior Marine officer of his day was plausibly capable of what he accomplished. Though predicting alternate futures is a dangerous endeavor, it is safe to say that today's Marine Corps would be drastically different absent Barnett's efforts.

As a reward for this, Barnett was abruptly relieved as commandant in the middle of his second four year term, in what one historian has called "the Barnett Putsch." His dismissal was the combined effort of the lame duck secretary of the navy, a disaffected and ambitious Marine officer and the influential congressman who was that officer's father. Despite the intended insult of the process, Barnett continued to serve until he reached retirement age in 1923.

In retirement, Barnett dictated the following memoir, stringing together his favorite stories from forty-five years of service. His childhood in small town Wisconsin. His years at the Naval Academy and the ensuing two year cadet cruise. His commissioning as a Marine, part of the first group of Annapolis graduates to join the Corps. Years of overseas service in Sitka, Samoa, Peking, the Philippines, Panama and Cuba. Encounters with Robert Louis Stevenson, Cecil Rhodes, the Meiji Emperor and the Dowager Empress of China. Barnett provides an unprecedented look at the Corps during the gap between the Civil War and the Spanish-American War. He died in 1930 without having finalized the text and it was closer to a transcribed oral history than a polished autobiography

After a delay of eighty years, the text has been edited and prepared for publication. The only additions made are the full names of those referred to originally by their last name or rank. The text has been edited for content and length, omitting rhetorical flourishes, conversational asides and

Major General Commandant George Barnett (Library of Congress).

other peripheral content. Some sections have been rearranged. Photographs, captions and chapter headings were not part of the original documents. Barnett's original title, *Soldier and Sailor Too*, has been changed to *George Barnett, Marine Corps Commandant: A Memoir, 1877–1923*. With these exceptions, the narrative is as Barnett dictated it. Scholars should continue to use and cite the original documents.

There is much that Barnett left out of his memoir. If he couldn't say something positive about the Corps, he chose to say nothing at all. This is an admirable trait but frustrating to a reader or historian. Additionally, he often fails to provide background which was common knowledge in his day, but which no longer is. The editor has addressed these deficiencies in brief notes after each chapter.

Andy Barnett, Editor

Chronology

December 9, 1859	Barnett born in Lancaster, Wisconsin. His family moved to nearby Boscobel in 1860, where he was raised and attended the local schools.
July 22, 1871	Lelia Sinclair Montague born. She grew up in New York and Baltimore.
June 27, 1877	Entered the U.S. Naval Academy.
June 10, 1881	Graduated from the U.S. Naval Academy. Spent the next two years on his cadet cruise aboard the USS *Essex*.
July 1, 1883	Appointed a second lieutenant in the U.S. Marine Corps.
August 31, 1883	Assigned to Marine Barracks, Navy Yard, Brooklyn, New York.
October 30, 1883	Assigned to Marine Barracks, Mare Island, California.
July 14, 1884	Joined USS *Pinta* and commanded the Naval Guard at Sitka, Alaska.
August 5, 1887	Assigned to Marine Barracks, Navy Yard, Washington, D.C.
May 1, 1888	Assigned to Marine Barracks, Newport, Rhode Island.
September 28, 1888	Assigned to Marine Barracks, Navy Yard, Washington, D.C.
May 26, 1889	Joined USS *Iroquois*.

September 1, 1890	Promoted to first lieutenant, after seven years as a second lieutenant.
July 30, 1892	Assigned to Marine Barracks, Navy Yard, Washington, D.C.
May 6, 1893	Assigned to Marine Guard, Columbia Exposition, Chicago, Illinois.
December 18, 1893	Assigned to Marine Barracks, Navy Yard, Washington, D.C.
April 4, 1896	Assigned to Marine Barracks, Portsmouth, New Hampshire.
June 15, 1896	Joined USS *Vermont*.
December 12, 1897	Joined USS *San Francisco*.
April 25, 1898	Assigned to the USS *New Orleans* when the U.S. took possession of the former *Amazonas* in England. Barnett served on her throughout the Spanish-American War.
August 11, 1898	Promoted to captain after nearly eight years as a first lieutenant.
November 30, 1898	Joined the USS *Chicago*.
March 3, 1901	Promoted to major.
July 9, 1901	Assigned to Marine Barracks, Newport, Rhode Island.
October 14, 1901	Assigned to recruiting duty, Philadelphia, Pennsylvania.
September 13, 1902	Joined a Marine battalion in Panama, Republic of Columbia under the command of Lieutenant Colonel B.R. Russell.
January 8, 1903	Assigned to Marine Barracks, Navy Yard, Washington, D.C.
January 24, 1903	Joined the 1st Marine Brigade in the Philippines.
July 22, 1903	Assigned as Fleet Marine Officer, Asiatic Fleet. During this assignment he served on the USS *Kentucky* and the USS *Wisconsin*.
December 6, 1904	Took command of the 1st Marine Brigade in the Philippines.

Chronology

February 28, 1905	Promoted to lieutenant colonel.
July 20, 1905	Assigned to Marine Barracks, Navy Yard, Washington, D.C.
June 15, 1906	Assigned to Naval War College, Newport, Rhode Island.
November 8, 1906	Assigned to Marine Barracks, Navy Yard, Washington, D.C.
January 11, 1908	Married Lelia Montague Gordon in Baltimore.
March 3, 1908	Took command of the Legation Guard, Peking, China.
October 3, 1910	Assigned to Marine Barracks, Philadelphia, Pennsylvania. This command included the recently created Advanced Base School.
October 11, 1910	Promoted to colonel.
March 8, 1911	Commanded 1st Marine Regiment in Cuba through June 22, 1911.
May 25, 1912	Commanded 1st Marine Regiment in Cuba through August 5, 1912.
February 19, 1913	Commanded 1st Marine Regiment in Cuba through May 2, 1913.
December 23, 1913	Advanced Base Brigade activated with Barnett as its first commander.
January 1914	Advance Base Brigade undertook exercises at Culebra, Puerto Rico.
February 21, 1914	Appointed major general commandant of the Marine Corps for a four year term.
August 29, 1916	Promoted to permanent brigadier general.
February 1918	Re-appointed major general commandant of the Marine Corps for a four year term.
September 1918	Sailed to France on the troopship USS *Leviathan*. Hospitalized for influenza and pneumonia before returning to the U.S. in December.
June 30, 1920	Relieved as major general commandant. Reverted to previous rank of brigadier general.

October 12, 1920	Took command of the Department of the Pacific, San Francisco, California.
March 5, 1921	Promoted to major general in one of the first acts of the Harding administration.
May—June 1921	Class of 1881 held its Fortieth Reunion, hosted by President Harding.
May 1922	Accompanied a delegation headed by Secretary of the Navy Denby to Japan, returning to San Francisco in September.
December 9, 1923	Retired from active duty.
April 27, 1930	Death of George Barnett at Washington D.C.
April 3, 1959	Death of Mrs. George Barnett.

CHAPTER I

A Western Boyhood

Forty-six years of active service in the navy and Marine Corps of the United States, forty-two of which were spent as an officer on the active list of the United States Marine Corps, are the underlying reasons for the selection of the title, "Soldier and Sailor Too," from the title of Rudyard Kipling's famous poem about the British Marines.

The regular U.S. Marine, must indeed, be a "soldier and sailor too." In my case, this was particularly true, because my class of 1881 was the first graduating class of the United States Naval Academy, Annapolis, from which second lieutenants of the Marine Corps were commissioned.

When asked upon graduation to submit in writing my individual preference for assignment, Line—Engineer Corps—or Marine Corps, I made my first choice "Marine Corps." This decision I have never regretted.

With pride and a thousand thrills, I have seen the United States Marine Corps grow from a small organization of about two thousand men and seventy-one officers to the large World War Corps of some seventy-five thousand men and three thousand officers.

I consider myself fortunate in having been in the Corps during this growth, and finally at the most important period of its history, selected as its major general commandant, in which position I served from February 25th, 1914 to June 30th, 1920.

My duties in the Corps have taken me to all parts of the world. I have sailed the Seven Seas under its symbols, globe, eagle and anchor, and through it has come what success I have won in life. The one prayer of my heart, where the United States Marines are concerned, is Tiny Tim's "God bless them, every one."

Early in my naval career, I learned the value of keeping an accurate mental record of events. As I have had a rather unusual life, I decided to jot down in more or less chronological order the principal happenings in my life. In this way I meant to preserve them in permanent shape for the members of my family. In my twenty years of travel outside the United States, either on board naval cruising vessels or on foreign duty on shore, I kept no diary or notes. What I write of those years is entirely from memory. It is written in the fond hope that it will lead Americans to a fuller realization of the glories and achievements of the U.S. Navy and Marine Corps.

I was born in Lancaster, Grant County, Wisconsin on December 9th, 1859. When I was two years old my family moved to Boscobel, Wisconsin, where I lived until I entered the U.S. Naval Academy. I attended the public schools of the town.

My home was a good, comfortable one of the type that was a "home" before that splendid American institution went out of fashion. Therein I was taught to fear God, to love my Country and to strive toward a useful manhood. I thank God that my dear mother lived to know of any honor I won in the naval service. She died in 1921 when eighty-seven years old.

A half century ago, the life of a boy in the west was far different from what it is now, not only in the west but elsewhere. While we were encouraged in all kinds of sport, especially sleighing, skating, hunting, fishing, riding, base ball, etc., we were required to do many things a boy would now resent. We were impressed with the fact that we could not be drones but had to do a reasonable amount of useful work. We had to shovel snow, bring in wood, kindling, etc. in winter, besides attending to the cows and ponies. We all had ponies but on condition that the boys of the family attended to not only theirs but their sisters'. We also had what seems to be almost lacking now—that is, respect for our parents and our seniors. The words of our parents and of our teachers in school were more respected than most laws are now. Not only did we have to do work as indicated above, but we had to cut grass, attend to the vegetable garden, hoe corn and potatoes, pick currants and berries and do a thousand and one useful chores about home. After work we could play and no country ever furnished more sport for a boy. The streams were full of trout and the river of catfish and there were many splendid swimming holes. Our ponies furnished a never ending source of amusement and for weeks after a circus the youngsters of the town tried hard to copy the stunts of the circus riders. My practice in horsemanship as a boy has stood me in good stead all my life.

In the same town of Boscobel lived the Honorable George C. Hazelton, member of Congress from the Third Wisconsin District. As my boyish ambition was to go to West Point, I was interested in the man who could send me there. Mr. Hazelton was elected to Congress in November, 1876. As he was a neighbor, I asked my father if he would speak to Mr. Hazelton and request an appointment for me to West Point, but fate had other things in store for me. My father did not wish to ask Mr. Hazelton this favor. The subject was dropped. Up to that time I never had thought of the Naval Academy. I never had seen a graduate of Annapolis, and living so far inland, I had no opportunity of knowing anything of salt water or of life on the sea.

Going home from school to lunch one April day in 1877, I met Congressman Hazelton. He stopped me, after my greeting, and said, drawing an official looking letter from his pocket: "George, how would you like to go to the Naval Academy at Annapolis?" I was thrilled and could hardly credit my good luck. Then he told me the letter was from the secretary of the navy informing him that there was a vacancy at Annapolis from his district. I accepted, contingent upon my parents' consent. Then I turned and ran all the way home.

Boy though I was, I saw what a changed life this appointment would mean to me. My parents, at first, were not inclined to allow me to choose a naval career. But I solicited the help of certain excellent friends of my family and my father and mother were finally convinced and gave their consent. I have often thought of what my life might have been if I had not met Mr. Hazelton that April day, or if Mr. Hazelton had met some other boy of the school, and he had been the lucky one. If I had not gone to Annapolis, I probably would have followed in the footsteps of a large percentage of the graduates of high schools in Wisconsin, and attended the State University at Madison. At least, that was my idea at the time. If I had graduated at Madison, it is impossible for me to say now what my life would have been thereafter.

Not long after I received my official appointment from the Navy Department, I started for Annapolis. It was a great adventure, for I had never been away from home for more than a day at a time. To start for a strange place nearly twelve hundred miles away seemed to me a gigantic undertaking. I learned from the newspapers that a boy from Milwaukee, Michael J. Donnelly, was leaving for Annapolis at about the same time. I wrote to him and we arranged to go together. My father thought of accompanying me, and would have done so but for the fact that Lieutenant Joel A. Barber, U.S. Navy, of Lancaster, Wisconsin, was at home on leave about that time. He told my father that it would be far better for me to go alone because, if I had anything in me it would be better to put me upon my own resources at once, and that, in his opinion, during the examinations at Annapolis, parents of prospective candidates rather injured their chances.

Lieutenant Barber also gave me several pieces of advice as to my conduct during the time I was to be at Annapolis. First, he told me to remember that I would have four years of very hard work; therefore, he recommended great energy and application. He also warned me that one of the foundations of the service was absolute truth. "In fact," he remarked, "in the service truth and honesty are not comparative terms; a man is either truthful or he is a liar. And he is honest or he is a thief."

He gave me another piece of advice which I put in practice not only at Annapolis but have used to advantage all my life. He said that when an instructor asked me a question during recitation I should look him straight in the eyes while answering. He said he felt assured (having been an instructor there himself) that a boy who followed that advice would get better marks than a boy who allowed his eyes to wander about instead of looking at the instructor. In that connection I remember an incident which came to my notice forty years later. I heard an officer of very high rank in the service trying to convince the secretary of the navy of the wisdom of a certain line of action which the secretary was questioning. I noticed that the officer's eyes were wandering all over the room. Instantly the advice of Lieutenant Barber came back to me. I was not surprised when the conversation was over to find that the officer had lost out on his argument.

Editor's Comments on Chapter I

The title Barnett chose for his memoir is significant. It refers to the poem "Soldier an' Sailor too (The Royal Regiment of Marines)" by Rudyard Kipling. The Royal Navy set a standard that the United States Navy aspired to and Kipling's depictions of military life were popular on both sides of the Atlantic. Barnett was also aiming deeper. Throughout his career, he envisioned a Corps that could serve as both sailors and soldiers, able to undertake amphibious operations and fight in the trenches.

The Barnetts came to the Wisconsin Territory from Pennsylvania in 1845. George's father, James Barnett (1823–1907) was involved in several hotels, as well as livestock brokering. Part of a large and politically active family, he served as Boscobel's first mayor in 1873–1876. One side effect of James' efforts as a livestock broker was that his son became an accomplished horseman, which served him in good stead.

George's mother, Elizabeth A. (Eliza) Callis Barnett (1833–1921) was born in Tennessee, though her father, Henry Callis, was from Wilmington, North Carolina. The family came to Wisconsin soon after the Barnetts. She and James married on November 13, 1855.

The most intriguing figure in George's childhood was his uncle, John Benton Callis (1828–1898). Callis sought gold in California with James Barnett and managed a plantation in Central America before returning to Wisconsin. There he married Martha Barnett, James' younger sister. With the advent of the Civil War, the North Carolina native helped form a company of the 7th Wisconsin Infantry, part of the famed Iron Brigade. Due to casualties among the senior officers, Callis commanded the regiment at South Mountain, Antietam and Gettysburg. While the Iron Brigade was saving the high ground for the Union at Gettysburg, Callis was shot through the chest and lay wounded on the battlefield until the Confederates withdrew three days later. Near death, he was retrieved by relatives and returned to Boscobel, where his family was living with James and Eliza Barnett. Surviving his wounds, Callis returned to service, eventually reaching brevet brigadier general. After the war ended, he served in the Army of Occupation in Alabama. Mustered out, he was elected to a term in Congress from Alabama before returning yet again to Wisconsin. In 1874–76, he served a term in the Wisconsin Assembly. It is likely that Callis was one of those "excellent friends" who convinced James Barnett to allow his son to pursue a military career. There can be no doubt that his example made quite an impression on young George Barnett.

George Barnett's siblings were:
- Martha (Mattie) Barnett (1857–1949). George's older sister graduated from the University of Wisconsin in one of the early coeducational classes. After a brief career in education, she married Arthur F. Nixon (1854–1936) in 1888.
- Charles H. Barnett (1863–1933). George's younger brother pursued a variety of business ventures around the country.
- Laura Ethel Barnett (1872–1910). George's much younger sister graduated from the Baltimore Conservatory of Music. She moved to Washington, D.C. and married Dr. Emory William Reisinger (1871–1937) on September 27, 1898. She was the only Barnett to produce a surviving child, her daughter Laura Natalie Reisinger.

Barnett was a well connected young man, as were most service academy appointees. That college was a family expectation is a further sign of the family's status in the community. His father's and uncle's connections would have mattered a great deal at a time when a congressional election could be won with 13,000 votes. Congressmen didn't just happen to meet a schoolboy on his way home and offer him an appointment to Annapolis. It was an

John Benton Callis—49er, Civil War hero, congressman. Barnett's uncle was severely wounded at Gettysburg and nursed back to health in Barnett's home. Callis was a powerful role model to Barnett (editor's personal collection).

Charles, Martha (Mattie) and George Barnett. Barnett barely mentions his family, probably because he had no amusing stories about them. He did write to them from his overseas deployments and some of those letters are preserved in the local newspaper (editor's personal collection).

asset used to cement local alliances. For example, Lieutenant Joel Barber was the son of rising politician J. Allen Barber, who later served two terms in Congress. Appointees still had to pass admissions examinations, survive four years of schooling and undertake a two year cruise before commissioning, but without the right political connections, appointments didn't happen.

Barnett's insistence on the value of absolute truth and honesty may seem like a platitude, in line with his nostalgia for the bygone days when children respected their elders. It is not. It was a principle he lived by throughout his career. His mention of it here foreshadows several implied rebukes later in the memoir.

Suggested Reading

Holford, Castello N. *History of Grant County, Wisconsin, Including Its Civil, Political, Geological, Mineralogical, Archaeological and Military History, and a History of the Several Towns.* Marceline, Mo: Walsworth Pub. Co, 1976, c1900.
Nolan, Alan T. *The Iron Brigade: A Military History.* Indiana University Press, 1983.
Ray, William R. *Four Years with the Iron Brigade: The Civil War Journals of William R. Ray, Co. F, Seventh Wisconsin Infantry.* Cambridge, Mass.: Da Capo Press, 2002.

CHAPTER II

A Young Man at Annapolis

So I left home and started on my great adventure with a light heart and the enthusiasm of youth. I was dressed in the best suit of clothes I had ever had. I felt that life had little more to give me at that particular moment. The trip was without particular incident, although everything was novel to our young eyes. In Pittsburgh—it was during the terrible railroad strike of 1877—troops were guarding the railroad yards. They were United States Marines. They were the first Marines I had ever seen. Little did I dream that after my graduation at Annapolis I would spend nearly my whole life in the Marine Corps.

At Baltimore, where we registered at the old Barnum's Hotel, we were amazed by the number of colored people there. I had seen but few colored men. It was hard for me to understand that there were so many colored people in Baltimore. I had thought that they were all concentrated in the far south. The waiters at Barnum's were all colored. Our first meal was dinner. As we sat down to the table, the blackest man I ever saw, about six feet four inches tall, came to wait on us, and handed us the menu card. We did not bother about looking at the menu because we knew what we wanted. Natives of the west, at a time before cold storage was as plentiful as it is today, we never had eaten any real raw oysters, except very small ones sent out from Baltimore frozen, in tin cans. We had discussed this on the way east and were ready for some real raw oysters. This we told the waiter. He asked us how many we wanted. Having in mind the small ones we had seen in Wisconsin, we told him about three dozen each. He smiled and went away. We noticed that on his way to the kitchen he stopped and spoke to other waiters and they all laughed. Presently he came back, another waiter with him, each carrying the largest trays I ever saw, filled with oysters on the half shell. Each oyster seemed as large as a hand. Not only our waiter but the other waiters in the dining room were all smiling. We saw the joke on us and only ate a small portion of our large orders.

II—A Young Man at Annapolis

The next morning we wandered about Baltimore and saw the sights of interest. We had never been to Washington, and as it was considered a perfectly marvelous place by western boys, we were anxious to visit it. The day being Sunday we found we could not get to Annapolis (the railroad facilities were poor at the time). So we decided to spend the day in Washington and report in Annapolis on Monday morning. We were wonderfully impressed by the necessity of getting to Annapolis as soon as possible, and found we could reach Annapolis as quickly from Washington as from Baltimore. Before we left, we asked our waiter what was the best place in Washington to get sea food. He told us "Harvey's." And he advised that the best thing Harvey's served was "steamed oysters." That Sunday afternoon we drifted into Harvey's and ordered steamed oysters. The colored waiter asked us how many we wanted, a peck or a half bushel. That was new lingo to us. We concluded that the waiter in Baltimore had communicated with a friend of his at Harvey's as to our break the night before. So we were chary about ordering in that quantity. By questioning the waiter we learned that a peck would be about right as he explained, "that they were measured with the shells on." We found that they were quite as delicious as they had been represented and for us, that meal put Harvey's on the map forever.

The next morning we started for Annapolis. Upon arrival, we went to the Maryland Hotel, registered, and then went to the Naval Academy as soon as possible. We had heard of "hazing," so it was with fear and trembling that we entered the academy gates. Neither of us had ever seen salt water. One of our chief desires was to swim in it. That evening after dark we went into the academy grounds again. No one stopped us and we made our way to the sea wall. There, behind a pile of coal, we undressed. Fortunately for me, young Donnelly undressed faster than I did and jumped in. The result of this jump made me decide not to go in at all. He went too near the gas house and the water was covered on the surface with coal tar. Out he scrambled very quickly. I tried to rub the tar off of him with our towels without much success. I did get off enough of it so he could put his clothes on. We returned to the hotel and spent the greater part of the night trying to remove the remainder of the tar from poor Donnelly. The next day we went down to the sea wall near the Catholic Church and had a real swim in salt water. While we enjoyed our swim, it resulted in a terrible earache for me, the agony of which I remember to this day.

Our first bills at the hotel were too high for our purses so we soon located in a boarding house not far away and worked on preparations for the entrance examinations. A couple of days after this, I met the young man who was afterwards my roommate for four years in the academy and my lifelong friend,

John W. Weeks of New Hampshire, afterwards a member of Congress from Massachusetts; later United States senator and later, secretary of war. Weeks and I were congenial from the first and decided that, if we passed the examinations, we would room together. It was the custom at that time for cadets to choose their roommates as far as possible. Weeks and I were about the only pair in our class to room together the whole four years.

Finally the time came for the examinations. It was a nerve racking time for all of us. When they were finished, we were told to assemble in front of the Gunnery Building at nine o'clock on a certain morning where the results would be made known to us. A couple of hundred applicants assembled on time, a bright morning in May and the academy band was playing. The late Professor William W. Fay, in the Department of English, read off the names of those who had passed. By a strange coincidence thirty-five years later William G. Fay, a son of this same Professor Fay, was an officer in the Marine Corps and was one of the first aides I had on my staff as major general. Claude Fay, a daughter of his, married a classmate of mine, General Charles A. Doyen, and I was best man at the wedding. Mary Helen Fay, another daughter of his, married Joseph H. Pendleton, at present a major general in the Marine Corps, and my friend to this day.

There were a good many candidates who did not pass. Just as Professor Fay finished reading off the names of the fortunate ones, the band played "Home Sweet Home." Although a delightful piece of music at the proper time it must have made the losers even more sad than they naturally would have been. My name, beginning with "B," appeared very early in Professor Fay's reading. I at once started on the run to the telegraph office about a mile away to telegraph my family the glad tidings that I had passed. Young Donnelly

John W. Weeks, USNA 1881, congressman (1905–1913), senator (1913–1919), secretary of war (1921–1925). Weeks was Barnett's roommate for all four years at Annapolis and an important political supporter of Barnett, the navy and the Corps (Library of Congress).

found he had passed; also Weeks, and Weller, afterwards senator from Maryland. Our class, including those who passed the examinations and those turned back from the previous class, numbered one hundred and twenty-nine. As we ran for the telegraph office that morning, we were not thinking of the future greatness of the members of the class; we were only anxious to inform our parents, as soon as possible, that we had passed the examination.

Before going on the USS *Santee*, we were all assembled in the office of the secretary of the academy, Mr. Richard M. Chase, for the purpose of taking the oath of allegiance. We had to state our ages. Since that time it has been of no use for any of us to try to cover up our exact years because there it is in black and white sworn to in our youth. After leaving the secretary's office, I happened to see a man I thought must be the Superintendent of the academy because he wore more gold lace than I thought anyone could wear on one suit. In addition, he had on an immensely high beaver hat covered with gold lace. I was awestruck. Later I found that this apparition was none other than Andrew Denver, the Drum Major of the Naval Academy Band. It was not until later that I saw the real Superintendent, that splendid sailor man and gentleman, Rear Admiral C. R. P. Rodgers, who was an officer well worthy of the admiration and emulation of the youngsters under his command.

The USS *Santee*, our first ship, was a queer old relic. The old frigate type of sailing ship had been made over into what was practically a floating house. Her lower decks, however, were much the same as in former days. It was a novel experience to sleep in hammocks, especially for boys from the Mississippi Valley, who had never seen a ship. Our first instructions were in slinging a hammock. It was given by a fine type of sailor man of the old navy. Many of that type had long white beards and seemed to be really ancient. They knew their business, however, and were qualified to impart to us the knowledge necessary for ship life.

After hammock slinging was mastered, mattresses were issued, and our hammocks, after being properly stowed in hammock nettings were ready for the hammock call in the evening. My hammock hook number was just over the forward gun on the port side of the gun deck. My first night in the hammock was far from pleasant, because I was afraid of falling out. I finally went to sleep and did not waken until five a.m. Then I thought the world was coming to an end. The gun just under my hammock was the one used for firing at sunrise. When it went off, I jumped up so high I struck the deck above. Fortunately I landed on my feet upon the deck. Later on I always slept on, regardless of the morning gun, in the deep sleep of boyhood.

Our days were busy ones; we had setting up drill, boat drill, and each day swimming exercises from the USS *Dale*. The *Dale* was an old fashioned sailing ship, completely fitted out for the midshipmen's use in seamanship drills. As a part of the day's work, each midshipman had to go aloft over the cross trees and down the other side before going in swimming. I can assure anyone who has never tried it that the first trial thereof is a terrifying one for a dirt farmer from the west. I scraped my shins on every single ratline both going up and coming down. Like a cat, I held on, and finally learned the trick. At first we were allowed to go through the lubbers' hole in order to get into the top. Afterwards we were required to climb up from the outside, another terrifying experience, as it necessitated going up another rope ladder, the futtock shrouds, a great deal more nearly horizontal than the ordinary shrouds. We had not been very long at it before running aloft and down seemed to be a very ordinary routine matter. We soon learned that the quickest way to get down was to slide down the backstays. With many other midshipmen doing the same, this was sometime rather painful, because they would start above and come down too rapidly, forcing those below to slacken up on their hold and go faster. It was dangerous, however, to go too fast, for in trying to stop, we often burned our hands very badly by the friction on the backstays.

The *Dale* was a real old timer. She even had the old fashioned messenger gear for getting up anchor. In going over a ship of that kind, one is thoroughly impressed with the difference in sea going in the olden days, with practically no comforts whatever in comparison with the modern ships of the navy. The old timers had no steam, no cold storage, no electricity, no ventilating systems nor bathrooms. The cabins were exceedingly small. They were lighted by oil lamps or candles and were far from pleasant, especially in rough weather, when air ports could not be opened and the hatches were battened down, making the air below almost unfit for human beings to breathe.

Professor Matthew Strohm was our swimming instructor both on board the *Dale* and at the natatorium which was used for those who had to be taught swimming. The first day we were swimming from the *Dale*, a classmate of mine, John L. Rees from Michigan, dove from the side and shortly afterwards came on board very badly injured by sting nettles, an entirely new thing to the western lads who had only swam in fresh water. Thereafter we avoided the sting nettles as best we could.

While our summer on board the *Santee* meant hard work, we also had time for amusement. In recreation pursuits, catching soft shell crabs from the pier ranked high. We also enjoyed boating, and felt very proud when we were allowed to go out in the sailing cutters. At first we wore the white canvas midshipman sailor suits. Before very long we had issued to us the blue uniforms and everyone was proud of his first uniform and soon had photos taken in them to send home. Towards the end of the summer, and while all the

Even as U.S. warships converted to steam, midshipmen were trained to handle a sailing ship. "Knowing the ropes" and bringing in the sails were essential on the outdated ships Barnett served on early in his career (from *The United States Naval Academy* by Park Benjamin).

other midshipmen were away on their summer cruises, we were given a short leave before the beginning of the academic year. It was with great pride that we started off in those wonderful new uniforms. By that time a lordly second classman had borrowed my fine suit of clothes and I have never seen it since.

After enjoying our stay at home for a few weeks, we returned to the academy on the first of October, and started in our first year's work. The first step was to visit the Midshipman store where all the necessary equipment for our rooms, clothing, books, etc. were issued to us. We had to carry them to our rooms. From the first, I was particularly impressed with the idea that I was among total strangers, who took no particular interest in my affairs. This impressed me because it was so entirely different from what I had been used to in the public schools of my own town, where every teacher had a personal interest in each scholar. It seemed to me, at first, that the instructors were there simply to hear us recite. Very few of them seemed to give much instruction. We learned afterwards that this was not as much so as it seemed at first. However, the instructors did not bother to inquire whether or not we had spent our time profitably in study. That was our affair. The marks at the end of the week would show whether or not we had applied ourselves. For the first month, we were arranged in sections alphabetically. Through the whole course thereafter midshipmen were arranged in sections according to their previous month's standing in each subject.

After the opening of the yearly course, when all the midshipmen were back at the academy, I remember our first supper because of an incident which fastened it in my memory. One of the midshipmen at the same table with me pared his potato and then began eating it with his knife. The word passed like magic. In less than ten minutes it appeared as if every waiter in the room brought forks to this midshipman. A hundred forks were soon piled around his plate. It may have been a rude lesson, but one, I am sure he never forgot. No one ever saw him eat with his knife again.

Immediately after supper, we of the fourth class, who were quartered on the third floor of what was then called the new building, in order to get to our quarters, had to pass through the corridor of the third classmen. In doing so, we were in constant fear of hazing, as we had been told that there was much of it going on. As I reached the third floor the first day, a third classman spoke to me and said, "Youngster, what is your name?" I told him, and he said, "Sir." I caught on and afterwards when I repeated my name it was followed by the word "Sir." In fact, I learned very quickly that it was necessary to use the word "Sir" more than almost any other word. This midshipman then asked if I could repeat the preamble to the Constitution of the United States. Having so lately prepared for my entrance examination, I told him that I could. He made me stand on a chair before practically the whole third class and repeat the preamble. Then they let me go. After supper each day I had to do this same stunt, while others of my class were grilled in various ways, some in public, some in midshipmen's rooms. I heard many stories about hazing but saw or experienced nothing that amounted to much. In fact, I witnessed very little of it, as I was too busy doing my own stunt night after night.

As the first term wore on, I found the lessons were very hard and long, and required hard and earnest work. I had had no special preparation other than my attendance in public schools. Therefore, it seemed almost hopeless to me. But I plodded on as best I could, only doing fairly well until Christmas. Then I began to get terribly homesick. I never had been away from home at that time, and the week before the holiday I was homesick indeed. I recognized that I was doing very badly in mathematics. The midshipmen at that

A staged demonstration of hazing at the USNA from 1890. Hazing was enough of an issue that Barnett was aware of it before his arrival. It sometimes rose to levels that prompted congressional inquiries and mass expulsions (editor's personal collection).

time got a dollar a month spending money, principally to buy postage stamps as we could supply our ordinary needs for other things on requisition from the midshipmen's store. I had done so badly in mathematics that as the Christmas holidays approached, I was very blue. I told Weeks, my roommate, that I was sure my name would appear among those posted on Saturday morning as being unsatisfactory in mathematics. In order to cheer me up, he bet me his monthly dollar against mine that I would not be posted. I felt sure of winning his dollar, because I knew how badly I had done and he did not, but I took his bet. When Saturday morning came, I went to the bulletin board and expected to find my name near the top of those posted but to my great joy and surprise, it was not. I was glad to pay Weeks the dollar he had earned. Yet that evening I was blue again, as it was Christmas Eve. Christmas morning I was cheered up when a wonderful box from home, containing all sorts of good things to eat, was brought to me. A great many midshipmen also received boxes, so it meant a real feast just as long as the boxes lasted. At the academy during the four years, the food was wholesome in every respect and ample in quantity, but all of us, and especially the youngsters, missed the little dainties to which we had been accustomed at home. Even the receipt of this wonderful box did not banish my homesickness, but on the contrary, probably helped to increase it.

The next morning being Sunday and Christmas, we had no studies, and while sitting in my room, I heard a knock on my door. When I opened it, I found a colored boy with a note for me, addressed in a woman's handwriting. I was never more surprised in my life, because I knew no one there except the members of my own class. I could not imagine who would be writing to me. With shaking hands I opened the note, and found that it was from Mrs. Rittenhouse, wife of Lieutenant Hawley O. Rittenhouse of the navy, who had been my instructor in mathematics during the last week. He was a real instructor, for he not only heard the midshipmen recite, but assisted them by kindly instruction. He evidently had seen that I was homesick and blue, and had mentioned it to his wife. She had written asking me to join them for Christmas dinner. I was so affected that I had hard work answering the note, but I accepted. After the boy left, I sat down at my table, leaned over, my head on my hands and cried as I have never cried before or since, just for joy. That afternoon I went out to the Rittenhouse home and enjoyed a wonderful Christmas dinner. They had children in the family and it was a real Yuletide gathering with a tree and gifts and other things which make Christmas joyous and happy. From that time on, I never knew another homesick day, and my standing at the academy gradually improved. I lay it largely to the thoughtfulness of Lieutenant Rittenhouse and his wife. I feel that Lieutenant Rittenhouse made it possible for me to graduate from the Naval Academy. Out of the one hundred and twenty-nine who entered and the seventy-two who graduated, I was one of the fortunate ones.

In this connection, at the beginning of the last academic year at Annapolis, a nephew of mine entered the academy. As soon as I heard he had passed his examination, I took the occasion to write to several friends of mine on duty at the academy and asked them to send for this young fellow and simply let him know that in case of homesickness or trouble he could come to them for advice. They all responded so generously that I am sure his first few months at the academy have been much pleasanter than mine were. However, this might have been so without the letters I wrote, because midshipmen now are granted leave Thanksgiving, Christmas, New Year's and Easter, which is absolutely contrary to the practice in my time.

The summer practice cruise at the end of the first year was another novel experience. We had drilled on the ships at the academy from time to time throughout the year, and so had learned the names of the standing and running rigging, and the sails, and the names of the different parts of the ship as well. We thought we knew a great deal about a sailing ship. On our first cruise we soon learned a little about it in reality. As we left Chesapeake Bay, a heavy swell was running. I got terribly seasick, but I was not alone in that. I was on watch from midnight to four in the morning. It was raining hard, but I hardly knew it, as I was too miserable. By the end of the four hours, I was completely soaked. Just when the seasickness was at its worst, it became necessary to take in some of the sails, and never will I forget the horror of going aloft into the black darkness, and so sick that I hardly cared whether I lived or died. But I held on until the work was finally completed.

During our cruise on the USS *Constellation*, we visited many places on the New England coast. This was extremely interesting to us. Each week we spent at sea with drills and exercises, but always spent Sunday in port where liberty was granted unless we had gotten too many demerits. We came back to the academy after this cruise improved in spirits and in health, thoroughly tanned and hard as nails, and ready for our next year's work.

I think in many ways the second year at the academy was the hardest year of all, for we took up new studies which went far beyond instruction in the public schools at home. In the second year we were allowed more privileges, and it was our turn to do what hazing and running there was to be done. There was no hazing, theoretically. As a matter of fact there was considerable, at least in a mild form. My class decided that as we had had our share of it the year before, it was up to us to do our part of hazing that year. In fact, we were convinced by that time that a reasonable amount of hazing was good for fourth classmen as it took away their freshness and impressed upon them the necessity for showing respect to their seniors. Nothing particular happened during this year except hard work. We constantly had before us the expected pleasure of leave to be granted at the end of the second year and looked forward to the glorious time when we would be first classmen.

While I was home during my second class leave my mother conceived the brilliant idea of putting up a whole lot of preserves, jam, pickles, etc. for me to take back to the academy. She had special tin cans made for this purpose and carefully packed thirty of them in my trunk. Shortly after my arrival at the academy, I was sent for by the assistant commandant of cadets, Commander Willard H. Brownson. I wondered what I had done. I soon found out. As I entered his office he pointed to a trunk and demanded "Is that your trunk?" "It is, Sir" I answered. It was leaking jam from every opening, and when I unlocked it I found that twenty-nine out of thirty jars had broken. For many months after that everything I used was stained with jam. The whole contents of the trunk had to be emptied into a sheet and taken to the laundry.

One time, while we were second classmen and living in the so called new building, the late Rear Admiral Samuel Very was officer in charge. About twelve o'clock at night some midshipmen smuggled a half dozen sixteen pound shot into their quarters and also a bedraggled cat to which a tin can was tied. They let the cat go at one end of the corridor and down she went toward the other end, the sixteen pound shot after her until she reached the other end, when down stairs they rolled. It made a terrific noise and everybody was looking out of his door. Lieutenant Very had the call sounded for assembly in the lower corridor and a motley crew it made in all sorts of regalia. As we were formed in line, Lieutenant Very said, "I take it for granted that no second classmen did this." The second classmen were in charge of the squads. The officer in charge then announced that we would stand there until the culprits acknowledged their guilt. A short time before this Lieutenant Very had taken the part of the admiral's orderly in the wonderful rendition of the comic opera "Pinafore." When Lieutenant Very asked what had caused the noise, someone at the end of the line was heard to say, "It was the cat." "Yes," said Very, "it was the cat, but who started the cat?" After we had been standing there about two hours several of my class acknowledged their guilt, and were promptly marched to the prison ship *Santee*.

About this time another incident in midshipmen life, which was also rather detrimental to the perpetrators, took place. We had all spent the forenoon at seamanship drill on the *Dale*, and were dressed in our white sailor clothes. It was the day that our sailor clothes were turned in to go to the laundry. Some brilliant member of the class conceived the idea that it would be great fun to sew a pair of the trousers to one of the blouses, fill it with others, make a head and paint a face on it with charcoal, and then throw it over the banister where it would land with a dull sickening thud right near the table of the officer of the day. Then other midshipmen, properly instructed in the scheme, were to run down stairs and assume that a midshipman had fallen over the banister, form a circle around him, and call out "Give him air." It all happened just as planned, but we had forgotten there might be another act. The officer of the day was the late Rear Admiral Leavitt C. Logan. When the excitement had calmed down, he had this dummy taken into his office, torn apart, and took the names of every midshipman whose clothing had formed a part of the dummy. We were all marched to the *Santee*.

The battalion of midshipmen was ordered to Washington March 4, 1881 to take part in the inaugural parade. It was snowing hard when we left Annapolis, and very cold, so we wore overcoats, rain coats and arctic overshoes. By the time we reached the Capitol the sun was shining and the streets were deep with slush, so much so that in some places it was over our overshoes. One of the most delightful incidents of the inauguration was the fact that we had our dinner served at the Riggs House, then at the corner of 15th and G Streets, just across from the Treasury. We stacked arms at 15th street and proceeded to the feast. It was certainly one and it was a wonder a midshipman survived. We did not do a thing to that splendid menu but order everything from oysters to dessert.

After reforming, for some reason or other, we halted just at the corner of 15th and New York Avenue for some time. While we were standing there, a great many colored people came selling candies, chicken, etc. but after our dinner at the Riggs, we wanted none of it. One fat old colored woman who was very persistent, was such a funny looking object, so big and so fat that someone said to her, "Mammy, do you see that cadet officer out in front?" She answered, "Yes, Sir." The midshipman then said, "If you do what I tell you, you will make more money than by selling sandwiches. That dapper young fellow out there is the adjutant of the battalion, Cadet Lieutenant Houston Eldredge. If you go out there and without arousing his suspicions, throw your arms around his neck and kiss him, we will give you a dollar." And it all happened as planned, much to the disgust of the adjutant.

During our first class year the present Captain William H. Stayton, president of the Baltimore Ship Building Company, had quite a novel experience with the Department of Seamanship. Stayton was always a little unruly, and I have always thought that he put up the job so it would happen just as it did. On one of the examinations in ship building, in answer to a certain question, he wrote out word for word one complete page of the book we had been studying, even correct as to the punctuation. When the papers were examined, one of the instructors noticed this, and called it to the attention of the head of the department. They all concluded that Stayton must have been "gouging," that is using unauthorized assistance. Stayton was sent for and accused of this. He pretended to be very angry when asked if he would object to sitting down and writing that answer over again. He said that of course he objected, but out of respect for Commander Henry Howison, head of the department, he would do it. He sat down and wrote the identical words he had written during the examination, Needless to say, Stayton had a wonderful memory and he also had the laugh on the instructor.

I wonder if many of the class remember an incident that happened while we were living in the so-called new building as second class men. For some infraction of the regulations some members of the class had been quarantined, and so missed their Saturday afternoon liberty in town. A number of the culprits got together, each one contributed a sheet from his bed, they sewed all the sheets together and on the sheets printed in letters about two feet high, "Give us liberty or give us death." This they hung out on the front of the new building which faced towards the Superintendent's house. Just about the time they finished their work the Superintendent, Rear Admiral C. R. P. Rodgers, came out of his house and as he walked towards the new building, he saw the sign. They didn't get any liberty. I remember well that the ring leader in this affair was Lauchheimer, afterwards adjutant general of the Marine Corps. All those implicated got theirs good and plenty.

Another incident in cadet life when a first classman was at the time the battalion of cadets came to Washington April 27, 1881, for the ceremonies in connection with the unveiling of the statue of Farragut in Farragut Square. Lieutenant Commander Charles M. Thomas was the officer in charge of the battalion ordinarily, and an excellent drill instructor he was. We thought so much of him in this capacity that we were all more than disgusted when Captain Henry B. Robeson, Head of the Department of Gunnery, under which department infantry drill came, personally took command of the battalion for that day. We did not know his voice nor did we know his manner of giving orders. As a matter of fact he had little manner about giving them, as he did not know what to give. Therefore, many mistakes were made and our part of the parade was not as satisfactory as it should have been. Again this proved the truth of the old saying, "You should not swap horses while crossing the stream."

After the ceremonies Robeson turned over the command again to Thomas. Late in the afternoon as we were marching down Pennsylvania Avenue going to the railroad station, a street car passed and as it passed we saw Captain Robeson on the rear platform. As he saw the cadet battalion, he conceived the idea of joining them, but unfortunately for him and much to the joy of the cadets, he did not wait for the car to stop before getting off. While the car was still going he jumped off backwards with sufficient momentum to throw him to the ground and roll him in the dust, at the same time breaking his full dress sword belt. We all felt he was well repaid for spoiling our parade that day.

Another incident in midshipman life happened with reference to one of our classmates, William W. Russell, always known as "Pete" Russell. He spoke French very well indeed when he came to the academy so it was not necessary for him to study or pay much attention to his recitation in French. Professor A.V.S. Courcelle was one of our instructors, and a delightful old Frenchman he was, but very old. He always wore a long black frock coat, out of the rear pocket of which there was always trailing a red bandanna handkerchief. When Pete Russell was called on and given a subject on the blackboard, he always took the one directly in the rear of the Professor. Several times during the recitation Pete would extract this bandanna from Courcelle's pocket, walk around in front of him, bow low and in excellent French present it to his preceptor, who always thanked him profusely. So far as we knew, he never caught on to the fact that it was a joke on Pete's part.

Once during midshipman life Pete was given a subject in geometry to demonstrate on the blackboard. He went there and had no knowledge whatever of the subject assigned. He stood with his face to the wall, head bowed down, looking at the floor. Professor W.W. Hendrickson, head of the department, entered the room in the meantime and seeing Pete keep this position so long, said to him "Mr. Russell, what are you looking for?" He said, "I am looking for a perpendicular I have just dropped." Needless to say, Pete did not get a big mark for that recitation.

I suppose all academy midshipmen before and since have felt as we did, that to be a first class man was about the biggest thing in the world. Our second class year passed as the third class one had, without any particular happenings except that we were getting nearer and nearer to our goal. Before our graduation, we were all excitement, ordering our graduation uniforms and our civilian clothes for our graduation leave. The custom at the academy then was that out of our yearly pay five dollars per month was retained by the paymaster and called "retainer pay," so at the end of the four years the graduating midshipman would have sufficient money for his outfit.

Finally the great day approached. The joyous news came that our diplomas were to be handed to us by the president of the United States, James A. Garfield. We graduated on June 10, 1881. Much to our disgust, it was a very rainy day, but that did not change the arrangements in the least. The battalion was formed and the diplomas were delivered by the president, without regard to the rain. As the president handed me my diploma, he said to me, "What district are you from?" When I told him I was from the Third Wisconsin District, he said to me, "Then you were appointed by Mr. Hazelton?" That impressed me then, and it has ever since; it showed what a wonderful memory he must have had, if he could, as in my case, remember the congressman's name from whose district each midshipman had come. This may not have been true, but I like to think that he was so familiar with the members of Congress.

During the four years, the midshipmen looked forward with anticipation and pleasure to the June ball, always given by the new first class in honor of the graduates. When the time came for the ball, Fate ruled against us. The Superintendent of the academy, Commodore Foxhall A. Parker, was very ill and particularly so the first week in June. He had made a request that all the ceremonies were to go on as usual regardless of his illness. Not only on account of our fears that the ball might be prevented, but because he was a

USNA cadets being reviewed by President Garfield on June 10, 1881 shortly before his assassination. Garfield was the first president to give the commencement address at the USNA (from *Frank Leslie's Popular Monthly*, October 1881).

lovable character, we hoped for his improvement. But at dinner formation graduation day, the commandant of midshipmen, the late Rear Admiral Frederick V. McNair, was seen approaching the midshipman officer in charge of the battalion. We feared the worst. Immediately Commander McNair removed his cap and announced to the battalion that the commodore had just died, and that the ball was off. We did enjoy supper that night which was already prepared and the graduating exercises were carried out as usual. The diplomas we received on June 10, 1881 stated that we had successfully completed our four years course at the Naval Academy. But we still had two years to do as midshipmen before our final graduation in 1883. Immediately after graduation, we set off for our homes with joy in our hearts, and with anticipation of a well earned rest after four years of hard work.

After I had been home about a week I had a very serious accident, caused by my horse stumbling. I sustained a broken arm, shoulder and knee out of joint, which laid me up for four months. It is strange that my accident happened on the very day that President Garfield was shot. My last and only view of him was on the day he handed us our diplomas. I remember his saying in his speech that if he could change ages with us, he would gladly change positions with the lowest member of the class. Little did he or any of us think that on that day he was making what was practically his last public appearance.

I have from time to time heard criticism of the Naval Academy, but the more I think of it, the more I think that it was and is now a splendid institution for giving an excellent ground work for a naval education. One cannot expect any institution to provide a complete education and especially one where so many technical subjects must be included. At the same time, it gives a good foundation, and as with all other colleges, it should be counted a success if it accomplishes the task of planting the desire for learning in the minds of the students. I know of no college more successful in teaching honor, truth, uprightness, sobriety, respect for others, and all of the many qualities which go to make up the character of a gentleman. The best test of all is results and I am sure the academy has amply justified its existence by the results achieved.

As I said earlier, there were one hundred and twenty-nine cadets in my class the first year and seventy-two graduates, and about twenty-five were commissioned after graduation. It may be of interest to speak for a moment about a few of the class, just to show into what fields they drifted and in many cases what success they attained.

Charles H. Lauchheimer, was a second lieutenant in the Marine Corps and rose steadily in that service until he became brigadier general and during the World War was my very efficient adjutant general. He died in 1919.

The same advance in the Marine Corps was made by James E. Mahoney; that is from second lieutenant to brigadier general, and he is now dead.

Charles A. Doyen, who entered the Marine Corps as a second lieutenant, went to the brigadier generalship and was the first commanding officer of the Marine Brigade in France. He died in 1918.

I entered the Marine Corps as a second lieutenant and became its major general commandant and was commandant of the Corps during the World War.

William L. R. Emmett joined the General Electric Company after he resigned, and is now the chief engineer of that company. He designed all the electric drive machinery for our latest battleships and is an engineer of world-wide note.

William H. Gartley joined the United Gas Improvement Company of Philadelphia and for many years has been its chief engineer, and is one of the leading engineers of this country.

Oliver Shallenberger joined the Westinghouse Company and died as its chief engineer.

Edward E. Capehart went from ensign to captain in the navy and died several years ago.

Robert P. Forshew entered business in Brooklyn, New York and for many years has been commanding officer of the New York Naval Militia, on the staff of the Governor with the rank of commodore and rear admiral.

Uriu Sotokichi, one of the Japanese students in our class went from lieutenant to admiral in the Japanese navy and was lately made Baron and a member of the Japanese House of Peers.

Yenosuki Enouye, another Japanese student, also made the grade from lieutenant to rear admiral in his country's navy and was naval aide to the Emperor of Japan for many years before his death.

Tusuka Serata, a lieutenant, rose to a captaincy and died shortly after the Japanese-Chinese war, where he distinguished himself.

All of my class who entered civil life after graduation maintained an active interest in naval affairs and were largely instrumental in helping to build up the navy from 1885 to the present time. Many of them served during the Spanish and World Wars.

In after years when Weeks had made a great success of life, I asked him what in his opinion had contributed most to his success, and he said that without doubt it was his training in the service, where he had learned to appreciate the value of self discipline, energy, honesty, truthfulness, and system. Such remarks have convinced me that it would be a very wise thing for the Naval Academy to be kept full to capacity at all times even if all graduates could not be retained in the service. They would make splendid reserve material to be called into service in case of need.

Editor's Comments on Chapter 2

The entrance examination for the academy was quite stringent and based on specific textbooks. The questions were published by the academy in the *Annual Register* and later as a separate document. Despite this, fifty per cent of the candidates commonly failed either the physical or academic examination. A deficient score in any single subject was sufficient to eliminate a candidate. The educational background of candidates was very uneven and even good students might be unfamiliar with the required texts. Four of Barnett's classmates were fourteen years old

Admiral Baron Uriu Sotokichi, of the Imperial Japanese Navy and USNA Class of 1881, commanded a squadron during the Russo-Japanese War, most notably at Chemulpo Bay. He and his wife, a Vassar graduate, were lifelong proponents of better relations with the United States (Library of Congress).

when admitted, while another ten were fifteen. Barnett, like most of his classmates, arrived early and spent time preparing for the test. Candidates did not get a second chance to take the examination. Those who failed were sent home without even travel expenses.

John Wingate Weeks was a fortunate acquaintance for Barnett. After Weeks did not rank high enough in the class for a commission, he made his fortune in finance before turning his attention to politics. He was a senator by the time Barnett was appointed commandant and served as secretary of War in the Harding administration. Weeks was a consistent supporter of the navy and Marines and would play a key role in Barnett's career.

Barnett characterizes his hazing as innocuous and there is evidence that hazing was less serious during his time there. At other times it became a matter of national discussion and a serious disruption at the academy. An outbreak in 1874 attracted Congressional attention and prompted a law making it a court martial offense. The resulting frequent court proceedings had a negative impact on the honor code, as both the hazer and his victim had reason to minimize any event, even if under oath. *Fag-Ends from the Naval Academy* includes several songs and poems bewailing the crackdown on hazing. Applying military discipline to teenage boys in groups turned out to be a considerable challenge.

In academic work, practical training and daily oversight, the instructors at the academy were strict, but distant. They were military officers, after all, and mainly veterans of the Civil War. They were used to giving orders and having them obeyed. This may have been poor preparation for teaching English and algebra to teenagers. It also left the younger students at the tender mercies of their older classmates, who were in positions of authority over them.

George Barnett wearing his USNA sword (editor's personal collection).

Barnett displays sincere affection for the academy and always valued the friends he made there. He had life-long relationships with many of his classmates, especially those who joined the Marine Corps. The Class of 1881 was remarkably close knit, with an active alumni association and regular reunions. This may have been because of the difficulties they faced at the end of their cadet cruise. Barnett was very active in the association and the five year reunion booklet consists of letters to him from his classmates. They managed to reserve a section at Arlington National Cemetery, where Barnett, Weeks and others are buried.

A similar pleasant view of the academy was expressed by Cyrus Brady (USNA 1883) in *Under Tops'ls and Tent*. Recalling only good times, Brady recounts some of the same anecdotes as Barnett, including the "forks in the mess hall" story.

A less rosy view of the times can be found in Park Benjamin's *The United States Naval Academy*. The title of the relevant chapter is "The Academy in Era of Naval Decay." The problem was less with the USNA than with the navy as a whole. The country had little enthusiasm for a blue water navy and many of the ships were embarrassingly obsolete, as will be evident from Barnett's later cruises. The USNA academic and technical programs were quite good, but when instruction turned to practical matters, midshipmen spent their time re-rigging the USS *Dale* (commissioned in 1839) and practiced their gunnery aboard the USS *Nantucket*, a Civil War era monitor. Meanwhile the major naval powers were converting to steel, steam and fast firing rifled weapons.

In passing, Barnett mentions his nephew's recent admittance to Annapolis. This refers to Vice Admiral Lloyd Mustin (1911–1999), who entered the USNA in 1928. This indicates when the memoir was dictated.

SUGGESTED READING

Benjamin, Park, and G. P. Putnam's Sons. *The United States Naval Academy: Being the Yarn of the American Midshipman (naval Cadet) ... Paid Out*. New York ; London: Knickerbocker Press, 1900.
Brady, Cyrus Townsend. *Under Tops'ls and Tents*. Scribner, 1917.
Drew, Anne Marie. *Letters from Annapolis: Midshipmen Write Home, 1848–1969*. Annapolis, MD: Naval Institute Press, 1998.
Homer Lee Company. *Fag-Ends from the Naval Academy*. New York: H. Lee and Co., 1878.
Moeller, Peter W., and Franklin Moeller. *The Naval Academy at Annapolis and Hazing: Or, the Vindication of an Honest Name*. New York: Burr, 1884.
Soley, James Russell. *Historical Sketch of the United States Naval Academy*. Washington, Government Printing Office, 1876.
United States Naval Academy. *Annual Register of the U.S. Naval Academy*. Government Printing Office, 1883. Other editions available.
United States Naval Academy. *Misdemeanor Book, U.S. Naval Academy*. Annapolis, Md., 1877.
United States Naval Academy. *Regulations of the United States Naval Academy, as Approved by the Secretary of the Navy*. Washington, D.C.: Government Printing Office, 1876.
Washburn, Charles G. *The Life of John W. Weeks*. Boston: Houghton Mifflin, 1928.

Chapter III

Cadet Cruise—Africa

After I recovered sufficiently from my accident, I was ordered to the USS *Essex* which was fitting out at the Philadelphia Navy Yard and after this was completed, we started on our first foreign cruise. We thought we were getting a very good ship. I wonder what a midshipman now would think if, for his first ship, he was ordered to something similar to the *Essex*. Although she had auxiliary steam power, except in a few minor cases, she had no more comforts than the ship of revolutionary days. But with the enthusiasm of youth on this first foreign cruise, we thought little and cared less about the lack of comforts.

Our quarters were in the "steerage," a small room outside the wardroom bulkhead with a stateroom on each side, each stateroom containing four bunks, two lower and two upper. As there were nine of us, one of the midshipmen had to sling a hammock over our table. Our dining table was in what was called the "steerage country" and just under the wardroom ladder leading to the deck above. Nine of us lived in those close quarters for the cruise. I am sure the entire space would be considered only ample for two people on shore.

We had one small store room. I was caterer of the mess. It was my duty in Philadelphia to buy stores for the trip. I did not have much idea as to quantity. When the stores were delivered the lieutenant, Morris R. S. Mackenzie, laughed at my purchases and asked me what I was going to do with a barrel of vinegar too large for the tiny store room. I explained that I had gone to the retail groceries and their prices were so high, I went to wholesalers. There I had to take articles in their original packages or not at all. The store room was packed from deck to deck. It is no exaggeration to say that we had to eat our way into it. All the same, we had the joke on the wardroom officers several months later down on the Straits of Magellan. Dr. Melancthon L. Ruth, afterwards White House physician for President Cleveland, was caterer of the wardroom mess. He bought his stores at retail at very high prices, and in smaller quantities than I had. We were at sea longer than expected and the wardroom stores ran out. They were glad indeed to borrow from us. I suppose the duty of catering came to me because I had been caterer of the midshipman mess on our two cruises on the *Constellation*, and a terrible time I had. The midshipmen wanted to live on nothing, so they might save their money for leave after the cruises.

When the ship was ready, the crew went aboard at Philadelphia. Then we went to Norfolk Navy Yard to complete our fitting out. We were there about a month. We spent a very happy Christmas there. Norfolk then was comparatively small, but it had many delightful people. One of the class of 1881, and a shipmate, George P. Blow, was from Norfolk, so he and his family outdid themselves in making our stay there pleasant. On the tenth of January, 1882, we left Norfolk, crossed the North Atlantic Ocean and arrived at Funchal, Madeira, after a very stormy passage. Never will I forget my joy on reaching my first foreign port.

While our trip had been cold and stormy, we now found ourselves in a perfectly beautiful place with summer weather. The midshipmen got liberty and went ashore. We reveled in the beauties of the place, the wonderful sun-

The USS *Essex* sometime in the 1890s. Commissioned in 1876, she was typical of American warships of the era. She mainly sailed rather than steamed, was unarmored and usually operated independently. Valuable for showing the flag, she was no match for the armored warships becoming common (Library of Congress).

shine, the mountains and the strange sights. We got horses and rode to a convent far up on the mountainside and came down in a few minutes where we had been hours going up. Our journey down was on sleds with greased iron runners, on a roadbed of small round cobble stones, very slippery from constant use. The owner of the sled stood up in the rear of one of the runners and guided it with a steel point of a rod used as a rudder. In Funchal, the streets were so steep and hilly that the principal mode of transportation was large sleds drawn by oxen.

During our stay we were invited to luncheon and afternoon dance at the residence of the British Consul who lived very handsomely. We were particularly impressed with the palms in his grounds. They were the first real ones we had seen. The luncheon was large and formal. There seemed to be a waiter for each guest, and several times during the luncheon, much to my disgust, my plate was removed before I had finished the course, because of my talking to my neighbor on my right or left. I remember in that way I lost about two thirds of a plate of delicious strawberries, the first I had ever seen in January. An incident at the dance after the luncheon also remains in my memory. George Blow, who, by the way, was always very dignified, was dancing with an English girl who did not reverse. As the dance went on, he did not wish to say he wanted to stop because he was dizzy, but when the music stopped, he was so dizzy that he reeled. The young lady, thinking that he had been drinking, was much insulted, and said, "Sir, you have been drinking. Take me to my seat."

In Madeira liberty was granted to the crew. At that time, in the service, little was thought of the fact that many of the enlisted men, while on liberty, got drunk. Many overstayed their liberty and were locked up in the native jails. I was sent ashore in a boat with money to pay their fines and orders to bring them to the ship. I paid the fines and started down to the landing with the overtime men. Many of them were still under the influence of liquor. It had not been impossible to get more supplies, even in jail. About halfway down to the landing some of them demanded permission to enter a saloon for drink. When I refused, they went anyway. I applied to the police, and a detail was sent to assist me in getting them to the dock. On the way a drunken bluejacket grabbed my sword from behind, pulled it out of the scabbard and tried to attack a policeman. I finally got them to the dock where a ship's boat was waiting. A dozen bluejackets jumped into it and shoved off, leaving me on the dock alone. I signaled to the ship and reported my difficulty, and another boat with a Marine guard was sent to assist me. The drunken men in the boat, seeing they were about to be captured, jumped overboard and swam to the beach where they were picked up by the police, more or less exhausted, as they landed.

At that time it was not considered much of an offense for an enlisted men to get drunk ashore. When he returned to the ship he was given time to sober up and that was nearly the end of it. Later on in the cruise when we neared the flagship, the men who had committed the offense in Funchal were tried by general court martial and all convicted, regardless of the fact that they denied every charge and specification. They all got severe sentences. I mentioned above that getting drunk then was not serious just to show the difference between then and now. There is so much work on ships of the modern navy that the men must be industrious and sober. Without any Volstead Act or Eighteenth Amendment, the navy today would still be as sober as it is, because of the necessity of clear, active brains.

After about five days in Funchal we went to Santa Cruz de Tenerife where a few delightful days were spent and where I had my first view of beautiful Mount Tenerife, the first snow capped mountain I had ever seen. It seemed to rise abruptly and directly out of the deep blue ocean. We had a chance to go ashore there.

One evening I was boat officer and was sent ashore to bring off the officers who were on liberty. The water was very rough and the boat officer had to be careful in bringing his boat alongside the stone mole, or it would be crushed by waves. W. L. Emmett, a class mate, was apparently the only officer who wanted to come off. Bill was always very absent-minded. As the waves surged the boat in towards the mole I called, "Stand by and the next time the boat gets near enough be quick and jump." As the boat came in Emmett was star gazing, and he did not think quickly enough. When he jumped, the boat was about thirty feet off. Naturally, he landed in the water. We pulled him out and got him aboard none the worse for the plunge.

Our next port was Port au Pray, Cape Verde Islands. Shortly after we anchored there, native canoes came alongside filled with oranges. I gave a colored steward a quarter, and told him to go to the gangway and purchase me some oranges. He came back and said, "Lord, Mr. Barnett, I have to get a basket or a bag; the fellow in the canoe wants to give me a whole bushel for a quarter." Everyone bought a great many and orangeade was the rule for many days.

After a few days we sailed for Cape St. Vincent, Cape Verde Islands. There we found little to interest us except that it was a port of call for ships sailing between South America and the west coast of Europe. From Cape St. Vincent we sailed for Monrovia, the capital of Liberia. We anchored outside the bar, as it was very rough. In order to run the ship's boat with safety, native crewmen were employed who understood the running of the bar where the waves were high and dangerous. These men would back water on their oars until just the proper wave came along. Then we would rush in on the back of a wave until we reached the smooth part of the river just inside the bar. One day the midshipmen got permission to go ashore in native canoes, which were little more than ordinary dugouts. The natives were wonderfully expert in handling the boats. We landed on the hot beach to find all the natives of the village assembled; then we went in swimming and had our fill of tropical fruit.

Among our number was one of the best fellows who ever lived, the late Martin Bevington, who at that time was assistant engineer. He conceived the brilliant idea of digging holes in the sand well above high tide mark and taking a dozen or so native children, burying them in the sand with just their heads out. These twelve little black heads sticking out of the sand not only amused us, but the natives, whose pleasure was equal to our own.

The captain of the *Essex*, Alexander H. McCormick, had orders to take the president of Liberia and the secretary of state, both colored men, from Monrovia to Cape Palmas for consultation. Much to our surprise, they lived in the cabin of the captain which was highly proper according to his orders, even if it did seem strange to us. After attending to the business at Cape Palmas, we returned the president and his secretary of state to Monrovia. Then we started on our long trip to Montevideo, Uruguay.

While we were at Cape Palmas on the African west coast, one of the officers secured a wonderful young chimpanzee and brought him aboard ship. He soon became a pet of everyone from the captain down, and particularly the executive officer, Lieutenant Mackenzie. Wherever we went after that, the first thought of all as we dropped anchor was to get fresh fruit for "Peter." Peter would take an orange, stick his finger in the end of it, then suck it until I do not believe a steam roller could have gotten juice from it. The sailors and Marines were not long in providing Peter with a complete outfit of sailor and Marine uniforms. At general muster Peter stood by the side of the executive officer, holding on to his sword, dressed as a sailor or Marine. At every port where we stopped, the ship was crowded with children anxious to see and play with Peter. "Drop the handkerchief" seemed to be the best amusement. Peter would drop it on the deck, walk away for a distance, apparently taking no notice whatever, but at the same time keeping his eye on the children. If any one of them started for it, Peter would have it before the child could reach it, no matter how nimble.

Peter belonged to the junior officers' mess where he sat in a high chair, had his own dishes and took his meals with us. He also had a place at one of the forward messes of the men. When mess call was sounded he would get his cup, pan and spoon and put them on the table where he belonged. He had an abnormal appetite for coffee and all day long he would drink it, if he could get it. When you gave him a cup of coffee and removed it before he finished it, he was extremely angry and literally tore his hair. When drinking coffee, Peter sat on the rim of a bucket and anything he spilled went into it. If, while sitting in his high chair at our table, one of the cadets would pretend to strike his neighbor, he would jump up regardless of anything in the way and rush across the table and take a hand in the scrap, but always against the one who had started it. Peter slept in a regular hammock, and was counted as one of the crew.

He had a little wash tub and wash board and would go through the motions of washing his clothes and wringing them out. He was a great friend of the captain of the hold. The latter made him a little barrel pump. He would fill one of the breakers with water and arrange the pump. Peter would pump away as long as there was any water in the breaker. Given a tack hammer and tacks he would drive tacks all over the ship. If given a screw driver, he would go along the deck until he found a gun track with screws in it, insert the screw driver and try to turn it, which he was not strong enough to do.

His only enemy was the quarter gunner of the after eleven inch gun. This gun was very highly polished and was the pride of the gunner's life. He would not allow Peter to come near, for fear he would scratch it, and would box his ears if he approached. When the gunner was away, and left his pet uncovered, Peter would deliberately jump on it and scratch a piece of lacquer out of the body of the gun. Then seeing the quarter gunner coming, he would take to the rigging and make his escape.

Peter was very fond of raisins and prunes. One of the amusements on board was to put these in a glass of sherry. He would eat them and soon be tipsy. I mentioned his fondness for coffee before, and his anger at having his cup removed before he finished it. One day this was done to tease him. He screamed with anger, flapped his arms on his chest many times, folded his arms, put his head down, pushing himself by his hind feet all the time screaming with rage. We called it, "walking off on his ear."

Another day a young goat was brought aboard. It seemed very friendly, and Peter tried to get acquainted with him, but his method was unfortunate. He would stick his finger in the goat's side and then smell his finger. When he got tired of this, he pulled the goat's hair. The goat, tired of his attentions, turned on him and butted him out in one round. Always after that Peter had a high regard for the goat. When the goat was on deck Peter liked nothing better than to be taken by the hand and help chase the goat about the deck, screaming with delight all the time.

Very often Peter would do things for which his ears were boxed. He would defend himself from a blow as well as he might, with his arms and hands. At one time, while one of the officers was in the gangway reading, Peter came along, reached up and tore a leaf out of the book. The officer boxed his ears good and plenty. Peter fought back as best he could, but when he saw he was getting the worst of it, he walked away with a very sad expression on his face, glancing back at the officer. The officer, noticing this, reached toward Peter and said, "Peter, let's be friends." Peter slowly returned, took his hand and instead of jumping into his lap as he usually did, he pulled the hand down toward him and bit one of the fingers very badly. The next minute he was on the foreyard, out of all reach.

As we went through the Straits of Magellan, it was very cold. Peter was a quaint sight in his little blue Marine overcoat with collar turned up. He would walk around in the cold water and snow, and soon caught a cold which affected his lungs, and he displayed every indication of consumption. Every morning at the regular time Peter would wait on deck at the top of the wardroom ladder for the doctor. He paid no attention to other officers as they passed, but when the doctor came, he would take his hand and go to the sick bay and take his medicine like a little man. Every week Peter was shaved by the barber. He wore side whiskers only. A queer object he was with his monkey face, side whiskers, and a little short stemmed pipe in his mouth, and dressed either as a sailor, a Marine or a brownie.

Peter never lapped anything. He put his finger through the ring of a cup and drank as a human being might. Poor little fellow, as his cough got worse, towards the end, he would hold his sides and cough and expectorate in a very human fashion. While in Callao, Peru, Peter died. Everybody on board ship felt his loss as that of a shipmate. He had a regular military funeral which was attended by the whole crew. As I remember it, nearly every boat in the ship was filled. He was buried on San Lorenzo Island in the harbor of Callao, Peru. At that time it would have been hard to make anyone believe that Peter was not pretty close to being the "Missing Link."

Editor's Comments on Chapter 3

The USS *Essex* tells us many important things about the navy of that time. She was commissioned in 1876 and was considered one of the finest ships in the fleet during Barnett's time on board. Even so, the *Essex* was an unarmored wooden hulled sailing ship with auxiliary steam power, i.e. she mainly sailed and only occasionally relied solely on her engines. This made her much cheaper to operate and allowed for a greater range. As the navy lacked both funds and overseas bases, these were necessary compromises.

As Barnett mentions, she had little in common with a "modern" warship. No armor, radio or refrigeration, but with broadside batteries, sails and black stewards. Crew men helping a chimpanzee chase a goat around the deck completes the setting. Just six years after Barnett served on her, the *Essex* was decommissioned and served as a training vessel for the remainder of her career.

One thing the *Essex* had in abundance was officers. She had a captain, paymaster, two engineers, Marine Lieutenant Otway Berryman, six other lieutenants, two passed midshipmen and seven naval cadets. The ship's total complement was only 190. An earlier accounting showed 24 officers and 175 enlisted men. The navy was top heavy, at one point reaching a ratio of one officer for each four enlisted men, which kept many officers ashore. Congress continued to appoint young men to the USNA, which continued to graduate and commission them. This would have consequences for the Class of 1881.

Naval cadets, as the graduates were known, were an ambiguous class. They were most definitely not enlisted men. Nor were they much like the traditional "youngsters" employed by navies in the Age of Sail. Yet they were not commissioned officers either. Barnett was fortunate in that his captain gave him a taste of responsibility, even if it involved retrieving drunken crewmen from a jail. After completing their cadet cruise, they would be promoted to midshipmen. After four years at the academy and two years of cruising, they could begin their wait for someone ahead of them to die or resign. By 1881, the backlog of Annapolis graduates awaiting commissions as ensigns had grown to over two hundred, with an expected delay of eight years before they might achieve that exalted status.

The president of Liberia mentioned was Anthony W. Gardiner (1820–1885), who served as president 1878–1883. Gardiner was born in the United States, but his family relocated to Liberia in 1831. Liberia became a republic in 1847 and had the unique status of a Black colony in Africa. Due to its ties with the United States, the U.S. Navy sometimes assisted and protected the young republic.

Barnett and his classmates were surprised to see the president of Liberia being treated as a dignitary and superior to a navy captain, as would most white Americans of the day. The end of Reconstruction brought a resurgence of White supremacy and the U.S. became increasingly indifferent to the fate of Blacks in general and Liberia in particular. The first African-American was appointed to the USNA in 1872, but was attacked and beaten by the other cadets before withdrawing. Five more brave cadets faced similar resistance over the years. It would take until 1949 for the first African-American to graduate from the USNA. He roomed alone for four years.

Around the World with the Blue Jackets provides a rosy portrait of what serving in the navy was like at the time, complete with a visit from King Neptune. It has the further advantage of taking place on the USS *Iroquois*, a ship that Barnett will later serve on.

Suggested Reading

Rhoades, Henry E. 1843–1934. *Around the World with the Blue Jackets, Or, How We Displayed the American Flag in Foreign Waters.* Boston: D. Lothrop Company, 1890.

Chapter IV

Cadet Cruise—South America

The trip from Monrovia, on the west coast of Africa, to Montevideo, Uruguay, was long and tedious especially through the doldrums. We depended almost entirely on sail except when leaving and entering port.

During the trip, we crossed the equator, and entered Neptune's domain. The old sailor men on board got up a wonderful entertainment to celebrate the crossing of the line. They built a large canvas tank on the quarter deck and filled it with salt water. Neptune and his crew of assistants, dressed in fantastic costumes for the occasion, were ready to initiate all who had not been south of the equator before. Each of us who had not crossed the line before received a printed summons from Neptune, signed by him, ordering that the greenhorns appear for initiation into his domain at the proper time.

On a platform above one side of the tank Neptune's barber had his chair. As each novice presented himself, he was put in the barber's chair. The lather was applied by the barber with a large paint brush, and he was none too careful to keep the lather from the eyes and mouth of his victim. He then pretended to shave him with a huge tin razor. Just as this was finished, the barber touched a spring with his foot, the chair tipped backwards and dumped the victim into the pool, where he was properly ducked by Neptune's assistants, who waited for him there. On this trip there were so many novices that finally Neptune and his crew became exceedingly tired, so much so that, towards the end, the fun rather turned in favor of the novices, who spent their time ducking Neptune and his crew. One young fellow of our class, DeWitt Redgrave, objected to being ducked, and refused to obey the summons, and went aloft the maintop to escape. From there he appealed to the executive officer against what he called barbarous treatment. The executive simply laughed at him and said to the crew in a low voice, "Go, get him." They brought him down and of course his treatment was no less severe than the others had gotten.

After a long trip of thirty-five days, we reached Montevideo, There we anchored in the river about three miles off the city. Ordinarily boating to the shore was not at all uncomfortable, but frequently with only a few moments' notice, a "pampero" would start blowing, and in a very short time transportation between shore and ship was almost impossible. These pamperos did not indicate any storm, but simply very high winds coming from the pampas or prairies of Uruguay and the Argentine. Very often we went ashore in the late afternoon for dinner, intending to come off that night. By the time the dinner was over the wind was so high that passage to the ship was impossible. Sometimes we had to spend a day or two on shore in evening clothes, not being prepared for a change.

Ninety miles up the La Plata River from Montevideo is the city of Buenos Aires. We had heard much of it and were delighted to go there. Buenos Aires had a population of about five hundred thousand, mostly Spanish and Italian, with a sprinkling of English and German. It was called the Paris of South America and well deserved this title. It was noted then for its splendid horses. No one spent any time on shore without being impressed by the handsome horses and carriages everywhere. The Argentinos are fond of racing and we had the pleasure of witnessing races at Palermo Park while there. The city was a wonderful market for furs brought in from the mountains of southern Argentina and Patagonia, and from the mountains further west. I remember particularly the marvelous chinchilla skins I saw and I was sorry that I was unable to buy a lot of them.

After a month there, we started on our cruise to Valparaiso via the Straits of Magellan, instead of around the Horn. We reached the eastern end of the straits early in July, midwinter in that latitude. The mountains were covered with snow and lakes and streams were frozen, especially on the island of Tierra del Fuego. The passage through the straits was very picturesque, and in some places quite dangerous, owing to the narrowness of the straits, the currents, and the strong winds tearing down the valleys from the high mountains. They were called "williwaws."

About half way through, we stopped at the port of Punta Arenas for coal. We happened to be there on the Fourth of July. Some of us youngsters spent most of the day skating on a lake back of the town. Here we saw the first Fuegons or natives of Tierra del Fuego, who came along side in their miserable dugouts to sell us furs, principally guanaco and vicuna skins or robes. The guanaco skin has soft silken fur, white and lemon yellow. It is exceedingly light and very warm. The natives were of an uncivilized type, very dark and ugly looking, and seemed to have almost none of the comforts of life. The guanaco robe I bought I sent to my mother, who had it made into a sleigh robe and a good one it made for many years thereafter.

During the trip through the straits, we stopped at several islands about which we knew nothing. A lot of us midshipmen landed on Elizabeth Island for the purpose of shooting geese on the ice covered lakes. Geese were plentiful, and we had a couple of very good days' sport. Much to our surprise, we found ordinary domestic sheep on the island. Unfortunately, one of the midshipmen, Robert Dashiell, shot the first he saw, thinking it was a wild one. We soon found out, however, that an Englishman had a sheep ranch there and he was not long coming aboard ship and claiming remuneration for his dead sheep.

On this island I was wonderfully impressed with the quiet of the place; I had a queer feeling of being so far away, almost at the southern end of South America. This thought took me back home and reminded me of the time there when no one could have convinced me that I would so soon be at the uttermost parts of the earth.

We finally steamed to the westward past Cape Pillow, and entered the Pacific Ocean for the first time. Just outside of Cape Pillow, we had one of the heaviest seas I have ever encountered. Great rollers came for thousands of miles and they were so high and heavy they did some damage to the ship. Finally we reached Valparaiso, Chile, and anchored there in about forty fathoms of water. This anchorage is rather a roadstead than a harbor. Nearby were many merchant ships which ran between Chile and England. They were all anchored head and stern in lines, and as they rose and fell with the waves, their anchor chains were exposed at great length. A great deal of chain had to be let out and the bow anchors dropped well ahead of where the ship was to lie, because of the deep water.

A very laughable incident occurred in connection with these big merchant ships. The USS *Alaska*, commanded by Captain George Belknap, was also there. On board that ship was a classmate of mine, midshipman Samuel Bryan, and an ensign several classes ahead of us, Albert N. Wood. Wood was captain's clerk, and he was sent ashore one day by the captain to take the Christmas mail to the post office, in time to catch a steamer that would reach the U.S.A. before Christmas. Midshipman Bryan was boat officer of the steam launch and took Wood ashore. Wood was senior to Bryan and took it upon himself to advise as to the handling of the boat. As they came near one of the big merchant ships, her bow rose in the air and left a very large space between the anchor chain and the bow of the ship. As Wood was in a hurry, he thought he would go close to the ship and save distance, instead of going outside the long chain reaching to the anchor ahead. His speed was pretty fast, and just as he neared the ship, the bow of the ship went down with the waves and the chain cable raked the steam launch fore and aft, taking off her smokestack and canopy and making her useless for the time being. A boat from one of the ships put off to her assistance and Wood put the mail into this boat and proceeded towards the shore, leaving Bryan to do the best he could with the disabled launch. As he left Bryan he called out: "Good-bye Bryan, won't the old man give you hell." Wood, not to be caught in the same way, attempted to pass well ahead of the next big ship, intending to go outside instead of between the chain and the bow. But he did not go far enough, and unfortunately for him, and for the boat, just as he got over the cable, the bow of the ship rose rapidly, the cable caught the boat about midships, lifting it high in the air and breaking it in two, dumping the whole crew with Wood and the mail into the water. Bryan called out: "Oh! Wood, I <u>know</u> the old man will give you hell." Which he did. Anyone who knew Admiral Belknap will realize that this description is no exaggeration.

Valparaiso is a wonderful city built on the numerous hillsides overlooking the roadstead. The population is largely Spanish, with many English and Germans also. It is one of the principal business cities of South America. Here again we enjoyed the racing season, and had many fine afternoons at Viña del Mar, where we not only saw splendid horses but many beautiful women, for which Chile is noted.

During the time the ship was at Valparaiso, five of us had the rare opportunity of taking a trip to Santiago de Chile, which is ninety miles back in the interior, and reached by a railroad passing through some of the most beautiful scenery in the world. We climbed nearly all the way and finally went through a pass in the mountains and came into view of the city of Santiago. In my opinion the situation is the most beautiful I have ever seen. It is on a plain surrounded by snow capped mountains from fifteen to over twenty thousand feet in height, Mount Aconcagua being the king of them all, twenty-three thousand feet high, one of the highest in the world. From what we could hear, it seemed to be the Chilean idea of life to make sufficient money in Valparaiso, and then to build a residence, almost a real palace, in Santiago. The principal street there is the Alameda. It is wide enough for two streams of running water, two separate car lines, several walks and drives, and many rows of trees. While in Santiago, we not only enjoyed the sights, but went at night to the grand opera, really good and at popular prices.

After our leave in Santiago, we returned to Valparaiso and shortly thereafter the ship sailed for Coquimbo, a port which is noted for its large shipments of copper. While in Coquimbo both officers and men had a gay time on shore and spent the days most delightfully. On the same bay and a few miles away, was the town of La Serena, where we attended many dances. At Coquimbo and La Serena we saw the Chilean dance, the "Cueca," somewhat similar to the Tango which we had seen in Argentina. Of course, we all learned it, or imagined we had. In fact during the cruise we danced in all languages.

After leaving Coquimbo, we went to Iquique, Peru, where a great deal of the nitrate of the world is obtained. It is this province surrounding Iquique that has caused so much trouble since the Chilean-Peruvian war in 1880. After the war this province, originally Peruvian, was held by the Chileans for many years. This was objected to by the Peruvians, as a large share of their revenue came from the province.

We next visited Arica, and we saw there what remained of the USS *Wateree*, one of the American ships wrecked by a great tidal wave in that harbor twenty years before. At the same time the American ship, *Fredonia* was completely engulfed and lost; likewise a Peruvian ship, the *America*. The *Wateree* was a side wheel steamer, a relic of Civil War days. She was standing right side up and almost perfectly level. From what we were told, the tidal wave picked her up and put her down bodily quite a distance inland, and a second tidal wave brought her back to within a half mile of the beach where she still is.

After Arica we went to Callao, Peru, where we stayed a long time. This was just at the end of the Chilean-Peruvian war; in fact Lima, Peru, was still in the hands of the Chilean army of occupation; the commanding general being Patricio Lynch, who ruled with a very heavy hand. Not far from Lima was the town of Chorrillos, which before the war had been the Newport of Peru. This town was almost totally destroyed, and the evidences of battle were still visible in the town and surrounding country. In the town of Callao, we saw three ships which had become famous during that war, because they had fought the first battle between real ironclads. These ships were the Peruvian *Huascar* and the Chilean *Cochran* and *Blanco Encalada*.

While in Callao, we made numerous visits to Lima, an attractive city located at the base of the Andes Mountains with the river Rimac running through the city. In Lima, the capital of Peru, we were particularly interested in a church where we saw the tomb of the famous Spanish Pizarro, who conquered Peru from the Incas. There we read with a great deal of interest Prescott's *Conquest of Peru*.

Besides our ship, two Italian ships were in the harbor. There were many entertainments on board the ship and on shore. At one given by the Italian Minister to Peru, I wore my social intercourse uniform (military evening clothes) and a classmate of mine, Cadet Gartley, who had not provided himself with either social intercourse or full dress, borrowed my full dress uniform. When the party ended, a number of American and Italian officers were on the dock, waiting for the ship's boats. An Italian officer did not notice that the lower step of the ladder was missing. Unfortunately for him, he took one step too many and landed in the water. He was pulled out and was very angry. As we youngsters started down the ladder when our boat came in, I suppose I was thinking of my full dress uniform. I cautioned Gartley, who was wearing it, to be careful and not repeat the Italian officer's mishap. His reply was, "You must think me a d—fool. I am not going to fall in; I am not going to follow in his footsteps." He had hardly finished this remark, when he took one step too many and I saw my uniform disappear under the water. We pulled him out and no others made the mistake. I worked for hours on my uniform, washing all its gold lace with fresh water to minimize as much as possible the injury done by the salt water. Later on when my clothes had been dried and pressed, it was found that no harm had been done.

The end of our cadet cruise was drawing to a close. In April we received orders to take passage to New York by mail steamer and go back to Annapolis for our final examinations. Not only the midshipmen from our ship, but those from the USS *Pensacola*, took passage on the same ship, making about fifteen of us in all. We sailed from Callao and stopped at Paita, Peru, and Guayaquil, Ecuador.

We finally reached Panama, which at that time was filled with French, who were attempting to build the Panama Canal. The headquarters of the Panama Canal Company was in what had been the old Grand Hotel. The few days that we were in Panama convinced us, even as youngsters, of the futility of attempting a canal as the French were working on it. The workmen on the canal were dying like flies of yellow fever, and yet no serious attempt had been made to check the yellow fever by eradicating the mosquitoes. This was because it had not yet been demonstrated that yellow fever was carried by the mosquito.

The harbor at the Atlantic end of the Canal was at that time called Aspinwall, which is the present Colon, and we spent several days in there because the steamer from San Francisco was late in arriving in Panama, and the New York steamer was waiting for the passengers from San Francisco. They finally arrived and we went on board the New York steamer.

In Aspinwall, we met a very queer character, an Irishman, a citizen of the United States, named Thomas Hughes. He had made a lot of money in mining in the far west, and had gone to South America in the hopes of discovering other mines there. He had not seen Americans for some time, and seemed delighted to see all of us youngsters. He had plenty of money, and nothing pleased him better than to spend it on us. He insisted on buying Panama hats for several of us. I wore mine for years thereafter.

On board the New York steamer there was an exceedingly pretty girl on her way from San Francisco. There was also an American railroad engineer, and his young wife, Mr. and Mrs. Wesson. Through some of the other passengers we learned that a young fellow had been very attentive to this girl on a trip from San Francisco to Panama. We decided to make life rather a burden to him. The plan was not to let him see her alone for the remainder of the trip. We never left her one minute of the day or during the evening, much to the annoyance of the young man and to the pleasure of all the plotters.

Also on board the steamer was a Mr. James R. Partridge, who had been the American Minister to Peru. It was reported to us that he thought our conduct with reference to the young lady and the young fellow very reprehensible. So, boy-like, we decided to give him something worth talking about. We took Mrs. Wesson into our confidence. She loaned us an outfit of her clothing. That evening after dark we dressed one of our classmates up in these clothes and in a place where the American minister could not help seeing us during his walks, different cadets made violent love to this supposed girl, much to the disgust of Mr. Partridge, who said we were a lot of young ruffians.

We finally arrived in New York and as we had been nearly the whole cruise in warm weather, we made a queer looking outfit. We all wore straw hats, and as it was a long time before the season for straw hats in New York, we were jeered by the small boys in the streets until we provided ourselves with proper head gear.

Chapter V

Graduation and the Marine Corps

We proceeded to Annapolis, and there continued our studies preparatory to final examinations. We were the first of our class to arrive in Annapolis, but others soon began to wander in from all over the world. When we all met after having been separated for two years, we had much to talk about, as some of the class had been to almost every part of the world. I am sure they were all impressed as I was with the wonderful opportunity naval life had given us so far. Travel is always one of the best means of education. We had visited many countries, and observed many different races and classes of people and our cruises had only whetted our appetites for further travel. I was so much impressed with this that it had a certain effect on my whole life, because whenever I had a chance, I took sea duty in preference to shore duty, and never on the home stations, but always, if possible, on a ship going to the uttermost parts of the earth.

In Annapolis and waiting for our final examinations, we lived in boarding houses. I lived at Mrs. Iglehart's. One night I went to bed about ten o'clock and at one was aroused by a messenger from one of my classmates. This note was from R. P. Forshew. I know he will deny it, but it is true. He asked me to please come to the house of a Justice of the Peace and get several of the class released. They had been arrested for causing a disturbance down near the water front, in a place kept by a man called "Left Arm Brown," because he had no right arm. The Justice of the Peace was a Mr. Thompson, known to the cadets as "Turkey" Thompson. I do not know why. I went to his house and heard what they all had to say, and then pled with the Justice to let them go. I finally succeeded, not, however, until after he had imposed a fine on each of them. Of course, they had no money, nor did I. But I was persuasive enough to get Turkey Thompson, the Justice of the Peace, to lend me the money personally on condition that I would be responsible for it. I paid the fines and we left the house. One of the cadets found that by mistake he had taken a hat belonging to the Justice instead of his own. He said in order to get even with the Justice, he would kick a hole in the hat, which he proceeded to do. Afterwards he had to pay not only the fine but for the hat. I suppose he likewise will deny this, but I hadn't been on the party, and therefore can probably remember more than he can.

When graduation day came that year, we found that the second class, soon to become first class, had gotten into difficulties with the superintendent, Commodore Francis M. Ramsay. The commodore had decided that they could not give the customary graduation ball. Annapolis was full of people in town for the graduation ball, and our class decided that it would have an unofficial ball. We got together as many of the girls as possible and enlisted their services. We roamed over the fields about the academy and picked thousands of daisies and other flowers to use in decorating the gymnasium. Our ball was really worthwhile, much to the satisfaction of all concerned, except the second class.

Finally our examination came, and all those who passed were given diplomas of graduation from the academy. While we were at sea, in fact on August 5, 1882, a bill was passed by Congress stating that thereafter only such number of graduates could be retained in the service as there had been vacancies created during the previous year, but providing that ten at least of each class should be retained in the service. Those who resigned and those mustered out entered civil life. They took with them the training they had received, and also great interest in the service, and I have no doubt but that the graduates of my class, and those of classes following who entered civil life, had great weight in molding public opinion in favor of an increase in the navy, which in 1883 was at about the lowest level it ever reached. Nearly all of those graduates joined the Naval Militia of their states and did splendid service, and during the Spanish War and the World War, their services were very valuable. As I remember, the number we retained that year, according to this law, was about twenty-three or four. Among those who graduated high enough to remain in the service, several resigned, thus making vacancies for others. I remember those kept in the service were ten for the line, twelve for the Marine Corps, four for naval constructors and four for engineers. Seventy-four had passed. So about fifty were given $1,000 each and honorably discharged.

After our final graduation, we were granted leave to await the decision as to which branch of the service we would be assigned. Before leaving the academy, each cadet to be retained was obliged to sign a paper showing his preference for the several branches of the service. I chose the Marine Corps first, and a short time after I reached my home, I received notification that my request had been granted, and that I was appointed a second lieutenant in the Marine Corps from July 1, 1883. I was further ordered to the Marine Barracks, Brooklyn, New York, for special instruction. All others who had been appointed second lieutenants were also ordered there, and we assembled at Brooklyn shortly thereafter. These included: Francis Sutton, Lincoln Karmany, William Stayton, Charles Doyen, James Mahoney, Henry C. Haines, Charles Lauchheimer, Charles Rommel, Franklin Moses, and Barnett. A little later on, Rommel exchanged with Con Perkins who had been assigned to the Engineer Corps.

During our stay at the Brooklyn barracks, we received instructions as junior Marine officers, especially in the line of infantry drill and of our duties aboard ship. While on liberty, we bought high hats, except Sutton, who never had any money. One evening several of us wished to go out in Brooklyn and make some calls. Sutton was one of the number going. As I said, he had no high hat, so, as Lauchheimer was officer of the day, Sutton borrowed his hat, but without permission. While we were calling, it started to rain hard. We had no umbrellas, so we got thoroughly soaked, high hats and all. Sutton put Lauchheimer's hat in its proper place without a word, and the next day Lauchheimer was angrier than I had ever seen him.

During our short tour at the Marine barracks, I was again caterer of the mess. On the first of October I collected the full mess bill for the month. About the 12th of the month we all received orders detaching us and sending us to all parts of the earth. I had a half month's mess bill left for each one. At luncheon that day we took a vote as to whether I should turn this money back or give a farewell party. It was unanimously decided to give a party, and I was requested to make the necessary arrangements. It was a real party and many guests, young officers from the ships, were present. I will not go into the details of this party, as it might embarrass some of those who were then present, but who are now dignified officers of the service. About two o'clock in the morning, we decided to call on the commanding officer, Major Charles Heywood. We did so, and asked him to come over and join our party, which he did. While he was there, we proposed his health as the next commandant of the Marine Corps. This pleased him, and ever after that he seemed to have a soft spot in his heart for all of us. When the next vacancy occurred, he was appointed colonel commandant of the Marine Corps, and was afterwards promoted to be brigadier general commandant, and afterwards major general commandant. He served in the position of commandant twelve years during which time he saw many improvements in the Corps. I am sure that our association with General Heywood did us good during all our subsequent service, as he was a splendid man and officer who had served in the Marine Corps all during the Civil War. He was on board the *Cumberland* at Hampton Roads when that vessel was sunk by the *Merrimac*, and later on, he was with Farragut to the end of the war.

I found that my orders and those of Lieutenant F. J. Moses were to proceed to the Marine Barracks, Mare Island, California. We left on October 16, 1883 and arrived at Mare Island five days later, where we reported for our first regular tour of duty in the Marine Corps. The commanding officer at that time was Major George W. Collier, an enormous man and very powerful, and on account of his strength he had been called Sam Collier after a prize fighter of that name. I remember once when as commanding officer, Major Collier went to San Francisco, as was his custom once a week, to swear in recruits. I heard from the first sergeant that two men, who had each been given bobtail discharges the day before, were laying for the Major on his next visit to San Francisco. I thought this was of sufficient importance to telegraph the Major at the recruiting office, so I telegraphed him to beware of so and so, who were laying for him. The Major telegraphed back, "Never mind, if there are only two of them."

The Major was afraid of snakes, both real and imaginary, and there were quite a number of rattlesnakes on Mare Island at that time, so one day the Major passed word around that any enlisted man who killed a rattlesnake would be given a week's furlough. The next day a trumpeter by the name of Ruges brought the Major a long rattle, and the Major immediately gave him seven days' furlough. After he came back and had been at the barracks two or three days, he again brought the Major a rattle and again got a week's furlough. After this had taken place three times, and the Major had spoken of what a wonderful snake hunter Ruges was, I asked the Major if it ever occurred to him that Ruges could bring the same rattle to him every time. He sent for Ruges and took away the rattle, and after that Ruges seemed to have a hard time finding rattlers, as he did not bring any more to the Major.

The Major's family went east to spend a couple of months, and he asked us if, during their absence, he could mess with us, Lieutenant F. J. Moses and me. We told him that we would be glad to have him. He asked us what the mess bill would be and we told him, $25. At the first meal, we found we would be bankrupt if we attempted to feed him on anything like an ordinary mess bill. It was nothing unusual for him to eat six eggs, a pound of steak, three cups of coffee and endless hot cakes for breakfast. He had quite a chicken farm in his garden and used to sell the eggs, so we decided on a scheme which may not have been entirely justifiable, but seemed so to us, because we had in mind that when we agreed to feed him for a certain price, he should eat a reasonable amount; so every morning before the major was up, we would go to his chicken yard and get about four eggs, so the major ate two of our eggs and four of his own each morning. Shooting was not allowed in the inhabited part of the Island, but the island was full of California quail. We found a very good scheme was to buy an air rifle and while we were after the Major's eggs, pick off two or three quail that would feed with his chickens, so we had quail often and lived very well regardless of the Major's appetite. At that time the tule swamps north of Mare Island furnished splendid duck and snipe shooting, and we had no trouble in keeping our table amply supplied with all kinds of water fowl, especially canvasback ducks.

Shortly after this, Captain Charles Williams was ordered there for duty. He was a great musician, playing on several instruments and made a great addition to the post. He was likewise a painter of considerable note, and used to spend most of his spare time in a room he used as a studio. Several of us, Moses and myself and Stayton, who was attached to one of the ships at the yard, used to go into his room and have fun with Captain Williams, criticizing his painting. One day we found the door locked, although Captain Williams was inside. For three days this continued, and finally on the fourth day, the door was opened and we entered to find him painting as usual. He had painted a good-sized picture of three asses with their heads together and the picture was named, "The Three Critics." Then we learned what he had been doing during the three days he had kept the door locked.

Williams was a great shot and used to join us going to shoot ducks. He got a wonderful layout of rubber decoy ducks in San Francisco, and the first day he received them we went duck shooting. We separated and had not been apart long before I heard two shots in rapid succession. I also heard the worst cursing I ever heard in my life. Moses had sneaked up and had seen those decoy ducks, and had taken them for real ducks. He fired both barrels into them and got the whole bunch. This was particularly offensive to Captain Williams, not only because he lost his ducks which were of rubber, but because Moses always claimed that no real sport would shoot ducks on the water, but would wait until they flew and get them in the air.

Editor's Comments on Chapter Five

The final examinations were the culmination of six years of effort, counting for 24 percent of the final grade. Final rankings mattered immensely, as they determined seniority and seniority governed promotion. Karmany and Doyen ranked ahead of Barnett on the seniority list in 1883 due to their class ranking, an advantage they would retain even after he was appointed commandant. Commandants held higher rank ex-officio, with their permanent rank and seniority unchanged.

Promotion in the navy and Marine Corps was strictly based on seniority, with the Corps not eliminating that practice until the 1930s. The retirement of a colonel meant a promotion for the senior lieutenant colonel, major, captain, first lieutenant, second lieutenant and even a commission for a candidate on the waiting list. Every officer was acutely aware of their position on the seniority list. Citations and medals could provide a boost up the list, but fitness was not a consideration.

An overcrowded officer's corps with no provision for fitness-based retirements created an unsustainable situation for the Corps. Junior officers waited years for a minor command and even outstanding officers suffered from stagnant careers. The lack of advancement was breathtaking. Robert Huntington commanded a Marine battalion in Cuba during the Spanish-American War, but spent twenty-five years as a captain. Three of that battalion's captains were in their fifties. Lieutenant Otway Berryman of the *Essex* spent twenty-two years as a lieutenant, as did future Commandant George Elliott. That was how promotions worked in the period between the Civil War and the expansion preceding the Spanish-American War.

As Barnett mentions, an 1882 law restricted the number of USNA graduates commissioned. This change addressed the proliferation of officers without impacting existing officers or limiting Congressional appointments to Annapolis. The same law created new positions in the Marine Corps and made them available to USNA graduates. The top graduates got their choice of navy or Marine commissions, until all the available slots were filled. Three of them chose discharges, perhaps disenchanted by their cadet cruise or the bleak prospects for advancement. The remaining two-thirds of the class were discharged.

The Class of 1881 did not meekly accept this. They formed a lobbying group to protest the law, but to no avail. The effort formed the basis of later reunions and helped create an exceptionally close and unified class.

Some of the graduates ranked in the top ten of their class chose the Marines, perhaps hoping for quicker advancement. The navy had a long list of midshipmen waiting for an ensign's slot to open up, while the Marines would be immediately commissioned. Barnett states that he made the Marines his first choice, but the navy positions were all taken when his turn came. Despite his rank in the top third of the class (23rd overall), he owed his military career to a higher ranking classmate who requested a discharge.

Before 1883, no Marine officers were USNA graduates. Between 1883 and 1897, all new officers were USNA graduates. The impact of these "Fabulous Fifty" on the Corps is hard to overstate. Notable Annapolis graduates commissioned during this period include: Joseph Pendleton (1884); Eli K. Cole (1890); John Lejeune (1890); Wendell Neville (1891); Ben Fuller (1891); Charles Long (1891); Albertus Catlin (1892); Dion Williams (1893); and John Russell (1894). All commandants between 1914 and 1936 were USNA graduates and members of the Fabulous Fifty.

Despite their advantages, the Class of 1881 was not uniformly successful. It was a long and uncertain path to positions of authority. Sutton (1889) and Moses (1914) died in the line of duty. Stayton resigned in 1891. Lauchheimer and Haines moved into staff positions, which removed them from the command track. Perkins,

Doyen and others could charitably be called "hard drinking," as alcohol abuse damaged their careers. Only Barnett achieved prominence.

The Marine Corps was in desperate need of a new mission. As the navy modernized, their shipboard roles were becoming irrelevant. Small arms were useless in battle. The increasingly highly trained crews did not require Marines to prevent mutinies. Though Marines were often injected into situations to protect American lives and commerce, they had not developed any particular expertise or doctrine for amphibious landings, expeditionary operations or combined arms. There were serious and ongoing efforts to eliminate the Corps throughout the 1880s and 1890s, led by powerful politicians and senior navy officers. It would take until 1903 for the Corps to get a commandant who wasn't a Civil War veteran, which delayed changes in doctrine and practices. As Marine Captain Henry Cochrane noted, "The Navy is undergoing a complete revolution, but the Marine Corps slumbers."

The Corps that Barnett joined was not only endangered, but small, fractured and ossified. In 1880, it totaled only 2,000 enlisted men and 78 officers, who were rarely gathered into units as large as modern companies. Desertion rates were as high as 25 percent and re-enlistments were rare.

With the paucity of formal instruction or permanent formations, mentors and protégés played an important role in developing Marine officers. Ben Fuller served as naval cadet on the *Iroquois* with Barnett. Fuller would later choose the Marines and served as commandant (1930–1934). "Pete" Ellis served under Barnett on the *Kentucky*, but his drinking endangered his career. Commandant Barnett overlooked his alcoholism and sent him to the Naval War College, where he became a pioneer of amphibious warfare. Clifton Cates nearly resigned after World War I, but Barnett convinced him to remain, promoted him and made him an aide. Cates went on to a storied career, capped by serving as commandant (1948–1951). Future Commandant Thomas Holcolm (1936–43) served under Barnett in Newport and again in Peking. Similarly, Smedley Butler was Littleton W.T. Waller's protégé, and followed him when possible.

The circumstances surrounding the cancellation of the graduation ball were without parallel in USNA history. The 1882 law hit the Class of 1881 hard, but they were done with their studies. The classes still at Annapolis could see that years of work would go to waste for most of them. This led to a breakdown of discipline and a near mutiny. It reached a head during the 1883 graduation ceremony, when Superintendent Ramsay arrested the entire graduating class and had them marched to the *Santee* for imprisonment.

Suggested Reading

Millett, Allan Reed. *Semper Fidelis: The History of the United States Marine Corps*. New York: Macmillan, 1980.
Shulimson, Jack. "Military Professionalism: The Case of the U.S. Marine Officer Corps, 1880–1898." *Journal of Military History* 60, 2 (April 1996): 231–242.

Chapter VI

Sitka

In August, 1884, I received orders to join the USS *Pinta* and proceeded to Sitka, Alaska, to command the guard of Marines stationed in that place. On the way north, we anchored for a day or two in the harbor of Esquimalt, British Columbia, and had the pleasure of visiting Victoria, an attractive Canadian city nearby. We then proceeded on up the Inside Passage and arrived at Sitka, Alaska, in due time, where I relieved Lieutenant Howard Gilman. I moved into the same quarters that Gilman had occupied and made arrangements to take my meals at the hotel in Sitka.

I found the first task of my Alaskan service was to take charge of two thousand Indians of the Sitka tribe. I had never been associated with Indians before and they were a distinct novelty to me, but I was eagerly interested in them. My first night in Sitka, I was sitting in front of a fire, reading a book, Bulwer's *Strange Story*. Just as I reached the most interesting and blood curdling part, my dog was aroused from sleep and jumped up, barking furiously. Thinking it meant some commotion among the Indians, I jumped up also. But nothing happened and we both subsided. I admit I was frightened, though, for a moment or two. In fact I had been reading too long and was nervous.

Shooting has always been a favorite pastime of mine, and Alaska with its wonderful deer shooting was ideal for the indulgence of this desire. One of the Indian policemen, to whom I confided my wishes, advised me to wait until the first light fall of snow. One cold morning at 4 a.m. he called me. I dressed, drank some coffee, and off we started. For two miles we tramped up the Indian River, then started to climb Mount Verstovia, a mountain about three thousand feet high. It was very steep and hard climbing. When we had reached the plateau near the top of the mountain, I was very warm. There we found a small place, about two acres in extent, entirely free of trees, but surrounded by heavy firs. Just at the edge of this clear place, the Indian pre-

The USS *Pinta* was a former harbor tugboat converted for service in Alaska. Only 420 tons and 137 feet long, she persevered in Alaskan waters until 1897. The Marine detachment in Sitka was mustered as part of her crew, but she was often elsewhere. Here she is celebrating the Fourth of July, 1886 in Sitka (Alaska State Library, ASL-P91-66).

pared a place to sit down behind a log. I asked him why he did this. His reply was, "wait for deer." I was very warm, and the wind was blowing, so I feared I would catch cold if I joined him. I asked him when the deer would come and he answered, "Ne no save; if he no come today, he come tomorrow." I started out on my own hook, looking for deer tracks. Needless to say, the Indian got a deer, and I got none. It was my first deer hunt. Afterwards I was more successful and bagged many a wonderful specimen of this game.

The Indians and their welfare took up most of my time and interest. Naturally, being in charge of the Indians, I was invited to all of the Indian events. They were peaceful and provident, for Indians. The Indian town of Sitka contained about two thousand Indians in the winter time; in the summer it was almost deserted, except for the very old people and children. The rest of the Indians, male and female, spent the summer at different places, hunting and fishing, and securing the winter supply of fish and game which was dried for future use. They likewise saved large quantities of herring oil and seal oil for winter use, and dried a great many berries for the same purpose.

The Alaskan Indian tribes are made up of different families, presumably descended from different animals, such as the fox, mink, seal, boar, deer, etc.

The head of each family is called, the "father of the mink," the "father of the deer," etc. They always wore something distinctive, to show to which family they belonged.

The Indians lived in roughly made wooden houses of large size, with a raised platform, in the nature of a transom, built on three sides of the house, and a vacant place in the center for a fire, and a small hole in the roof. The entrance was a comparatively small opening at one end, which was generally covered with a mat or some kind of skin for keeping out the wind. The place on this platform was divided by matting or skins into what might be called small state rooms for the different members of the family. Dances took place in the vacant space in the center around the fire. When any big dance was scheduled, they always held it in the largest house of the tribe. A more detailed description of one of these dances may interest my readers.

Anahootz, chief of the Sitka Indians, was building a new house. The building of a house, especially for a chief, was a community affair, and all hands help with the task. As the chief's house was nearing completion, he sent invitations to the next nearest tribe of Indians, the "Killisnoos," ninety miles away, and invited the whole tribe to come to his house warming, called a "potlatch." This invitation was accepted, and one morning about eight

A group of potlatch dancers in Sitka, circa 1905, posing in front of Anahootz's house (editor's personal collection).

VI—Sitka

o'clock practically the whole tribe of Killisnoos, with the exception of the very aged and the young children, arrived off the Indian town Sitka, in their canoes. It was the Indian custom that when visiting another tribe, the visitors could only land at low tide, because it was the custom to have dances of welcome participated in by those of the tribe residing there on the beach, and return dances were given by the visitors as they landed. It was high tide and snowing hard and very cold, but they waited in their canoes until low tide, according to custom.

Meanwhile different heads of families on shore appeared at the water's edge from the different houses, dressed in costume and made long-winded speeches to the corresponding family out in the canoe. For instance, the "Father of the Minks," the oldest of the Sitka Indians at that time, made his speech, he being all dressed up in mink skins. He was answered by the father of the visiting "Minks." Then the old fellow on the beach scampered away towards his house, in a manner he thought was mink-like, thus indicating to the canoe minks that they were invited to his house. This continued all the time until the hour came for the dance of welcome on the beach.

They were all properly gotten up according to their custom, and the dance was most interesting, being a great deal like a theatrical performance with different acts. During the singing and dancing, the women formed the chorus and several older men beat on native drums. Finally the visitors landed and had their return dance, after which they proceeded to the houses where they were expected. The next day the regular celebration was to start in Anahootz's house. This consisted of different performances for three days, the first day being devoted entirely to speech making. The talking man of each family made his speech, which was answered by Anahootz's talking man. These speeches were long-winded and very flowery, according to Indian custom.

The next day was devoted to dancing. Different dancing men of each tribe presented a dance significant of some part of the Indian customs. In the course of these dances Anahootz's talking men made speeches to the visitors, and a great many new Indian blankets were torn into strips six to eight inches in width, and distributed to certain members of the tribe as souvenirs, the talking man announcing they were in memory of the ancestors of the recipients, and he entered into long-winded and flowery recitations in praise of those ancestors. When I attended these functions, I always got strips of the blankets because, it was stated, I was in charge of the Indians and represented the Great White Father in Washington. In the course of the winter, after many dances, most of the Indians had accumulated many strips of various hues. They were not wasted, but were sewed together into beautiful striped blankets of many colors.

The last day of the dance was given over to feasting. It was just one round after another of dried fish, dried berries soaked in oil, herring oil, and seal oil, and very often of hard tack and pork exchanged at the enlisted men's mess for venison, fish and game. The farewell dance was given in the largest house in town and it was literally packed with Indians. This dance had five or six acts, each act being a dance peculiar to some feature of Indian life, such as the Berry Dance, the Seal Dance, the Salmon Dance, etc. These dances were given in the hope that the supplies of the different commodities would be plentiful during the year. During this dance the Indians were in full regalia and gorgeously painted, and were more like one's ordinary idea of the Indians of the plains.

Once I had some friends with me who were passing through Sitka and could only stay for a day. When one of the young ladies saw an Indian in full war paint and feathers, she became frightened and fainted. It was hard to get her out into an open space, because the Indians cared nothing for women as women, and it required some hard-boiled Marine language to make a passageway for our little group, especially as we had the seat of honor at the end of the house farthest from the entrance.

I attended another Indian dance which was most unusual. The Indians believe that when a man is drowned, his spirit goes into the body of the animal from which he is supposed to have descended. An Indian of the seal family was drowned one day and his body was not recovered. The occasion was seized upon for a ceremonial dance. It took place in the largest house of the seal family, and the head man of the family, dressed as a seal, was the star performer. With him were other young men similarly dressed, who were the principal actors. They started their dance, the women in the meantime chanting wild songs of some kind. At stated intervals, the singing and the beating of the drum suddenly stopped, and the dancing party put their hands to their ears and listened. At that instant, we would hear a peculiar sound similar to that made by a seal. Then the Indians would start the song over again, and using Indian canoe paddles which they held in their hands, would go through the motion of paddling, and at the same time moving a few steps towards the place from whence this sound had come. This was repeated many times, until they got near the edge of the platform round the side of the house, where they tore off one of the boards, and from the inside they pulled out an Indian dressed entirely as a seal. This was supposed to represent as nearly as they could get it, the recovery of the body of the man who had been drowned. The dance from that point on was one of rejoicing rather than of lamentation.

I found much that appealed to me in the simple symbolism used by

VI—Sitka

these primitive people of the far north to express their joys and sorrows, and the important happenings of their lives. Their evident sincerity made their crude attempts at drama as exemplified by the dances, very interesting and convincing. In their native state they lived in a most primitive fashion. But the status of the individual families was well defined by their customs and traditions and they had a certain pride of descent that made for character.

An important feature of Indian life is their manner of conducting funerals. During illness the doctors attempt cures only by charms. The Indian doctor has quite an outfit of headdresses, masks, rattles, etc., to be worn during the incantations supposed to relieve the patient. In the presence of the sick person, he goes through a regular performance, often working himself into quite a frenzy. It was not uncommon for an Indian doctor, recognizing the fact that the patient was not going to get well, to accuse somebody of having bewitched the patient. Until this custom was broken up, they would take the one accused of witchcraft and torture him or her into a confession. The one accused often confesses that the food of the patient has been tampered with. Then they took the self confessed witch out, tied him or her to a stake and left the poor wretch to die. The Indian doctor is selected in youth, usually because of physical peculiarity, such as being hunchback or possessed of a bad eye, called the evil eye. From the time he is selected, he is coached by older Indian doctors in all the arts and tricks of the profession. From that time on, his hair is never cut, and from what I saw, never cleaned in any way, so that later in life the doctors appear with long matted hair, filthy beyond imagination.

When an Indian, other than a doctor, dies, he is cremated, but an Indian doctor is wrapped in matting and placed in what is called a dead house, which is a small structure placed on stilts about three or four feet high and tightly closed. In this house, with the corpse, is placed all of his paraphernalia, and even his canoe, most valued possession of an Indian, is hauled up and placed beside the dead house. Its future use is forbidden. If he possesses a Chilcat blanket, which is the most valued blanket known to the northern Indians, this blanket is fastened to the outside of the dead house, and stays there until it rots—unless some curio seeker gets it.

Now as to the patient. When a patient dies, he or she is wrapped in a blanket and dressed in full Indian costume and placed against the wall at one end of the house in a sitting position. There the corpse is left for two or three days in state, during which time many dances take place. A corpse is never taken out through a door, always through a window, if there is one; if not, through a hole made in the side of the house. It is considered bad luck to take a corpse through a door. When the corpse is passed out through the opening in the side, the body bearers take it on the outside, and immediately afterwards, the Indians inside take some live coals from the fire in the center of the room and throw them out through the opening, in order that the departed one may have warmth ever after. Then the Indian's hunting dog is thrown out through the same opening to accompany his former master to the happy hunting grounds.

Prior to all this, a funeral pyre has been built, back of the house. This pyre consists of dry wood, about the size of cord wood, built up about three feet above the ground, with a vacant space in the center, in which the corpse is placed. Then dry wood is put over the top, and over all this is poured oil of some kind. Standing by are two men, who, with long poles in their hands, are to act as stirrers, their function being to keep the fire going and stirred up until the body is completely consumed. After the body has been consumed, a few of the ashes are collected and put in an Indian box, which is closed up and placed in the family dead house. A dead house is a small wooden structure built to receive the ashes of different members of a certain family. If the Indian who died was a married man, his wife is taken by the female members of the family into a small house built of branches and placed about fifty or sixty yards from the funeral pyre where she is washed by Indian women, her clothes changed, hair combed, etc., after which she is considered ready for remarriage. During the time the cremation is going on, mourners of the family stand in a circle about twenty yards from the fire, beating the ground with long poles and chanting the funeral dirge. Very often hired mourners are employed.

Indian doctors' dead houses are generally placed on stilts on a promontory or on an island nearby, and all over southeastern Alaska one comes upon these dead houses. Most of the Indian curios in the different museums of this country came from these dead houses of the doctors. It may be indelicate to take curios from dead houses, but unless this had been done, such collections as we now have in museums would not be in existence.

A prominent Indian doctor of Sitka died while I was there. The usual custom was carried out, and a very fine specimen of Chilcat blanket was fastened on the outside of the dead house. I decided that it would be a shame to let that blanket stay there until it rotted. One very stormy night I went down through the Indian town, saw no one outside, went to the dead house, got the Indian blanket, and by a circuitous route back over the hills, returned home with the blanket. It came near being a serious affair, for while crossing a stream on a log, I slipped and fell into the stream. I fortunately got out none the worse, except that I was very cold. I put this blanket away in a secluded room and the next morning about daylight, nearly all the head men of the Indian village appeared and reported to me that this blanket had been taken. A thorough search was made but the blanket never found. A short time before I left Sitka, I packed that blanket and another I had bought, with my effects to bring home with me. Retribution caught up with me, because on the steamer between Sitka and Seattle, my box of curios was opened, and when my freight arrived in Washington, these two blankets were missing.

A lieutenant, George Emmons, on a ship attached to the Alaska station was a great collector of Indian curios, and the articles he collected form the principal part of the Indian collection in the Metropolitan Museum in New York. I went with him on many expeditions for Indian curios, and we were generally very successful.

One summer a party of explorers, headed by Lieutenant Frederick Schwatka of the army, and Professor William Libby of Princeton University, arrived at Sitka with orders from the Department for the *Pinta* to take them to Yakutat, at the base of Mt. St. Elias, from which point they were to attempt the ascent of the mountain. As we entered the harbor, we passed a fine specimen of an Indian doctor's dead house. Professor Libby, knowing that Emmons and I were collectors, remarked to us that no doubt we wished we were going to stay there, so that we would have a chance to see what was inside of this dead house. The next day was rainy and windy, so the commanding officer told Professor Libby and Lieutenant Schwatka that it would be impracticable to land the party that day. Emmons and I announced at breakfast time that we were going to lower our canoe over the side and go duck shooting. Everybody laughed at us for being so foolish as to go out in such weather, but we finally started in our canoe. After getting out of sight of the ship, we came in a roundabout way to the dead house where we made a wonderful haul. We got a canoe load of headdresses, masks, rattles and different implements. We loaded them into our canoe and started back to our ship. I was in the bow and my friend was in the stern, steering. I remarked that I did not think it wise to steer too close to the ship and get under the overhang, because it was rough and we might be swamped. He said that he would attend to that, but unfortunately he did not. He steered a little too close to the ship and we got under the overhang. Just as we got under the ash chute, someone from the engine room poured down a whole bucket of ashes, which struck us amidships and upset the canoe, and there we were in the water with our collection floating around. The only one who saw us was the Quartermaster. He lowered a rope and we collected our articles and got them on board where we secreted them. We landed our exploring party the next day and returned to Sitka. Six weeks later we went back for the party. Professor Libby, during his exploration, had visited the rifled dead house. He told us that he understood what our duck shooting trip had been, for he said he found nothing when he visited the dead house.

During my stay in Alaska, nearly all the officers and men were interested in prospecting for either gold or coal; in fact, we spent most of our spare time in this occupation, but without any adequate financial returns. Two of us, while on a hunting trip one day, located a vein of coal about fifteen miles back of Killisnoo. Although we got about twenty-five tons of fairly good coal from this vein, and located our claim, it never amounted to anything because we had no money for development work.

Killisnoo is the center of the herring oil industry, and in a lagoon back of this place, all winter long, they drag a seine, and get from six to eight hundred barrels of herring at a time. These herring are scooped out of the scows with an ordinary steam scoop and loaded onto lighters and taken to the factory, where the fish are steamed and the oil pressed out, after which the refuse is made into fertilizer.

The Indians are very fond of the fresh herring oil as an article of diet. I am sure that no one can picture what a run of herring is like unless one has been seen. I have seen what appeared to be a black river running for miles through a lagoon or harbor where the herring were so thick that it looked almost impossible to run a boat through them. The Indians catch thousands of them by running their canoes among the fish and then dragging through the water a pole with sharpened spikes along one side. They get at least one on each spike at each haul.

One time I found it necessary to go on official business from Sitka to Juneau, a distance of a hundred and eighty miles. I had a large Indian canoe and four Indians as a crew. We paddled ordinarily, and sailed whenever possible. It was cold weather and when I got in sight of Douglas Island, comparatively near Juneau, it was snowing very hard. Thinking that I could save a great deal of distance and time by going through the passage to the west of the island, and in that way reach Juneau without going around the island, I started through it, but the tide was running out too rapidly for us. The canoe grounded about half way through, and there we had to stay until the next tide, so instead of reaching Juneau about five o'clock as I had expected, it was midnight before I got there. I was cold and cramped from being in the canoe so long, so I made for the only light I saw, and found that it was a saloon. Fortunately in the center of the room was a big stove, red hot. I received permission to spend the night there, and I spread bear skins and blankets down beside the stove and spent a very comfortable night.

Another time, I had to make the trip from Sitka to Juneau, taking with me a Marine who had accidentally discharged his rifle and nearly shot off his middle finger. There was no doctor in Sitka at that time, so I had to put a tourniquet on this man's wrist to stop the flow of blood. It was necessary to do more, so I got out the surgical instruments I had at the post, and took off his finger, tied up the arteries, used disinfectant, and sewed up the wound. I dressed the wound twice a day for about a week and at that time thought it was not doing well, so decided to take the man to the nearest doctor, who was at Juneau. It was mid-winter and we had nothing but an old-fashioned navy steam launch with no condenser, so she had to be watered about every three hours. I picked a Marine crew but none of them knew anything about running a launch, so I had to act as engineer and pilot, using the chart that I had.

We had to cross about fifteen miles of open water in Chatham Straits where it was very rough. Three times we tried to cross this strait but the launch rolled so that it rolled all the water out of the tanks. Water we would get only by carrying it from some distance up small streams down to the launch. We evidently picked up some sand with the water, because one time we got about halfway across Chatham Straits when we found that the feed pump would not work, so I had to take it apart. We had to haul the fire, and there we rolled about while I was taking the feed pump apart. It was filled with sand. I cleaned it, and we restarted the fire and finally went ahead. During this time, the rolling of the launch made me very seasick, and it was in all a very uncomfortable trip. Finally we reached Killisnoo, and I found that as practically all the rest of the trip was in Chatham Straits, I would be unable to make it in the launch, so I hired a tug from the herring oil factory there, and we finally arrived at Juneau, where I put my wounded man in the hands of a doctor, and I returned to Sitka in the tug.

About six weeks later the wounded Marine returned to duty at Sitka all right, but minus a finger. He repaid labor and kindness to him by stealing five hundred dollars from me, which I had in my room, and deserted on the next steamer to Seattle. There was no telegraph in those days in Alaska, so he had two months start and never was caught.

During my whole stay in Alaska, I had the most wonderful fishing and shooting that anybody in the world could have. There were all kinds of salt water fish besides the marvelous trout in the numerous streams all over the country. At proper seasons, we succeeded in getting plenty of deer, grouse, ducks and ptarmigan. During this whole tour of duty I lived out of doors more than I ever have before or since. I enjoyed it all, and I think it did me a world of good physically, and stood me in good stead all of my life. Besides, it being my first real duty in the Marine Corps, I considered it a very valuable experience, because I was independent and had to work out my own problems.

I, of necessity, had to learn the Indian language sufficiently to get along with them. I made regulations for the government of the Indian village, made the Indians clean up their houses and whitewash them, clean up their streets, dig sewers, and in fact, required them to do a great deal in the way of sanitation, which was new to them. I held court every morning, decided all kinds of controversies between Indians, and would sentence them for everything except murder. In case of murder, I had to send the accused to the district court of Oregon. I only had one such case during my tour of duty there.

I had a jail in which Indians sentenced to confinement served out their sentences. The ordinary punishment was either a fine of so many blankets (Indian wealth being arrived at by the number of new blankets he had stored away in his house), or I would sentence them to confinement, during which time they had to have their hair cut and, in addition, had to cut wood. To an Indian doctor, the loss of his hair made him ridiculous to all other Indians, because his power as a doctor was gone, and while he was cutting wood, all the little boys would make fun of him and point fingers of scorn at him, and in this way the practice of doctors in connection with witchcraft was entirely done away with.

During my time in Alaska, civil government was established there, the first Governor being ex–Governor John Henry Kinkead of Nevada, with whom came the United States Marshall, the United States District Judge, the United States District Attorney, the Clerk of the Court, etc. All civil affairs were turned over to these officials. They added very materially to the small social life in Sitka. The District Attorney's family was particularly attractive people. He was Mottrom D. Ball of Virginia. They were direct descendants of the Washington-Ball-Lewis families. Mrs. Ball was a Miss Sallie Lewis Wright. Mr. Ball was a very highly cultivated man, and his wife and two daughters, Sallie Lewis and Caroline Linton Ball, were as charming as could be found any place in the world, and they did more than any other people in Sitka for the social life of that place. We depended entirely upon ourselves for our amusement, and among the pleasantest memories of my life is my association with these people,

Besides the Balls, there were Mr. Orris Baker and his family, Captain Byron K. Cowles and his family, and Doctor Zina and Mrs. Lura Pitcher, he being the Marine Hospital surgeon. With reference to the Pitchers, Mrs. Pitcher was a very beautiful young woman and came there as a bride from Michigan, as I remember it; and in this connection, a very strange thing happened only recently. I had not seen nor heard of the Pitchers since that time until the winter of 1918. A young lieutenant in the Marine Corps, Gwendell B. Newman, a Marine aviator, was killed from a fall in his plane near Wash-

Barnett and friends in front of the Marshall's office in Sitka, 1885, shortly after Barnett's arrival. From left: Mrs. B.K. Cowles, Laura Cowles, Kittie Baker, Lt. George Barnett (#6), Mrs. Vanderbilt, Dr. Martin, Tallis Ball, John Vanderbilt, Marshall Atkins (Alaska State Library ASL-P277-018-096).

ington. My family were very fond of young Newman, and learning that his only relative was a very old grandmother, Delia Barden, who lived in Michigan, and that she was coming on for the funeral, we decided to have the funeral from my house and I telegraphed his grandmother to come and stay with us during the time she was in Washington.

After the funeral, this old lady, who was eighty-five, just by chance remarked to me; "General, by any chance are you the same Mr. Barnett who was in Sitka about thirty-five years ago?" I told her that I was, and she said, "Then you knew my daughter, Mrs. Pitcher." I told her that I remembered Mrs. Pitcher with a great deal of pleasure. I learned that Dr. Pitcher had died and that Mrs. Pitcher had married Lewis Newman, the father of the young man who had been buried from my house that day. By a strange coincidence, I made arrangements for the funeral of Captain Cowles, who died during a temporary stay in Washington, and a little later Mrs. Lucy Cowles, his wife, died in Wisconsin and was brought on here by her daughter, and his funeral was likewise held from my house. Mr. Ball died years ago, but his family now reside in McLean, Virginia, and sometimes I see them, and always with a great deal of pleasure, remembering as I do, their unfailing kindness to me when I was a youngster in Sitka. Mrs. Ball died in 1923.

After three very pleasant years of duty in Alaska, I was ordered back to the United States proper, in June, 1888, and after a month's leave at my home in Wisconsin, I reported for duty at the Marine Barracks, Washington Navy Yard. Nothing of particular interest happened during this time of duty in Washington, my time being divided between the Marine Barracks at the Navy Yard, and the Marine Barracks, Washington, D.C.

Editor's Comments on Chapter Six

After a couple of brief training stops, Barnett was ordered to Sitka, the capital of the District of Alaska. Alaska had been purchased from Russia in 1867 and the army (1867–1877), Treasury (1877–1879) and navy (1879–1884) successively had jurisdiction. None of them proved adequate to the task. The Organic Act of 1884 established a small civil government of federal appointees.

This nascent government relied on the military to maintain law and order. As a result, Barnett possessed a modicum of power as commander of the only land force in the district. He could, and did, order jail terms and punishments for Natives. By his account, he was an honored guest of a friendly tribe, with local chief Annahootz serving as the head of a loyal Native police force. His classmates were envious, as most were assigned to antiquated ships where they had little status or scope. In the official crew listings of the day, Marine officers came after the surgeon, paymaster and chaplain, but ahead of the boatswain and carpenter.

Nevertheless, he remained a very junior officer at a very remote post. He had only twenty-five men under his command and was backed by the small and often absent USS *Pinta*. Many whites felt that only force, or the threat of force, kept the Natives in check. As the new governor noted "in the spring of 1879 ... a considerable portion of the natives at Sitka armed and organized themselves and attempted to march upon the white settlement with the avowed intent of massacre and plunder. They were prevented by the timely interference of Annahootz and his Kokwanton supporters." In addition, Governor Kinkead was at war with the Christian missionaries in Sitka, actively opposing their efforts. Though Barnett certainly enjoyed the posting and the independence it afforded him, it was not a plum assignment.

Frederick Schwatka was a noted explorer. In 1879 he led an expedition to Hudson Bay and in 1883 travelled the length of the Yukon River. Schwatka's lectures and books made him a celebrity. In 1886, the New York Times funded an unsuccessful attempt to ascend Mt. St. Elias, then considered the highest peak in North America, that included Schwatka, Professor William Libby and British explorer Haywood W. Seton-Karr. Seton-Karr left an account of the expedition titled *Shores and Alps of Alaska*.

Lieutenant George Thorton Emmons (USNA 1874) was assigned to the *Adams* and then the *Pinta*, where he spent the 1880s and 1890s studying Native culture in Alaska. Emmons was unusual in that he tried to establish friendly and equal relations with tribal leaders, usually buying or trading for artifacts. He sold massive and well documented collections to the American Museum of Natural History and other institutions, totaling about 11,000 objects. His work was not appreciated by most of his fellow officers, nor by his family. His first marriage ended after his wife's adultery while he was in Alaska. He then married Kitty (Katherine) Baker, daughter of Sitka hotelkeeper Orris Baker. After retiring due to ill health in 1899, Emmons published many scholarly articles, though his major work, *The Tlingit Indians,* was completed long after his death by Frederica De Laguna.

Emmons' influence on Barnett is evident. Barnett's views on shamans and zeal for Native artifacts mirrored that of the older officer. His descriptions of Tlingit customs was informed by Emmons' more detailed observations. Throughout his career, Barnett would display a lively interest in local customs, whether in Samoa, Japan or China. He was always ready for new experiences and approached local cultures with few judgments. Readers will note a lack of military detail in the narrative, but an abundance of amateur ethnography.

Suggested Reading

Emmons, G. T, Frederica De Laguna, and the American Museum of Natural History. *The Tlingit Indians*. Vancouver: Douglas & McIntyre, 1991.

Jackson, Sheldon. *A Statement of Facts Concerning the Difficulties at Sitka, Alaska, in 1885*. N.p.: n.p., 1886.

Seton-Karr, Heywood Walter, and John Bremner. *Shores and Alps of Alaska*. London: S. Law, Marston, Searle, & Rivington, 1887.

Chapter VII

Aboard the USS *Iroquois*

In the summer of 1889, I was again ordered to the west coast to command the Marine Guard of the USS *Iroquois*, which was being fitted out at the Mare Island Navy Yard. I reported there in May, but the *Iroquois* did not go into commission until September.

On the overland train from Chicago to San Francisco several officers going to the *Iroquois* were in the same car. There was a young staff officer who had just been appointed and so knew nothing of the service. We put up a job on him by asking him if he had telegraphed to the commandant of the Mare Island Navy Yard that he was en route. Of course he said he had not. We told him he must telegraph each morning, which he did. The commandant was Commodore John H. Russell, and when we all reported to him, he jumped the young officer and said he did not care where he was each morning. This officer later in life became the head of his Corps.

Early in September we sailed from San Francisco for Honolulu, and enjoyed our stay there very much indeed, although it was too short. We then sailed for Samoa, touching en route at the Marshall and Gilbert Islands. We arrived in the harbor of Jaluit in the Marshall Islands, a typical atoll, which is simply a projecting coral reef with a low land around, and the inside comparatively deep water, with a very narrow entrance through the coral reef. We only spent a few days in Jaluit, and then sailed for Butaritari, Gilbert Islands.

We dropped anchor quite a distance off the town; even our ship's boats could not get to the beach. We either had to land in canoes or be carried ashore by the natives. The only white person on the island was the wife of the American Consular Agent, Mrs. Adolph Rick, her husband being away on a cruise to San Francisco and back, for trading purposes.

One of the first days we were there the captain and five or six officers, myself being one of them, went ashore to call on the King of Butaritari, made

VII—Aboard the USS Iroquois

The sloop of war USS *Iroquois* weathering a storm off Japan. She was commissioned in 1859 and was of little value as a warship by the time Barnett served on her. That such an unseaworthy and antiquated ship was sent to Samoa in a crisis was a matter of some comment (from Henry E. Rhoades, *Around the World with the Blue Jackets, Or, How We Displayed the American Flag in Foreign Waters*).

famous by having been visited a short time before and mentioned by Robert Louis Stevenson in his writings. Our boats grounded some distance out, and we were carried ashore by the natives, each one fearing all the time that the native would stumble and drop him into the water. After we landed, we were joined by the wife of the Consular Agent and proceeded up through the only street in the town, which consisted of nothing but grass huts, to the King's residence, which was of simple construction and had a veranda about four feet high and four feet wide all around it. We were received in a large central room and all the natives collected on the veranda outside. During our visit, all of a sudden a crash was heard, and investigation disclosed that the whole veranda had fallen under the weight of so many natives. At the entrance to the king's grounds, we passed by a so-called soldier on each side of the gate, his uniform being simply a pair of ordinary white cotton trousers made of flour sacking, with a red stripe down the side; no other clothing. Each one presented arms with a wooden gun in one hand and saluted with the other hand.

The day after this, the King came off to return the call. He came in his state canoe, accompanied by about forty or fifty other canoes filled with natives. It appeared that the King, who was an enormous man, was rather well-to-do for a South Sea Island King, and during the visit of Robert Louis Stevenson, he told the King that he ought to have a kingly uniform, so the king was roughly measured and an order was sent to Litchfield & Company of San Francisco to make the King's uniform. The uniform was a typical Knight's Templar one, even including the chapeau, white feather and sword. This was the uniform he wore when he came off to the ship to return the captain's call. He seemed to be most unhappy in his uniform, because ordinarily he wore practically nothing and never wore shoes. His shoes were the largest I ever saw, and seemed to make him very unhappy. As he came over the side, just as he stepped on the deck, the salute of twenty-one guns was fired. This startled the king so much that we for the first time discovered that a very important part of his uniform had been neglected, as they had not furnished him with suspenders. He was so startled by the noise of the guns that his trousers dropped down around his ankles, much to the amusement of everybody. This was soon corrected by one of the midshipmen going below and getting him a pair of suspenders. A more ridiculous sight was never seen. The midshipman took off the King's coat, pulled up his trousers and put on the suspenders and replaced his coat. During all this time the salute was going on and I, with the Marine Guard, was presenting arms to His Majesty. Needless to say, everybody laughed.

The natives all came on board, and among other things, brought as a present a great big pig, which was sent forward to the forecastle. During the call the natives were provided with luncheon on the deck, much to their enjoyment. Before partaking of this, however, a blessing was asked, showing the influence of the missionaries in that far-off country. After the call was over, the natives went over the side and got in their canoes, and at last the King departed. Just as he shoved off from the ship's side, another salute of twenty-one guns was fired, and as the first gun was discharged from the forecastle where the pig was placed, he became frightened and jumped overboard, and before he could be rescued, drowned. I never saw Mr. Stevenson laugh more heartily than he did during a ride later on when I told him of the King's visit to our ship.

We finished our stay in Butaritari and started for Samoa, and were about thirty-five hundred miles southwest of Honolulu, in the strength of the southeast trade winds, when the piston rods of our engine broke completely off, and we were disabled so far as engine power was concerned, and started to sail back for Honolulu. The ship had to drag her propeller, and while we made good speed through the water, we made very little to windward.

One time during this famous trip we were comparatively near to Hong Kong, China, at another time near Yokohama, Japan, and another time within five hundred miles of Sitka, Alaska. We had started out from Honolulu expecting to arrive at Samoa within thirty-five days at the most, having left Honolulu on the eighth day of November. After we broke down, we sailed a little over twelve thousand miles, at one time as far as fifty degrees north latitude, where the weather was extremely cold, which caused considerable suffering by all, and we had the worst weather I ever saw at sea. Our provisions got very short, and we had to cut down to half rations and water allowance. We could not use coal for heating the ship, as we had to use what we had for distilling water. We were driven hither and thither and the whole time from the eighth of November until the eleventh of April, we never sighted a ship or a light. We finally cut down to quarter rations and a quart of water a day for all purposes. Finally, on the morning of the eleventh of April, we sighted land off the Straits of Juan de Fuca at the very northwest corner of the United States. A tug came off to our assistance and our captain asked the master what he would charge to tow us in to Port Townsend, Washington. He said, five hundred dollars. This seemed exorbitant, but the captain did not dare to refuse for fear that we might be driven off the coast again. There was a very light breeze at this time, and we had full sail set. The captain asked the tug master whether we had better keep our sails set and the tug master replied to keep them set, as the wind might help as we got into the straits. The tug master said he could get us in by twelve o'clock that night with good luck. We started on our way and the tug at no time tautened the cable between our ship and the tug; in fact, the tug had to steam hard to keep out of our way, and we reached Port Townsend about five o'clock in the afternoon, and as many as possible of us went ashore to get dinner. We had started out expecting to be at sea at most only thirty-five days and had provisioned for that time. We had made our stores last the one hundred and fifty-three days at sea, so no wonder we were on short rations.

I remember that Dr. Lucien G. Heneberger, Lieutenant Sumner Paine, and myself, went ashore together. I do not believe anybody in the world ever enjoyed Delmonico's in New York more than we enjoyed the "Delmonico" we went to there. We decided to spend the night there after a very good dinner, during which we ate everything the menu afforded. We got a room with a big stove in it, and I think we kept it red hot all night. We sat around it smoking until late in the night, fully enjoying the warmth which we had not had for over three months.

We tried to persuade the captain to stay ashore, but he thought he had better go back to the ship. The ground was covered with deep snow and he had ordered his gig in for him by ten o'clock. Going down to the dock, he was preceded by a member of the boat's crew with a lantern, and on account of the reflection of the light of the lantern against the snow, the captain did not see that a few planks were missing from the dock, so he fell through into the ice cold water. He was rescued by the crew, but had a badly dislocated arm, which was set by Asst. Surgeon Charles F. Stokes, later surgeon general of the navy.

As soon as we landed in Port Townsend, I sent a telegram to my father and mother, notifying them of my arrival there. The telegram reached them in the middle of the night. They could not believe it possible that I was at Port Townsend, as they knew that our ship had started for Samoa, thousands of miles in quite the opposite direction, so they had the telegram repeated. We had been reported missing for three months, and had practically been given up as lost, especially in Honolulu, where several of the wives of the officers had been residing, and services were held in the churches there for us on several successive Sundays.

Editor's Comments on Chapter VII

During this time, Samoa was a flash point, where German, American and British interests collided and sabers were rattled. In March, 1889, German and American ships were on the verge of battle and faced off in the narrow Apia harbor despite signs of a coming storm. Edwin Hoyt depicts the resulting disaster in his *The typhoon that stopped a war*. The Apia cyclone wrecked three American and three German ships, killing fifty-one Americans and ninety-six Germans. Short of options, the navy dispatched the recently commissioned protected cruiser USS *Charleston* and the obsolete *Iroquois* to Samoa.

The *Iroquois* was a Civil War era steam sloop-of-war. The *Hawaiian Gazette* called her "battered and unseaworthy" and reported that she could steam at a stately four knots—if the winds and tide were right. The *Iroquois* required a major refitting before she could attempt the voyage from San Francisco to Samoa and even then bets were taken that she would not survive the trip. Newspapers wondered just what mission "The Old Hulk" could accomplish, as she was more of a threat to her crew than to the Germans or Samoans.

The *Iroquois*' twelve thousand mile journey after breaking down was emblematic of the sad state of the navy. Shortly after this harrowing experience, her engines were repaired and the *Iroquois* set off again to Samoa. She lost part of her rigging outside San Francisco and was compelled to return for further repairs. Before these could be completed, forty of her crew of one hundred and sixty-six deserted. All told, the *Iroquois* would spend two and a half years limping around the Pacific, always on the verge of disaster.

The Samoan crisis and the Apia Cyclone provide an unlikely footnote to

Marine Corps history. Barnett's classmate, the promising Francis Sutton, died valiantly trying to save the USS *Vandalia* during the storm. Naval cadet John Lejeune survived the wreck by clinging to the beached ship's rigging for hours, witnessing his shipmates being washed away to their deaths. He was so impressed with Sutton's actions that he insisted on a Marine commission.

Stevenson and his party visited Butaritari in the summer of 1889. The king mentioned was Nakaeia, described by Stevenson as "a fellow of huge physical strength, masterful, violent, with a certain barbaric thrift and some intelligence of men and business." Barnett depicts him in a amusing anecdote, while Stevenson produced a character study of a South Seas despot.

Suggested Reading

Gilmer, William W. "The Cruise of the U.S.S Iroquois, One Hundred and Ten Days from Honolulu to Puget Sound, Bound for Samoa." 1937. Personal papers of John H. Russell, Jr., Box 1, Folder 9.

Hoyt, Edwin Palmer. *The Typhoon That Stopped a War*. New York: D. McKay, 1968.

Stevenson, Robert Louis. *A Footnote to History*. New York: C. Scribner's Sons, 1892.

Stevenson, Robert Louis. *In the South Seas: Being an Account of Experiences and Observations in the Marquesas, Paumotus and Gilbert Islands in the Course of Two Cruises on the Yacht "Casco" (1888) and the Schooner "Equator" (1889)*. New York: C. Scribner's Sons, 1896.

CHAPTER VIII

Stevenson and Samoa

From Port Townsend we sailed for San Francisco, and arrived there in due time, where our ship underwent repairs preparatory to again starting for Honolulu and Samoa. We arrived at Honolulu and were soon ordered to sail for Samoa, to relieve the USS *Mohican*. She had been there since the big storm in Samoa, which wrecked so many ships and cost so many lives among the Americans and Germans stationed there.

We finally arrived at Pango Pango on the island of Tutuila, Samoa. This is a beautiful little harbor with high mountains all around. There we found the *Mohican*, which sailed for Honolulu soon after our arrival. The natives of Samoa are magnificent people physically, and very good-natured. About the first thing we heard in the morning, and the last in the evening, was laughter from the shore. The first time I went ashore I was an object of curiosity to all the natives. My predecessor, the Marine officer of the *Mohican*, Otway Berryman, knowing that I was on the *Iroquois*, had told the natives that I was a peculiar person as I had a wooden leg, and I think that every man, woman and child in Pango Pango had to see my leg and pinch it before they would believe that I did not have a wooden leg. They never had seen a wooden leg.

It was the custom in Samoa that when anybody landed from a ship, the first native girl he met would ask, "Will you be my friend?" Naturally, the only answer possible was in the affirmative. Many officers, not realizing the importance of this answer, would, in many instances, find themselves in embarrassing positions, because, when promising a native to be his or her friend, it meant to him or her that he is the one selected to bring from time to time, presents of native fruits, fish, baskets, tapa, etc.; in return for which he is to receive such articles as soap, candles, food, etc. as may be given him. Therefore, to promise more than one native to be his friend would cause jealousy among the natives and probably trouble.

I remember a certain very good looking native girl asked Dr. Heneberger if he would be her friend, and he told her he would. A short time afterwards, the native girl threw off the doctor and took the captain's Chinese cook for her friend, as she found that she could get more table delicacies from the captain's cook than the doctor could furnish her. We had great fun with the Doctor about being deserted in favor of the Chinese cook.

All day long, every day, in the harbor, natives swam all the way from the shore to the ship, and came on board whenever they were allowed, and when they were not allowed on board, canoes were always around the ship. These people being filled with curiosity, seemed to find great amusement in looking through the air ports, much to our annoyance, as the *Iroquois* was an old-fashioned ship and each officer had to take his bath in his own stateroom.

Barnett in 1890, about the time he was promoted to first lieutenant. Taken in San Francisco, probably while the *Iroquois* was being refitted for a second attempt at reaching Samoa (editor's personal collection).

We were in the habit of going in swimming in the harbor, until one day a twelve foot shark was caught from the stern of the ship. This ended the swimming from the ship, especially as one of the crew of the captain's gig had taken French leave the night before, attempting to swim ashore, and in the morning his body was found considerably lacerated by sharks. It was very hot and wet in Pango Pango; everything mildewed, the equal of which I have never seen any place in the world. Our awning soon mildewed so badly that it was like a sieve.

Shortly after we anchored in Pango Pango, a canoe came off with a message that they were very anxious to have a doctor come to see a native who had been injured three weeks before. I went with the doctor and we found that the native had been shot through the knee, the wound had been neglected and exposed to flies, which were very numerous there, until his whole leg from his hip to his ankle was a bag of pus. I had been in the habit of assisting the doctor from time to time, and I attempted to do so in this case, but the stench was such that I soon fell over and the doctor had to give me a dose of brandy to bring me around. The wound was attended to, drain tubes put in, and in about six weeks time this man was on rapid road to recovery; although his knee was stiff, the visit of the doctor saved his leg from amputation and probably his life.

The native dance is known as Siva which is more like a performance of gymnastics than anything else. The people taking part in these dances either sit or stand on the ground, three on each side, with a girl in the center, and go through all sorts of movements with their arms and bodies, all the time singing a native song, following the girl in the center, who is the leader, and generally the leader is a very graceful and attractive girl from the native's point of view. Frequently we went ashore to witness these dances at night. The only thing they asked of us was that we bring plenty of candles, because they had nothing but oil dips in the way of lights, and it was a strange sight to see a row of footlights, made of candles, and the officers and natives sitting around in front of them, the natives simply wearing a breechcloth or short grass skirt, and the girls in addition to the grass skirt wore flowers and beads around their necks, wrists and ankles.

The mail steamer plying between Honolulu and Australia did not then stop at Samoa, but passed comparatively near the town of Apia, seventy miles distant from Pango Pango. So, once a month we used to get under way and go out to meet the mail steamer. If the weather was good we got our mail, and sometimes a small piece of ice from the purser, which was the only ice we had during our stay in Samoa. Whenever we went out to meet the mail steamer, we continued on and spent a few days in Apia.

Our first visit to Apia was particularly interesting because of the fact that we saw, for the first time, the wreck of the American and German ships caused by a great cyclone the year before. Some of these ships were upon the reef on their sides, and others were underneath the reef.

Shortly after we anchored for the first time in Apia [in August 1891], we were invited ashore to dinner by the German Consul. It did not seem the custom to introduce people, so I found myself at dinner seated next to a man I did not know, but who was very interesting. I soon learned that this man was Robert Louis Stevenson. His conversation was very delightful and I enjoyed being with him very much indeed. I have always congratulated myself for having recognized his marvelous conversational powers before I knew who he was. In general conversation, his use of different words to express minute differences in meaning was most remarkable. When a less gifted person might and probably would have used the same word repeatedly, he invariably used a different word which would more accurately convey his thoughts.

The next day he came off and called on the officers, and the day following, the ward room calling committee, of which I was a member for that month, went ashore to return his call. After landing, we went on horseback several miles back into the country to his place, called "Vailima." Mrs. Stevenson, his wife, was visiting in New Zealand, but his mother, a charming old Scotch lady, was there and served tea very delightfully on the veranda. After tea she asked us if we would like to see "Louis." We said yes, and she told us to walk upstairs, the stairs being on the veranda and not in the house. When we got upstairs and tapped on the door, a voice said, "Come in." We opened the door and at the opposite side of the room he was sitting in the position made famous by the Saint-Gaudens bas relief. He was reclining on a couch and had his writing board before him. He looked up, and seeing three of us, remarked, "Oh, Lord, I can only stand one at a time." So one of us went in, and after a reasonable time, the others went in in turn. This room was entirely surrounded by book shelves, filled with books. It had windows about six feet above the floor. They were all closed and the door was closed, so it seemed very stuffy to us, but appeared to be entirely satisfactory to him.

Stevenson was certainly a charming conversationalist and the time passed only too quickly. He talked principally of Samoa and the people and gave us much valuable information about the country and the customs of the people. Naturally I brought up the subject of his books and thoroughly enjoyed hearing his personal views. I asked him which of his books he thought his best, and he unhesitatingly said *Treasure Island*. He also mentioned *The Master of Ballantrae* most favorably. He seemed very bitter against actors who, he said, had used *Dr. Jekyll and Mr. Hyde*, without even thinking of his permission, and ignoring his claims to royalties.

We enjoyed our call very much, during which he asked us if we were fond of riding. We told him we were, and after that every time we were in Apia harbor, we used to ride with him, often returning to dinner with the family.

It was a queer household, composed of Robert Louis, his step-daughter, Mrs. Strong, her husband, Mr. Joseph Strong, their son Austin Strong and Lloyd Osbourne. Mrs. Strong was Mrs. Stevenson's daughter by a former marriage, and Lloyd Osbourne was her brother. After this first call, we saw Mr. Stevenson and the others very often. We were all fond of riding as were those of the family, and almost every day we took long rides, very often accompanied by Mr. Stevenson. During these long rides we learned more and more about the country and the people whom he loved and who loved him. We

Stevenson's home as it appeared in 1891, when Barnett was a guest. Stevenson is leaning off the upper balcony with his wife and mother below. Vailima was later expanded (from H.J. Moors, *With Stevenson in Samoa* p.40).

very often rode home with him for tea and sometimes for dinner. I have always remembered my first dinner there. As we were served soup, Robert Louis said he hoped we would enjoy it as he had prepared it. And so throughout the dinner some member of the family would remark about the course being served. Anything like real servants were conspicuous by their absence, but the natives he had doing work about the place seemed more like the feudal retainers of olden times.

Numerous natives were around willing to do anything wished by Mr. Stevenson, because they idolized him. I have often thought since that I was an extremely foolish youth, as I should have jotted down every word uttered when we were with Mr. Stevenson in his house, and during our rides.

I never met Mr. Stevenson without being impressed by his restlessness. He never seemed able to remain in one place but a short time, and when talking he would alternately walk up and down, and sit down, all the time smoking cigarettes; so much so that his fingers were decidedly colored by them. Although we could not help seeing that Mr. Stevenson was an ill man, his cheery good nature and deep interest in life seemed to completely do away with all thoughts of illness, and I am sure that none of us who often rode with him gave much thought to his illness, simply because it seemed far from his thoughts as he talked of the beauty of the scenery and the fascinations of the people. He was an enthusiast, and the beauty of nature never failed to charm him.

VIII—Stevenson and Samoa

Mr. Harold Sewall of Bath, Maine, was American Consul General in Apia, and he, together with the British Consul General Thomas Cusack-Smith and his wife, did a very great deal to make our stay in Apia most delightful. We rode, as I said, almost every day. It was always very hot and often very wet so we came back from our rides thoroughly wet and dirty. About a mile back of the town of Apia was a wonderful swimming pool. This pool was fed by a mountain stream fresh and delightful. It was our custom to keep an extra suit of clothing in a native hut near the pool. We would ride our horses into the pool, and wash our clothes, come out, ring out our clothes and hang them up to dry, and put on our fresh clothes, being thoroughly refreshed after the exercise and the swim. The pool was about eight feet deep, very clear and delightful. We soon noticed a queer custom of the natives, who were working on a road not far from the pool. Across on the opposite side of the pool was a gravel bed where the natives would fill baskets with this gravel, walk down to the edge of the water with a heavy basket in each hand, and walk across on the bottom of the pool and come out on the other side; all this as a matter of course, and it did not seem to them they were doing anything at all out of the ordinary.

During our stay in Apia, King Malietoa Laupepa gave a celebration which was attended by the natives of all the different islands and tribes. This celebration was in the nature of a pound party, in that everyone who came brought some kind of present to the King.

The King and his guests were assembled at one end of a large grass covered field under a matting roof and the natives arrived, appearing out of the woods, on the opposite end of this field and coming across it preceded by dancing girls. These girls were fantastically dressed in short grass skirts and flowers, and performed attractive native dances as they came, until they reached the presence of the King, when special dances were given. Then the talking man of each tribe made a speech to the King to which the King's talking man replied. After them came gift bearers from each tribe or family with offerings of eggs, chickens, fish, pigs, and fruits. This kept up until an enormous quantity of gifts were received. The speeches concluded, we sat down to luncheon under a matting roof with ferns spread about. There were thirty-six of us, white men and natives. Native girls served the meal. "Cava" was passed about in cocoanut shells, as the drink of the feast. It was made by grinding up cava root, soaking it in water and then draining off the liquid. It was not intoxicating, or at least only slightly so, and left a very clean, fresh taste, particularly good where drinking water was habitually so warm. The food was wonderful, the chief dishes being of fish and birds, wrapped in tea leaves, and cooked in hot coals and ashes, thus preserving the juices of the meat. The tea leaves were not of the tea plant as we know it, but of a native plant, the leaves being large and thick.

One native passed around a basket out of which the King took something and ate it with relish. The captain of the ship declined the dish when it was offered to him, as did every other white man present, but the natives ate from it with keen enjoyment. When it was brought to me, a wave of nausea passed over me when I saw the dish contained big fat wood worms, yellow and brown striped. They were alive and—well, no more, for even the memory is upsetting, and I nearly lost my delicious meal.

The King's headmen divided the gifts between the guests after the meal. I received a couple of chickens, a few eggs, several pieces of taro (a root like a sweet potato) and a small pig. We took our gifts back to our boat and made an odd procession as we proceeded on our way, the King's minions acting as burden bearers.

At this feast we met Tupua Tamasese Titimaea, the Chief of Apia, and his wife, whose valuable services to the survivors of the ships wrecked in the great storm had been rewarded by the gift from our government of a fine whaleboat. Tamasese and his wife were always honored guests on our ship. They came out in their whale boat. On their return to the beach he would not permit the boat to touch the ground, but always had a gang of natives to carry it on their shoulders to his house. Officers of visiting American warships in port made it their business to see that the boat was kept in splendid condition, painted and polished by the crews. Often we visited the old fellow's house where he served fruits and cava lavishly and had fresh mats prepared on which we could lie down and take naps in the heat of the day, while the native girls fanned away the flies.

Fanua, his daughter, at that time was what was called "the maid of the village"; that is, she was the most prominent and best looking girl in the town. She had many girl friends and they played casino with the young officers. However, they cheated outrageously, telling each other in their native tongue what cards they had.

An old American pilot, Elisha Hamilton by name, resident there for many years, had married a native woman and had native children by her. We often visited them, where we were always welcome.

Whenever we visited Apia, we purchased presents for our friends in Pango Pango. A German trader had a consignment of gaudily trimmed girl's straw hats and black lace parasols and I purchased one of each to take to my friend in Pango Pango. The other officers were so well pleased with my selections that they got the same selection next time they went ashore. The next Sunday when the girls of Pango Pango dressed up for church, they presented a laughable spectacle. They wore small grass skirts with flowers about their necks, wrists, and ankles, and each one had on her straw hat and carried her parasol. But they were the happiest girls in the world.

I have always been fond of fishing and when I arrived in Samoa in September one of my first questions was as to the prospect of finding good fishing. A native who spoke a little English told me that I should wait until the palolo came. I asked when that would be and he said it would be the morning after the full moon in October and November; that if there should be a good catch in October, there would be few in November, and if few in October, many in November. He said, however, it would be only early in the morning. I replied that I would be ready if it was in the middle of the night.

About three a.m. one October day, the orderly called me and said a crazy native was alongside in a canoe and said I was going fishing with him. I said that was correct, so I got up, dressed, secured a glass of milk and some bread, and went on deck. It was dark, so I took a lantern and looked for the fishing tackle. I saw nothing but two long-handled dip nets made of fine mesh mosquito netting. I did not want to appear too green, so I said nothing but took my place in the canoe and took a paddle as we shoved off. We paddled out through the entrance to the harbor which took quite a time. Outside we headed east and paddled for about an hour; then we saw a great many boats and canoes filled with natives. We paddled in among them and not a word was said by anyone in the boats. It was still quite dark. After a while there was just a faint show of light to the east, and I then noticed that all of the people looked over the sides of their boats. I did the same, but could see nothing. A little later just as the sun came above the sea horizon, they all began talking and laughing and grabbed dip nets similar to those in our canoe, and at the same time looked over the side again. This I did also, and I saw almost untold numbers of what looked like large angle worms coming up out of the coral reef. Some were red, some yellow and some green. The natives began dipping them up and dumping them into their canoes. I did the same and we soon had about half a canoe load. I saw a particularly large lot of them together and in reaching for them I upset our canoe and found myself in a sea of worms, which were crawling all over me, up my trouser legs, my sleeves, down the back of my neck, into ears, etc. In fact I was shedding worms from every hair. We tried to right our canoe but could not, so we swam to a large boat and climbed in, after which we were able to right the canoe and soon had another load. The natives ate these worms as they were, but took large quantities to the house to fry. Needless to say, I had enough of palolo fishing. I noticed that these worms broke into pieces as they rose to the surface and I learned that it was their breeding process. In about half an hour they went back into the coral reef from whence they came to remain for another year. I filled a glass jar with the palolo and sent them in alcohol to a museum in Honolulu.

We finally started back for Honolulu and arrived there without incident. It was particularly gay there because four American men of war and several English and Japanese ships were in the harbor. We greatly enjoyed several parties given by King Kalākaua. We also rode daily and attended many luaus. These are native feasts where native dishes are served and always poi. I tried poi once and never again as it reminded me of the way green wall paper paste should taste. The natives however, are very fond of it. It is very fattening. You eat it out of native wooden dishes by the primitive method of dipping one, two or three fingers in it, and then putting them in your mouth.

Horseback riding is one of the favorite sports in Honolulu, and everyone kept a horse and there were constant riding parties. One afternoon we rode down to Pearl Harbor to Dr. John S. McGrew's place for a moonlight supper and dance. We returned about three a.m. in the morning. This party I remember particularly because Dr. McGrew was a master in the art of mixing mint juleps. One of my fellow officers drank rather freely of them, and a friend of mine beckoned to me to go into the house and see a funny sight. I went in and in a window sat a very pretty girl and at her feet was the mint juleped officer making love in a very dramatic fashion, with about twenty people watching him and laughing. The joke was that the girl was a deaf mute and could not understand a word that he was saying.

Our stay in Honolulu lasted about a year and we were very loath to leave. I regard this as one of the most delightful times in my life. When we reached San Francisco, the ship went out of commission and I was ordered back to duty at the Washington Navy Yard in 1892.

Editor's Comments on Chapter VIII

Robert Louis Stevenson sailed through the southern Pacific in 1888–1889. Barnett comments on Stevenson's "queer household," which was an opinion shared by many. When the family arrived in Samoa in 1889, a missionary mistook the eccentric crew for a theatrical troupe. Stevenson bought land near Apia and planned an estate, living in a dirt floored shack or traveling while it was constructed. After Vailima was completed in 1891, Stevenson became an eager host. He was especially fond of the Anglo-Saxon navies and kept a list of all the warships that visited the harbor.

Barnett was a guest at one of the many dinner parties Stevenson gave for visiting ships' crews. Stevenson especially enjoyed riding, which provided another opening for Barnett to spend time with the author. No Stevenson family documents mention him by name, though Mrs. Stevenson's letters note both the dinner he mentions and the visit by the crew of the *Iroquois* in August 1891. While riding, building, writing and entertaining, Stevenson found time to be involved in island politics, opposing the Germans and their proxies. He died of a stroke in 1894 at age 44.

Beyond surviving after being given up for dead and meeting the most popular author of the day, Barnett had another reason to celebrate. He was promoted to first lieutenant on September 1, 1890, after a mere seven years.

Suggested Reading

Fraser, Marie. *In Stevenson's Samoa*. London: Smith, Elder, & Co., 1895.
Moors, Harry Jay. *With Stevenson in Samoa*. Boston: Small, Maynard & Co., 1910.
Stevenson, Margaret Isabella Balfour. *Letters from Samoa, 1891–1895*. London: Methuen, 1906.

Chapter IX

The Columbia Exposition of 1893

That fall I went with a battalion of Marines to the dedication of the buildings of the World's Fair at Chicago. The officers lived in a Pullman car and the men in a big room in one of the buildings. We thought it a splendid arrangement, especially as we paid nothing for our living, but the day before Christmas we were each handed a large bill for the individual share of the expenses of our car; a heavy tax just before Christmas. The main celebration was in the Manufacturer's Building which had seats for 180,000 persons and a platform for the presidential party. All the seats were filled. We escorted the president to the fair grounds, had our men stack arms and Lieutenant Thomas Treadwell and I went to the stairway leading to the presidential platform. Army soldiers were there and I asked what their orders were. They said they had orders to let nobody but Governors of states and their staffs pass. I then said, "Don't you think that two hungry Marine officers ought to belong to some Governor's staff?" He said, "I have no doubt of it." We walked up, got seats, and remained until a delicious luncheon was served, which we thoroughly enjoyed. Our fellow officers were disgusted on our return because they had not had the initiative to do likewise.

The next spring, I was one of the Marine officers ordered for duty at the World's Fair during the summer of 1893. It was a delightful detail. We had passes to all the concessions, lived in the grounds and passed a wonderful summer. Captain Benjamin R. Russell was in command, and Lieutenant Cyrus S. Radford was second lieutenant; I was first lieutenant. The Columbia Guard of the exhibits was made up of college students officered by regular officers of the army. Radford and I conceived the idea that it would be fine to be officers of this guard in addition to our other duties. It would give us additional pay and more standing in the fair grounds. Our commanding officer did not object and we became captains of companies. In the camp Radford was second lieutenant, at the Columbia guard camp he was Captain Radford and at the Kentucky state building where we often dined, he was Colonel Radford. He is a native of Kentucky. We attended all the functions at the different national buildings and they were entertaining and often amusing, as they also were at the state buildings.

When the West Point cadets were there, a ball was given in the New York state building. One of our officers was dancing with a girl, and another couple in dodging past them, went under their arms. The girl our officer was with had a bangle on her wrist which caught in the hair of the girl dodging under and pulled off her hair, as she wore a wig. The couple danced on, not noticing the scalp dangling from the girl's bangle, much to the amusement of all.

It was almost impossible to get good whiskey on the fairgrounds but we succeeded in getting a barrel of good Canadian Club sent in. We decanted it into stone jugs, each holding a gallon. I kept a number of jugs in my tent. An old couple from home were calling on me. They asked what I kept in the jugs and I said that we had to carefully store the oil for heating purposes. In rushed a friend, a lieutenant in the navy, and remarked, "Give me a drink, George, I'm nearly frozen." I replied, "You are crazy, man; you must think you are in the captain's tent." He caught on and withdrew and my home town friends thought it such a pity a fine looking young man like that felt he must have a drink. Needless to say there was no Eighteenth Amendment at the time.

One day while riding in an elevated railroad train in the fairgrounds, a man in front of me was the typical New York broker. He was very grouchy and just back of him was a young countryman, filled with enthusiasm and anxious to talk to everyone. The New Yorker responded by a grunt only to all his advances. Finally the train stopped at the California building and the youngster asked his gruff involuntary acquaintance, "Where do I go from here," meaning "where should I go." The old fellow rudely replied "You can go to hell if you wish." I took the young fellow in my care and showed him the sights for an hour or so and greatly enjoyed his enthusiasms.

My company of the Columbian guard was stationed in the art gallery. This was closed at night, and my special prerogative was that I could take friends through after nightfall, lighting up each room in succession, and showing them the pictures they could not have seen by day on account of the enormous crowds. Real crowds they were, too. On Chicago day there were 565,000 paid admissions to the Fair besides about 60,000 who entered on passes.

The Marine Guard took part in all official receptions of distinguished guests, and also did extra guard duty when required. There was a very serious fire in the cold storage building one day when the Marines were called upon to assist in keeping the people away from the fire. A newspaper man tried to get through the ropes, and the first sergeant of the Marine detachment told him he could not pass. The scribe persisted and the sergeant, after some argument, picked him up by the seat of his pants and threw him back over the ropes. Captain Silas Casey, USN, stood nearby and said to me, "Barnett, I am going in command of the USS *Newark* shortly and I want that Marine as first sergeant of my Marine guard." And he got him, too.

My quarters were in a large tent, with two beds in it, and I had different friends visit me during the summer. My invitations were eagerly accepted too, as quarters in Chicago were very scarce that summer.

At the close of the Fair, the Marine guard was retained to look after the packing of the government exhibit. They were such priceless papers as the Constitution of the United States, the Declaration of Independence, and the Emancipation Proclamation; all turned over to the Marines to return to the secretary of state at Washington; also the papers belonging to the Duke of Veragua, the original Columbus papers, which were priceless. This responsibility was very great and we never let them leave our personal touch. We sat with them, ate with them, and slept with them. Our relief was great when they were finally delivered in Washington. The Veragua papers were finally sent by special messenger on the USS *Detroit* back to Spain.

With sixteen men, I stayed for the final breaking up of camp just before Christmas. We slept in tents with the thermometer fourteen degrees below zero. We found it hard to keep warm even with blankets galore and oil stoves. Finally in order to dry the tentage for packing, we moved our men into a building vacated at the closing of the Fair. We placed the bunks like the spokes of a wheel with oil stoves at the foot of each one. There were thirty-one oil stoves and we were none too warm.

Editor's Comments on Chapter IX

The World's Columbian Exposition of 1893 was a coming of age party for the United States. Over twenty-seven million people were admitted to the fair. It featured two hundred temporary buildings, electric lighting, Cracker Jacks, the original Ferris Wheel, Frederick Jackson Turner lecturing on frontiers, Scott Joplin performing ragtime, and Little Egypt dancing. There were full sized replicas of Columbus' vessels, a Viking longboat and a U.S. battleship. The unnamed lieutenant in need of a drink may have been George Emmons, Barnett's friend from Sitka, who was overseeing an exhibit of Tlingit artifacts at the fair. After living in the futuristic "White City," Barnett found that his next posting lacked a bathroom.

Suggested Reading

Larson, Erik. *The Devil in the White City: Murder, Magic, and Madness at the Fair That Changed America*. New York: Vintage Books, 2004.

CHAPTER X

The USS *New Orleans* and the Spanish-American War

After reporting back at Washington, I was ordered to duty at the Portsmouth New Hampshire Navy Yard. Our quarters were in the old barracks there with only one bath room on the second floor, occupied by Captain William F. Spicer and his family of wife, two children and nurse. There was someone always in the bathroom when we wanted to use it, so I wrote to Washington for authority to put in another bathroom. The reply came back that there was no money available. So I wrote each day until the Quartermaster in Washington got tired of my persistency, and told me if I could get the work done on credit, he would pay it out of the next year's appropriation. I did so, and had one bath when I received orders to report on board the receiving ship at the New York Navy Yard where I remained on duty until 1897, when I was ordered to the USS *San Francisco*, Naples, Italy. Commander Arthur Nazro had received similar orders so we set out together from New York to Naples.

On arrival at Naples we found our ship had gone on to Asia Minor. So we set out by rail and ship to catch up with her. We enjoyed several days in Athens, particularly as it was my first visit. Our time was short, but I finally managed to get a fairly good idea of the historic city, because our steamer for Smyrna was delayed several days. When we arrived at Smyrna we found the USS *San Francisco* there and reported on board just before sailing back to Naples.

The night of the day we reported on the *San Francisco*, lying in Smyrna harbor, the wardroom officers gave us a dinner of welcome; the other guests of honor being the departing officers whose places we were to take. An orchestra played throughout the dinner and afterwards, the executive officer, Lieutenant Commander John van B. Bleecher, was called upon to respond to a

USS *San Francisco* dressed with flags, with the Italian ensign at her mainmast peak, possibly during her 1895–96 European Squadron service (Library of Congress).

toast. He was much embarrassed and got up just as the orchestra struck up loudly, so he just moved his lips, never uttering a sound, and sat down loudly applauded for his clever acting. How well it would be if many after dinner speeches were made in the same way.

There was quite a session after dinner and Mr. Volstead was by no means present. Lieutenant Blank was of the party. He was a great friend of mine and shortly after I retired I heard a knock at my door. "Come in," I said, and Blank entered. "Barnett," he began, "this is your first dinner on the ship and I just want to tell you that we don't do this every night." He then left, but twice the same night he came again and repeated the self same thing. I wonder if he remembers the incident.

We returned to Naples after a few days in Smyrna. There we made a carriage trip to Sorrento and from Sorrento down to the west coast of Italy, through Amalfi and then back to Naples, via Mt. Vesuvius, which we ascended to get as near to the crater as possible. Then we set sail for Villefranche, France, only a short distance from Nice on one side and Monte Carlo on the other. The social life there was very enjoyable, and at the famous gambling resort we participated unsuccessfully in the universal pastime of "trying to break the bank." But the delightful people from all parts of the world present recompensed us for our losses, and we charged them up to "amusement," taking care to have return railroad tickets in our pockets.

Lisbon was our next port of call and we enjoyed its beautiful churches, with their wonderful pictures, very much, and also visited the church where all the embalmed former rulers of Portugal as well as those of Don Pedro, former Emperor of Brazil, were kept. The Palace of Sintra in the mountains outside the city, a wonderful place of medieval architecture, remains in memory as one of the great sights of this trip.

We were privileged to be members of shooting parties that went to the shooting lodge owned by King Carlos I of Portugal. He was an excellent shot with both gun and revolver; one of the best I have seen. Democratic of spirit, he was as congenial and sociable as any ordinary mortal.

At Lisbon we heard of the sinking of the *Maine* in Havana harbor, and were naturally much excited. The next Sunday we held memorial services for those lost by the disaster. The American minister, Mr. Lawrence Townsend, and his beautiful wife Natalie, came aboard for the ceremony. Most impressive was the service, and the Minister's wife added a deal to the occasion by her singing. There we received orders to proceed to Gravesend, England, and take possession of the Brazilian cruiser *Amazonas*, just purchased by the United States in anticipation of war with Spain. About nine o'clock one morning we arrived and by noon had possession of the *Amazonas*, sent the Brazilian crew ashore and put an American force on board by dividing the crew of the *San Francisco*, and started homeward, as we dared not linger in England, because we could not leave the harbor if war were declared.

The ship was renamed the *New Orleans*. We took the northern passage home, not knowing when war would be declared. I volunteered for duty as watch officer and served in that capacity on the trip across the Atlantic. We were almost never dry and always very cold during the trip. The executive officer of the *San Francisco* was Lieutenant Commander Nazro and he served as commanding officer of the newly acquired vessel and Lieutenant Marbury Johnston as her executive officer and navigator.

All the storerooms, engine rooms, valves, etc. and in fact everything was marked in Portuguese, and before leaving port we got a lot of dictionaries in that language and spent considerable time while coming across, translating them into English, and also took a complete inventory of everything on board and marked everything in English. The ship had no heating plant, it was midwinter and the seas rough, so all onboard suffered greatly from cold. At times the ship seemed almost a submarine.

X—The USS New Orleans *and the Spanish-American War*

USS *New Orleans* at Brooklyn Navy Yard in 1898, shortly after arriving from England. A modern and partially armored cruiser, she would have been a valuable participant at the Battle of Santiago (Library of Congress).

At Halifax we found war had not been declared, so we proceeded to New York Navy Yard where alterations were to be made in the ship. She was armed with English guns, had smokeless powder in her ammunition and an excellent battery for a cruiser of her size and speed; she could make twenty-one knots. I foresaw war, and applied to stay on the *New Orleans* during it. My request was granted and I was in command of the Marine Guard of the *New Orleans* throughout the Spanish American War.

Soon we sailed for the West Indies, touching en route at Hampton Road. Off the north coast of Cuba we met some of our own ships and were nearly fired upon, as they did not recognize the *New Orleans* as an American ship because she was so different. Then we went to the south coast of Cuba and joined Admiral Winfield Scott Schley's squadron at the entrance of Santiago Harbor, blockading Cervera's ships inside the harbor. During this time we took part in several bombardments on shore batteries and also fired on the *Cristóbal Colón* one day when she came down near the entrance of the harbor. The ships that fired on her were the *Iowa, Massachusetts, Brooklyn* and *New Orleans*. The *Colón* should have been sunk that day but we steamed past her first at seven thousand yards distance from west to east, and then instead of turning with our helm to starboard and going nearer in, our helm was put to port and we went back at nine thousand yards distance and our shells were all ineffective. I did not understand the maneuvering nor have I since heard any satisfactory explanation of it. Whoever was responsible for it lost the chance of his life.

While transports were landing troops at Daiquirí, the *New Orleans* with several other ships was ordered over to superintend the landing, furnish boats, etc. and protect them. It was accomplished without any serious mishap save the drowning of a few horses and mules put overboard to swim ashore. Some of them turned seaward and thus were drowned. We fired a few shots at the small Spanish garrison and they quickly deserted it, so the landing was practically unopposed. Then we resumed our position in the blockading squadron off Santiago, having been joined by Admiral William Sampson on board the *New York*.

It soon became apparent that something would happen very soon, for the army was getting nearer and nearer to Santiago and Cervera's fleet must soon come out. In the meantime, our steam steering gear had broken down. One day our captain reported that the Spaniards were erecting a little battery of guns at Aguadores, a short distance east of Morro Castle, and Admiral Sampson signaled for us to go in and destroy it. Unfortunately our captain signaled back, "I am very short of six inch ammunition," so Admiral Sampson ordered the *Scorpion* to go in instead. She had no six inch guns at all.

To cap it all, a few days later our captain notified Admiral Sampson that our steering gear was broken, and we would not count on steaming at more than ten knots in case of battle. We were ordered to Key West to have it repaired, en route we made twenty knots and our steering gear worked perfectly. At Key West we found the battle of Santiago had been fought and we had missed it. We all felt that we should have tried out the steering gear while at high speed before reporting it to Admiral Sampson, and that if our ship had been in the battle, she would have been in many ways the most efficient of the fleet. We could have made four knots more than any other ship and she was the only one which carried smokeless powder and was armed with identically the same guns as the *Cristóbal Colón*, they having been made at the same place. Everyone on board felt that an unfortunate report had kept us out of the battle. We could have caught the *Colón* very quickly and it would have been a pretty fight between two ships with the same armament. I think that report cost our captain great success and promotion.

After repairs we proceeded to San Juan, Puerto Rico, to relieve the *Yosemite* from the blockade of that port. We had several exciting chases, captured a mail steamer which we sent to Charleston where the prize court failed to condemn her. We remained off San Juan until the signing of the protocol when we went inside the harbor and remained there while thousands of Spanish troops embarked for Spain. In October we proceeded north to Philadelphia where we took part in the peace celebration and parade, and then went to the New York Navy Yard.

Editor's Comments on Chapter X

After serving at the Columbia Exposition of 1893 and several uneventful years at naval yards, Barnett was assigned to the USS *San Francisco*, a protected cruiser. In the late 1880s, the United States started to modernize its navy and the result was a growing force of cruisers and coastal battleships. Armored cruisers had side armor, while protected cruisers had only partial armor shielding the engines and magazine. At 324' long, she carried twelve 6" guns and a crew of 384 and could make 19 knots. Though she too would soon be obsolete, she was a vast improvement on the *Iroquois*.

Barnett's discretion is on display in this chapter, as he names neither the lieutenant who had too much to drink nor the captain who missed a major battle. Lieutenant Blank was probably Marbury Johnston, who was a year behind Barnett at Annapolis. Johnston commanded Squadron 2 of the Cruiser and Transport Force during World War I, a handy person for a Marine wanting to get a regiment to France to know. The captain of the *New Orleans* was William Mayhew Folger.

One of the most modern warships of her day, the twin-screw protected cruiser *Amazonas* was nearing completion in England when rising tensions between the United States and Spain prompted the navy to acquire her from the Brazilians. On March 18, 1898, the *San Francisco* arrived at Gravesend and found *Amazonas* already flying the American flag. The new acquisition needed to leave before war was declared or face internment, thus the quick transfer of crew. After nine days, a scratch crew of 110 had the new ship (normally crewed by 366) underway, loaded with extra cordite and powder needed for the coming war. Preparing the ship and sailing it across the Atlantic under such conditions was a remarkable accomplishment.

Missing the battle was a sore point for Barnett, who was later criticized for his lack of combat experience. He was deployed to the Philippines, China, Cuba and Panama, all without earning the battle experience that so many other Marines enjoyed. For example, Marine Captain Littleton Waller, a future contender for the commandancy, served with great distinction at the battle Barnett missed. The *New Orleans* became a rarely mentioned footnote to the Battle of Santiago Bay.

Suggested Reading

Goldstein, Donald M. *The Spanish-American War: The Story and Photographs*. Washington, D.C.: Brassey's, 1998.
Leeke, Jim. *Manila and Santiago: The New Steel Navy in the Spanish-American War*. Annapolis, MD: Naval Institute Press, 2009.
O'Toole, G. J. A. *The Spanish War: An American Epic—1898*. New York: Norton, 1986.

Chapter XI

Seeing the World on the USS *Chicago*

The *New Orleans* had to have numerous alterations made, and as the *Chicago* was just about going into commission, I was ordered to that ship to finish my cruise. Rear Admiral Henry L. Howison was ordered to her also and we started on a cruise through the Mediterranean, around Africa over to Rio de Janeiro and back to the United States. This we enjoyed greatly and stopped at Gibraltar and Tangiers and at Port Said. While in the eastern end of the Mediterranean, a number of officers went to Jerusalem and others to Cairo. I was in the latter group and spent several wonderful days in the Egyptian city. I acted as paymaster of the trip and each officer furnished me with a certain amount of money for the bills. When we got back to the ship we sat around a ward room table squaring accounts, I remarked when we were squared up: "Here is a queer coincidence; I entered the service twenty-two years ago today and I have twenty-two dollars to the good." In any other walk of life, this would have meant the most complete failure, but I like that feature of the service in which the success or failure is not counted by money laid by.

While in Cairo, we saw all the sights for tourists and visited the Pyramids. This seemed too good to be true, and again I was glad to be in a service offering such wonderful opportunities for travel.

Our ship went through the Suez Canal down the east coast of Africa to Zanzibar and there we had a most interesting time. We visited the court of the Sultan of Zanzibar, a fine looking body of Arabs. All were gorgeously dressed and wore gorgeous belts supporting beautiful daggers and other arms. From Zanzibar we went down to Madagascar and from there to Delagoa Bay, Portuguese East Africa. The night before we left Delagoa Bay, a big bash was given for us at a prominent hotel. The next morning we were to leave in the private car of the Portuguese Governor for Pretoria and then to Cape Town where we would rejoin the *Chicago*. When the Governor came to take the admiral to the station, the admiral's aide was missing. I rushed into the courtyard to find him, and found the aide taking a bath in the fountain and singing loudly, "There's nothing in the house too good for Riley." The admiral said to me, "You come and be my aide and let him come along as best he may." Just as the train started the aide appeared and got aboard not feeling quite so hilarious, and all that day he must have felt considerably the worse for his gay night before, but not a sign did he give of anything but cheerfulness.

On the trip to Pretoria, all day we steamed along through the hot plains of Portuguese East Africa. When we went to bed at night, it was very hot, but the next morning we woke up nearly frozen. During the night we had climbed to a plateau about six thousand feet high, and everything was covered with heavy white frost. When we stopped at a little station about five o'clock in the morning I said to Paymaster Richard Ball, "There is a man I know; an American named Park." Park had come down from Pretoria to meet us. Ball had often wondered at my memory of people I had met, and could not believe that I recognized a friend in such an out of the way place.

After a short stay in Pretoria, Paul Kruger's capital of the Boer Republic, we proceeded to Johannesburg where we spent a most interesting week. Many American mining engineers were there. They would not permit us to go to hotels, but took us to their homes where they lived in most princely style. Splendid victorias and horses were put at our disposal, and we were not allowed to pay for a single thing. When I went back to the ship I had almost forgotten how to walk.

While at Johannesburg, Cecil Rhodes, then Premier of South Africa, telegraphed asking us to accept the use of his private car to Kimberly and Cape Town. The offer was accepted, and the car came in charge of Dr. Jameson, famous through his connection with the so-called Jameson Raid. It was fully equipped with commissary articles of all kinds, even to milk, liquor and cigars.

We were in Johannesburg the Fourth of July and the principal theatre reserved boxes for us. The theatre was beautifully decorated with American flags. When we entered, all rose and the orchestra played "The Star Spangled Banner." The audience showed its disapproval of any actor by throwing cannon fire crackers on the stage, which cleared it in short order.

We left Johannesburg in Mr. Rhodes' car and passed through Jagersfontein and Bloemfontein, on the way to Kimberly, where we arrived in due time and were met by Mr. Gardner Williams, Managing Director and Resident Governor of the de Beers Diamond Syndicate, the owners of the principal diamond mines in South Africa. Here we spent several days as guests of the diamond company, housed in its beautiful little hotel erected for the entertainment of guests. One afternoon we went hunting on the veldt and returned with six fine buck. At the Club House at Kimberly, there was the finest collection of animal heads I have ever seen. In the strong room of the De Beers Company we handled diamonds not by the single stone but almost by the bushel, certainly by the peck. We were all sorry our hands were not greasy so that some of the diamonds might stick.

After our most interesting stay at Kimberly, we went to Cape Town where we found the *Chicago* tied up. We saw a great deal of our Kimberly friends, especially Mr. and Mrs. Seymour, and Mr. Gardner Williams and his daughter, who had come down to enjoy the festivities. Mr. Seymour, on account of his splendid way of doing things, was called the Duke of Johannesburg. One day an orderly announced to the admiral, "Sir, the Duke and Duchess of Johannesburg are coming aboard."

During the stay there we visited Rondebosch where the famous Black Watch of England was stationed. We also lunched with Cecil Rhodes and often listened to his speeches in the House of Parliament. I considered him then and now as one of the world's greatest men and his wonderful will, providing for the education of the world's youth, shows the sterling worth of his character.

It was apparent that war between England and the South African Boer Republic could not long be deferred. Sir William Butler, the British commanding general in South Africa, believed it would be more serious than most Englishmen thought and was relieved of his command because he predicted it would take 50,000 men six months to end the war. As a matter of fact, it took 350,000 men two years.

Our stay at Cape Town over, we sailed for home with a stop at St. Helena where we visited "Longwood," the former home of Napoleon while captive on the island. It thrilled me because I have always believed that Napoleon was the greatest military genius the world has ever produced. It was with awe that I visited his house, the room where he died, and sat in the seat by the spring where he had spent so many long hours reading. I brought home twigs from willow trees near this spring, which I planted at home. The Governor of St. Helena gave a reception in our honor. His house was formerly occupied by Sir Hudson Lowe, the governor during Napoleon's stay there. The house contained many articles of furniture that had been brought from Longwood. I secured a knob from one of the doors to the room in which the great man died, and when I got back to Washington, I showed it to a friend of mine, a bishop, and a great collector of real curiosities. I told him if he would give me absolution in advance I would give him something rare for his collection. I gave him the door knob, much to his satisfaction, as he also was a great admirer of Napoleon

The rest of the trip to New York was without incident. There the admiral, captain and executive officer were relieved and, after a reasonable time in New York, we sailed on the 25th of November for Buenos Aires. Admiral Schley was our new admiral.

The day before Christmas we arrived in Buenos Aires, and went ashore for Christmas dinner at the famous Cafe Charpentier. After dinner our host called for cigars and the waiter brought Havanas. When the bill came they were $1 in gold each and our host had rather a rueful face. He was glad we had not taken several each as he had requested us to do.

From Buenos Aires we went to Montevideo where we spent some time anchored off the city. From Montevideo we went up the coast to Rio de Janeiro, and there I had the pleasure of meeting an old friend, Charles Page Bryan, then American Minister to Brazil. He was a great entertainer and thoroughly enjoyed giving parties at the legation in Petropolis, a city up in the mountains across the bay from Rio de Janeiro. It was a magnificent country place and he gave a big dinner for us upon our arrival, taking the guests by special boat and train from Rio de Janeiro. We had a wonderful time, one that lingers in my memory. During a forenoon's tramp in the mountains, I remember finding eighteen varieties of orchids. Afterwards Mr. Bryan took the admiral and five or six of his officers—I had the good fortune to be among them—to São Paulo, the capitol of the State of São Paulo, right in the heart of the coffee district. There I saw coffee raised on a large scale. It was a beautiful table land country and the city was very thriving; nearly everything there was done by electricity supplied by water power. Our trip was through the mountains and it was beautiful. At Rio de Janeiro we enjoyed the shops and the wonderful botanical gardens. While sitting on a bench there one day, a man came up to me and said he had noticed my Naval Academy ring, because he had a friend named "Weller" who wore one like it. It was my classmate, O. E. Weller, United States senator from Maryland, of whom he spoke. The man who greeted me was a Mr. Johnson and we became good friends, and I met his charming wife who was with him in Rio de Janeiro.

After our stay there, we made the trip north to Bahia, Pernambuco and Pará. Pará is about one hundred miles up the Amazon River from its mouth. I cannot say that I enjoyed the stay in Pará over much. It was too damp, hot and generally uncomfortable, and we were told that it was very unhealthy and that yellow fever was prevalent at that time. However, I was pleased that we had gone that far up the Amazon River. From there we went back to Montevideo, where with several others of the officers of the ship, I was detached and ordered home, our reliefs having come down by mail steamer.

We sailed from Montevideo on the Italian liner, SS *Marguerite* for Genoa, Italy. I persuaded the three officers, friends of mine, on board, that instead of sailing direct from Genoa for the United States, we should take a few days off and visit Italy. So we hurried through the customs at Genoa so we could make the night train to Rome. After we were cleared, one of my friends asked me if I thought it proper to give the Collector of Customs a tip, and I told him that I had tipped him for the whole crowd because he had shown that it was expected. I think I tipped everyone on the Italian ship but the captain and while in Italy, tipping seemed to be necessary early and often.

Arriving at Rome, we visited Cook's and made arrangements for seeing the sights of the ancient city. We made out our own schedule of places to be visited and gave them to the guide with the instruction not to waste time. He did not either and we saw everything there was to see in Rome, as far as our time allowed, and then visited Florence, Venice, Milan, Paris and London, and then went to Southampton, having managed to miss several boats but having seen a lot of Europe. Our delay was not noted and so caused us no trouble.

Editor's Comments on Chapter XI

The last chapters illustrate just how different Barnett and the other Annapolis graduates were from previous Marine officers. When the *New Orleans* needed a skeleton crew, Barnett stood watch as any regular navy officer would. When an admiral was short an aide, Barnett was an acceptable substitute. When Barnett joined the *San Francisco*, he was met by a long time friend. The Annapolis graduates had a social network that they could call on and the respect granted to peers. This changed the status of the Corps, much to its advantage.

Barnett sailed to Africa and around South America on his cadet cruise. He sailed the South Seas and then too much of the Pacific on the *Iroquois*. Now he got to see the world, with the advantage of his new rank, a modern ship and the improved reputation of his country and service. There were no civil wars, simmering disputes or armed expeditions on this cruise, just port calls and excursions at exotic locations. As part of Admiral Howison's party, he hobnobbed with Cecil Rhodes and was escorted by the celebrated Dr. Leander Starr Jameson. The 1895 Jameson Raid against the Boers in southern Africa was a fiasco and helped precipitate the Boer War, which erupted in October 1899. To make the assignment complete, Barnett was promoted to major before moving on to his next posting.

The navy's expansion during the late 1890s altered the Corps. More ships required more Marines, as did new bases. May 1898 found the Marines' authorized strength increased to 4,713 enlisted and 119 officers. In 1899, the Corps commissioned more new officers than it had in the previous two decades, many of them directly from civilian life. The expansion, coupled with retirements by Civil War veterans, accelerated promotions for Barnett and his classmates. He was promoted to captain on August 11, 1898, after fifteen years as a lieutenant, and to major on March 3, 1901. The next thirteen years would see him go from major to major general commandant.

Suggested Reading

Nalty, Bernard C. *A Brief History of U.S. Marine Corps Officer Procurement 1775–1969*, Moody, Ralph F., ; Joint Author. Washington, Historical Division, Headquarters, U.S. Marine Corps, 1970.

Chapter XII

The Philippines and the Asiatic Fleet

My next detail after reaching the United States and enjoying a month's leave, was on recruiting duty in Philadelphia, where I remained two years. Then I took command of a battalion of Marines sailing by army transport from San Francisco to the Philippine Islands. Arriving at Manila, I took the battalion to Olongapo and turned it over to the commanding officer there and returned to duty at Cavite. It was my first visit to Manila, and I fell in love with it and have liked it ever since. In the first place, I enjoy tropical weather. By the way, I found it necessary to take more exercise in tropical climates than in temperate zones and I think that is why men stand it better than women, because they lead a more active out of door life, which seems necessary in order to keep in good health in the tropics.

Not long after I went to Cavite, there was a vacancy as Fleet Marine Officer in the Asiatic fleet, and I was ordered to fill it. I went north on the USS *Solace* and joined the flagship *Kentucky* in the harbor at Chefoo, China, where the ships of the Asiatic fleet spent most of the summer. Quite a number of the officers were there with their wives, and we spent a very pleasant summer, as there was good riding and excellent swimming.

I reported on board ship the day before a great boat race which was to take place between a racing boat of the *Kentucky* and one from the *Wisconsin*. That evening I was walking up and down the deck with Admiral Robley Evans and he assured me that the *Kentucky*'s boat would win. Although the bets had been made, I badgered one of the officers of the *Wisconsin* into placing a bet with me for $150. He said he had wagered all the money he wished to place on the race, but at the same time he could not permit *Kentucky* money to go uncovered. I wished afterwards that he had not bet as next day our boat was beaten badly and I was the loser of $150.

XII—The Philippines and the Asiatic Fleet

From Chefoo, we went to Kobe, Japan, and I had the pleasure for the first time of going through the beautiful Inland Sea of Japan. A short time after our arrival in Kobe, I learned that the fall maneuvers of the Japanese army were to take place about sixty miles west of Kobe. Through the American Ambassador in Japan, I applied for permission to be one of the foreign observers with the Japanese army during the maneuvers. This being granted, I got the necessary orders to report on a certain day at army headquarters, where I was met by a Japanese officer who showed me to the hotel which had been taken for the accommodation of foreign officers. He told me my room was No. 4. I got to the hotel and found my room. The table at which I was to sit was No. 4; the horse I was to ride was No. 4; and my saddle was No. 4; in fact, during the twenty-one days I was with the Japanese army, I never went any place that I did not see No. 4 staring me in the face, and this was similar in the case of all other foreign officers. I mention this, simply to show the thoroughness of the Japanese and how they looked out for our comfort in every way.

The Japanese Emperor and his staff were at another hotel about six miles west of us. We had breakfast every morning at five o'clock, and then our jinrikishas would take us to the railway station, and we would proceed to the place nearest the emperor's residence and there await his arrival. After the reception was over, our horses would be brought and we would ride over the field of maneuvers for that day. We always lunched with the imperial party. In the evening we would meet and discuss the plans for the next day, the umpires meeting meantime and deciding the different actions for the day.

I was the only marine officer in the observers' group and they teased me greatly about horseback riding. Every morning I was asked if I had my anchor with me. One morning we were riding along a high bank between two rice fields covered with water. A German major turned in his saddle and asked me if I had my anchor with me that morning. In doing so, his horse made a misstep and in the twinkling of an eye he and his horse were floundering in the rice field. I politely asked if he wanted my anchor to assist him out and so the joke was turned nicely on him.

During the whole time of the maneuvers I was wonderfully impressed with the efficiency of the Japanese army. What impressed me most was the small amount of impedimenta they carried with them and the simple way in which the soldiers lived. I feel sure that an American army in peace times, living under similar conditions and working as hard as they worked, would at least have been tempted to grumble, but these Japanese were always on the alert, bright, cheerful and efficient, and all the observers felt that in case of war such an army would be sure to give a good account of themselves, as this same army did, later, in the Russian war.

The day the maneuvers ended we were all invited to a formal luncheon by the emperor, which was given in a beautifully decorated pavilion constructed for the occasion. More than twenty-three hundred Japanese officers and about thirty foreign officers sat at tables running lengthwise of the room, while at the end of the room facing all of us was the emperor, who sat at a table about four feet square on a raised platform. The foreign officers sat at one of the center tables near His Majesty. Three major generals and three rear admirals of the Japanese army and navy in full dress uniform stood at the right and left of the emperor. During the whole meal, they stood there as side boys or a guard of honor. One of the admirals, Yensuke Enouye, was a classmate of mine at Annapolis. I was enjoying a very good luncheon and he was getting nothing but glory. Several times I pretended to drink his health and he clenched his fist and seemed to say, "I will get even with you yet."

It was a time of royal feasting, for every evening the Japanese gave us a big official dinner. In the conference we had, I, being the only American officer, joined the British section, and discussions took place as to the possibility of war between Japan and Russia. We all agreed that war would come soon. Four Russian colonels present pooh-poohed the idea because General Kuropatkin, who had just visited Tokyo, had reported there would be no war. I believe these so-called maneuvers were for the purpose of getting as many Japanese troops as possible in southern Japan without causing comment, and I always have believed that the principal reason for our nightly official dinners was so they could account for foreign officers in Japan while they were at the emperor's residence, six miles away, discussing the question of war with Russia. Our prediction came true because war did come shortly after this.

I visited Yokohama, Nagoya, and Kyoto, the former capital of Japan, where the emperor resided while Japan was ruled by the Shoguns until 1868. At this time I met my old classmate, Admiral Baron Uriu, and he was a delightful guide for the sights of Tokyo.

I remember vividly the really wonderful Japanese dinner given us the last day of the maneuvers. It was served by Geisha girls, and was long but interesting. Of course we had to sit on the floor and with nothing to lean on, it was very tedious. The famous Marquis Oyama proposed the health of the senior foreign officer, a German major general, and we drank it in champagne. Oyama insisted on "bottoms up." Then he felt he must propose all our healths but did not insist on bottoms up; else the dinner might have been disastrous.

The *Kentucky* returned to Manila after my Japanese trip and then was ordered home, to be relieved as flagship by the *Wisconsin* in the harbor of Hong Kong. As my cruise was not completed, I was transferred to the *Wis-*

consin. Rear Admiral Yates Stirling relieved Admiral Evans and assumed command of the U.S. Asiatic squadron.

The Japanese Russian war was in progress, and an unusual incident occurred while the *Wisconsin* was at anchor at Woo Sung on the Yangtze River about fourteen miles from Shanghai. Four United States destroyers were at anchor near the *Wisconsin*. Rear Admiral Stirling invited me one Sunday to join a luncheon party in honor of friends of the family from Shanghai. In a sense it was a farewell party, because the admiral had learned he was to be detached. As he had been second in command, naturally he had hoped to be kept in command until he retired for age about a year later. The department, however, had decided that he should be relieved by a flag officer with sufficient time to serve out a full tour in command.

While at luncheon, an orderly reported to the admiral that a Russian torpedo boat was coming up the river. We went on deck to see the Russian boat turn and enter the Shanghai River, evidently heading for the city. About the same time we noted two Japanese destroyers coming up the river at very high speed. A big naval battle had taken place the day before near Port Arthur, and the Russians were defeated, so the Russian destroyer was seeking refuge in a neutral port. As we were ready to return to Shanghai, one of the U.S. destroyers was ordered to come alongside of the *Wisconsin*. The admiral and his guests boarded the destroyer and she started for Shanghai, only a short distance behind the Russian, and only a few moments ahead of the Japanese destroyers.

Newspaper representatives viewing the incident jumped to the conclusion that the American admiral was afraid the Japanese would disregard the neutrality of the port of Shanghai, and so had followed the Russian, thus placing his vessel between the belligerent forces in order to protect neutrality. I am sure Admiral Stirling had no such idea, and that it just happened in the ordinary course of events. However, the United States papers took it up, praised the action of the admiral and made so much of it that the Navy Department did not dare to relieve him, and he remained in command until his retirement age arrived.

Shortly after I joined the *Wisconsin*, the ship returned to Manila, and as the brigade commander in Manila had been detached because of illness, I was ordered to assume command of the Marine brigade in the Philippines. The quarters assigned me were in a fine old Spanish house in Cavite. The admiral of the Philippine squadron lent me three Chinese servants, extra numbers on the flagship, and as their services were not required during my stay in Cavite, I was very comfortably situated. I had a great deal of room to spare, so I invited a brother officer, William MacDougall, with a wife and two children, to share my quarters with me. They did so and Mrs. MacDougall took full charge of the house keeping, and I enjoyed their stay and became very fond of their children.

While on this duty I often spent the week ends at the Manila Army and Navy Club. Other times I visited the army posts, and one memorable Sunday I spent at Santa Mesa Barracks, just outside of Manila. It was a cavalry post, and a long ride was proposed. Horses were brought up, and I was given a very fractious horse as a joke, because I was a seafaring man. While crossing a dike, with rice paddies on either side, near a native shack which only boasted a roof made of palm leaves, some automobiles approached us from the rear. They passed us just as we got abreast of this shack and my horse gave a jump sideways and over we went through the roof of the shack. During this leap I thought, "what will these cavalry people think of me if I am thrown now." I was not thrown, but landed right side up, no worse for the jump. After that, I was welcome to any horse in the cavalry outfit.

During the rest of my Philippine tour little else of real importance or out of the routine happened to me. At the end of my tour there in the summer of 1905, I was ordered home by mail steamer. It was a delightful trip on the Pacific mail steamer *Siberia*. En route I stopped at Yokohama and at Honolulu. In Japan I spent a few days with my old classmate, Admiral Uriu. As I was very anxious to get some Japanese spaniels, he assisted me and I found some very high pedigreed dogs. I must say they were somewhat of a nuisance on the trip across, but I felt rewarded afterwards for they were fine specimens and greatly admired by my friends.

When I landed at San Francisco I found orders to report in Washington after a month's leave. Then I reported for duty as commanding officer of the Marine Barracks, Navy Yard, Washington, where I spent three very happy years.

Editor's Comments on Chapter XII

Fleet Marine Officer was a relatively new position, as was the notion of an American fleet as more than an administrative convenience. During the Spanish American War, Dewey defeated the Spanish at Manila, but lacked the necessary ground forces to occupy the city. One response to this was the establishment of a Fleet Marine Officer, to oversee the various ship's guards and potentially gather them into a sizable expeditionary force.

Even after the 1899 expansion, the Corps remained small and fragmented. Junior officers generally commanded ship's guards or small stations, while senior officers were stationed at larger navy yards. This affected the junior officers in several ways. Few married young, as they were at sea for years at a time. The lack of upward mobility reinforced this tendency. Many waited until they had sufficient rank and stability to consider marriage. They were often isolated, either commanding small outposts or the lone Marine officer on a ship. Some became excessively concerned with proper dress and discipline. Too many turned to alcohol for solace.

Before exiting this period, it is useful to review Barnett's position. He was no longer an unknown junior officer, but a potential commandant with a solid reputation. Despite his small town background and near continuous deployments, he had established important connections. His postings had given him a chance to demonstrate his ability to senior officers of the navy and Marine Corps. His former roommate, John Weeks, was an influential congressman, on his way to the Senate and a Cabinet post. Captain Archie Butt, the military aide to both Roosevelt and Taft, was a confidant. By 1910, he was on the short list for commandant.

CHAPTER XIII

Marriage and Honeymoon in Peking

On the night of December 9, 1906, the officers of the Washington Navy Yard were giving a ball. It being my birthday, I was having a supper party of about one hundred people. During the ball, a friend of mine came to me and said she was coming to my supper and would like to bring with her an attractive young widow from Baltimore and wished to present her to me. I said, "Certainly." She introduced us and the effect of the meeting was such that for two years I tried hard to marry her and finally succeeded. In 1908, just prior to my sailing again for the Far East on January 11th, I was married in Baltimore to Mrs. Basil Gordon, a widow with three children, two girls and a boy.

In this connection, up to the time shortly before I was married, I never had been mentioned in the Washington Post's "Town Topics." As stated above, my wife's name was Gordon, and after I had been trying to marry her for two years, Town Topics referred to me as "The Gordon Setter."

It may not be amiss to here mention that my wife, like all of her family, are quick at repartee, and one of her remarks certainly was at my expense. At our home in Virginia one summer we had quite a family gathering, consisting of my wife, her mother, her sisters, her children, and an aunt. All of the party except the brothers-in-law were southerners; the brothers-in-law were northerners. Each day we rode or drove about the country and passed many places where battles or skirmishes had taken place during the Civil War. The men called the others "Johnny Rebs" and the women called us "Yanks." One day we were near where the battle of Cedar Creek was fought, and my wife said, "Didn't the Rebs make you Yanks scratch gravel here?," and I replied, "They certainly did until Phil Sheridan came along and then you Rebs ran so fast there was no time to scratch gravel." I went on to say that I had noticed that the Johnny Reb women always made fun of the Yanks, but that as far as I could see from the present they always married Yanks. I hardly finished before she said, "Yes, my dear, we sometimes do as second choice." I had no more to say.

Another quick retort of hers was made shortly after the war and gained very wide comment. Franklin K. Lane, secretary of the interior, was about to leave the Cabinet. A big dinner was given in his honor and we were fortunately among the guests. My wife and Mrs. Lane had been working together in Canteen work during the war. After the men finished smoking they went to join the ladies. I happened to walk in with Mr. Burleson, the Postmaster General. As he entered the drawing room we found Mrs. Lane and my wife seated together and they were naturally talking of their war work. As we joined them Mrs. Lane said, "Mr. Burleson, what do you think of the work of the women during the war." He replied, "I don't think anything of it; the place for females is in the home." Mrs. Lane then said, "Do I understand that you don't think anything of our work" and he replied "Yes, that is what I said. I think that English females did good work, but American females wanted to put on a uniform, walk about and be admired." I saw my wife's red hair fairly rise on her head and I knew something was about to happen. She stood up and said "Mr. Postmaster General, it is evident to us that you know as little about the American females as you do about the American mails." He brought it on himself, for his remarks were at least improper and uncalled for, and our women do not like being referred to as females, and then again in France at least, our mail service had not been a brilliant success, if remarks of those at the Front are any criterion.

Being under orders to command the American Legation Guard at Peking, China, we had planned our honeymoon there, but Anne, the youngest child, was taken with pneumonia and could not be moved. So ten days after my marriage I had to leave without my new family. Not until the following September could they come out to join me.

Nothing of special interest happened on the trip to Peking. After relieving the retiring commanding officer, I took over his sparsely furnished quarters. Guessing at this condition, I had applied for proper furniture before I left Washington. It had arrived ahead of me and I had the quarters in good shape when my family arrived.

It was a joyous day when a cablegram came that my family had left San Francisco by army transport to come to China via the Philippines and Japan. I got leave and went to Nagasaki, Japan, to meet the transport on its arrival from Manila. But cholera on board had delayed its arrival and it was quarantined at Mariveles, Philippines Islands, therefore I waited about eight days in Nagasaki.

As the children were small, I secured two Japanese amahs to look out for them when they arrived. When the ship arrived, all the passengers were landed at the quarantine station and I was not allowed on board until the fumigation processes had been carried out. The passengers were taken out into the bath houses and had to take baths under the direction of the Japanese doctors, and after their baths, while their clothing was being fumigated, they were given Japanese kimonos and slippers. Finally, I was allowed in the enclosure of the quarantine station, and there I met my family dressed in kimonos and we had our first visit, sitting on bags of charcoal in the grounds of the quarantine station.

After the necessary formalities were gone through, the passengers were allowed to land and we all went to a hotel in Nagasaki. My wife and children were thrilled with all they saw in Nagasaki, as they had never been to Japan. We visited all places of interest in and about Nagasaki, and I remembered that Admiral Uriu, my classmate, was in command of the Japanese Naval station at Sasebo, which was only a few hours by rail, so I telegraphed him and he asked me to bring my wife there for luncheon the next day. We went by rail and arrived in due time. The admiral met us with two of his aides. Quite a crowd of Japanese were at the station, for the admiral was a great man to them and when I alighted from the car and slapped him on the back, consternation was visible on their faces.

We went by automobile to his house where we met Madame Uriu, who spoke excellent English as she was a graduate of Vassar. She was a sister of the wife of Marquis Oyama. We had a delightful luncheon, during which time a naval band played in the grounds. After luncheon we went in the admiral's steam barge for a trip around the harbor, which was filled with captured Russian ships. As we were steaming about, my wife said to the admiral that she had never seen but one Russian man-of-war, the *Askold*. "Have you ever seen that ship, Admiral," she asked. "Madame," he answered, rising from his seat, "I had the honor of sinking her."

In a few days we took a Japanese steamer for Shanghai, en route to Peking. The family greatly enjoyed Shanghai, particularly the Chinese city. A friend of mine there who wished to do something for Mrs. Barnett, asked me what I thought she would like. I told him I was sure she would like a real Chinese dinner. Two nights later she had her desire. Chinese dishes were served in the best Chinese way, and two young Chinese gentlemen were there. I had warned my wife not to ask them any questions, for if she did, she would get a direct answer. She forgot, and in the middle of the dinner asked a question that received a proper answer that startled the company. The Chinese have no false modesty and are given to calling a spade a spade without any

XIII—Marriage and Honeymoon in Peking

attempt to conceal their meaning. She asked no more questions. Chinese sing-song girls were the entertainment provided during the dinner. After each course, Chinese servants passed around hot towels to wipe ones hands and face.

It was the custom in China for all the business men to meet at the Shanghai club for a twelve o'clock luncheon daily. The day after the dinner I had an engagement with my wife for luncheon. Before meeting her I went to the Shanghai club and met so many old friends and had such a good time that she often wished I would go again to the Shanghai club, for after leaving there she said I had wanted to buy her everything in town.

That night we went to a Chinese theatre. It is difficult to describe the procedure as the plays last on and on, and it was a warm night, and the waiters were going up and down the aisles with steaming hot towels. Now and then one would raise his hand as an indication that he wanted a hot towel and the waiter would throw it much as a base ball pitcher throws a ball. Invariably it reached its destination safely, when the recipient would wipe his face gravely, roll it up and return it by a throw to the waiter who never missed it. Sweet meats were passed about in the same way, for the Chinese are real experts in making these dainties.

In Shanghai we met Judge Rufus H. and Mrs. Harriet Thayer, he being the Judge of the Consular Court there. We visited them later and today we possess five remarkable drawings of Chinese heads, the work of Mrs. Thayer, who was an artist of great ability.

A visit to Shanghai would not have been complete without a visit to the Astor House. Frequently we went there for luncheon and never missed the course of curry and rice, a specialty of the place and one always enjoyed. We learned there just how to prepare it and often have it at home.

After a few days in Shanghai, we took steamer for Tientsin. To get there we left the sea and entered the Peiho River. Our children were much interested in the natives on shore. They also delighted in the mud houses of China, and I joked with them by telling them our house in Peking was made of mud also. They asked me so many questions that finally they found out that the house was made of mud because it was brick and the bricks are made out of mud.

After a night at Tientsin without incident, we took train for Peking. There, upon our arrival, many of my friends were on hand to welcome us. The officers from the guard were there in a wagon drawn by two immense American mules, accompanied by two Chinese coolies with lanterns over their shoulders to show the way, it being dusk when we arrived.

The minute my family got inside the wall of Peking, they loved it. We drove to our house, which, as I said before, had been entirely refurnished. A hot coal fire was burning in the grate and a perfect dinner was ready and served by the most wonderful Chinese servants. The servants were all gotten up in beautiful Chinese costumes and this impressed my family very much.

Editor's Comments on Chapter XIII

Baron Uriu Sotokichi used his years at Annapolis to good effect. After winning glory in the Russo-Japanese War, he worked tirelessly for better Japanese-American relations. His wife, Baroness Iwako Uriu, was a Vassar graduate. Her sister, also a Vassar graduate, married Marquis Oyama Iwao. In 1909, Uriu and his wife traveled to the United States, where she spoke at Vassar's commencement and he attended a banquet in his honor given by the Class of 1881. They were generous hosts to their American friends, as witnessed by their multiple appearances in Barnett's memoir.

Lelia Sinclair Montague (1871–1959) was from an old Virginia family with a seagoing background. Her great-grandfather, Commodore Arthur Sinclair, was a hero of the War of 1812 and her grandfather, another Arthur Sinclair, sailed with Perry to Japan before opting for the South in the Civil War. Her Sinclair uncles, Arthur, William and George, served the Confederacy aboard the *Florida*, *Alabama* and *Merrimac*. Her father, Walter Powhatan Montague, also fought for the Confederacy, but the war ruined the fortunes of the family.

Montague moved his family to New York where one of Lelia's uncles had made good in the post-war economy. More children followed, but success did not. As Upton Sinclair, Lelia's first cousin, wrote "Pow wasn't much good at either making or keeping money, but he was the life of any party." Lelia grew up wearing hand-me-downs, though her mother didn't want her playing with the "common children" who shared their dingy apartment building. Her father became "increasingly indifferent to his domestic responsibilities," while her mother was losing her sight. Only better situated relatives kept the family afloat. Lelia graduated from hand-me-downs to sewing her own clothes. Eventually, the family moved to Baltimore to be closer to supportive relatives.

It was while they lived in Baltimore that another refugee moved in with them, Leila's first cousin Alice Montague. Alice would later marry Teackle Wallis Warfield, who died shortly thereafter of tuberculosis. Alice and her young daughter, Wallis, had several benefactors, the Barnetts among them. The Barnetts launched Wallis into Washington society in 1914, with a dance at the Marine barracks. Wallis met her first husband, Earl Spencer, while visiting Lelia's sister, Corrine Mustin in Pensacola. Corrine and Lelia later help facilitate her divorce from Spencer. On several occasions, Wallis traveled with Mrs. Mustin or Mrs. Barnett's daughters, Anne and Lelia Gordon, whom Wallis referred to grandly as her "Montague cousins." While Wallis was not a major actor in the Barnetts' lives, they were an important factor in her pre–Duchess of Windsor life.

It was in Baltimore that Lelia met Basil Gordon. Gordon was eleven years older and suffered from tuberculosis of the spine, but was brilliant, financially successful and from a prominent family. He was enchanted with her and they consid-

Mrs. George Barnett with her daughters, Ann Hamilton (left) and Lelia Sinclair Gordon (standing) (Library of Congress).

ered marriage despite resistance from his family. After nearly calling it off due to his precarious health, they married in 1895.

A son, Basil Jr., followed in due course. Following a continental tour, Gordon's health declined. The family sought refuge at Saranac Lake in the Adirondacks, where he was under the care of Dr. Edward Trudeau. Trudeau had treated Robert Louis Stevenson and his Adirondack Cottage Sanitarium was nationally known. In one of the "cure" cottages there, their second child, Lelia Sinclair Gordon, was born, with the mother being attended by the local veterinarian.

A third pregnancy took place under more difficult circumstances, this time in Baltimore. Basil Sr. remained seriously ill, his mother was failing and Lelia nearly died delivering twin girls, Ann Hamilton and Catharine Douglas Gordon. The elder Mrs. Gordon lived just long enough to see her new grand-daughters. Despite a return to Saranac Lake, Basil died soon after that. Tragedy was not done with Lelia. A year later the family was vacationing at Saranac Lake when a tent housing the infant twins and a nurse caught fire. Lelia rushed into the flaming tent and all four of them were burned, with young Catharine dying.

After that, she took her remaining children to Europe, seeking time and distance to recover. After rejecting several marriage proposals there, still in mourning and unmoored, she returned to the United States. The young widow split her time between Wakefield Manor in Front Royal, Virginia, and Washington D.C.

In Washington she made new friends, including Mrs. John McLean, one of the social queens of the city. McLean had been a close friend of Leila's mother-in-law. On that basis, she was admitted to the upper reaches of society. Soon after that, two of her young friends insisted that she chaperone them at the Navy Ball. This was how she met Lieutenant Colonel Barnett, who was immediately smitten. In turn, she found him "a wonderful dancer and a man of great charm and personality." He sent her flowers the next day and every succeeding day until they married.

Barnett seems an unlikely match for the wealthy widow, who had rejected offers by a count and a baron while in Europe, but the Sinclairs had a military tradition and she would prove well suited for the duties of an officer's wife. She didn't need to marry for financial security or position. She too had lived a nomadic life and wasn't afraid of adventure. While older, Barnett was the same age as her first husband. He was a rising star in the Corps and his days of deployments to Sitka or on leaky wooden ships were over.

Mrs. Gordon was also an unlikely target for Barnett's affections. After a long bachelorhood, Barnett pursued a woman quite unlike most officers' wives. He married her after a long courtship and was well aware of his wife's strengths and flaws. Throughout her life, Mrs. Barnett spoke her mind, was politically active and did not suffer fools. He was clearly proud of her, even when her wit did him no good politically. Such a marriage of strong personalities was not common in the military or in Washington.

Barnett describes himself as "being under orders" for Peking, but Mrs. Barnett recounts a more interesting story. He had a choice between commanding the Marine contingent on the Great White Fleet's epic journey around the world or the legation in Peking. Informing the reluctant Mrs. Gordon that he was about to be deployed and nothing could change that, he was able to end the long courtship and obtain her hand in marriage. Commandant Elliott then delayed Barnett's orders so the wedding could be properly arranged and assigned Barnett to Peking, a much better location for a honeymoon with young children. The wedding featured John Weeks as best man and a portion of the Marine Band.

Mrs. Barnett wrote a harrowing account of her trip to Peking. In the Philippines, her severe headaches were mistaken by a doctor for cholera and she was quarantined away from her children. Only the intervention of an officer's wife righted the situation. As she prepared to sail from the Philippines, she spent the last night as a guest of the Governor General, while her children and nurse boarded the transport. When she went to her ship the next morning, it was under a cholera quarantine. She was able to rejoin her children, but they had to wait until passengers stopped dying before the ship could depart. During the ten day delay, a hurricane struck and the boat put to sea to ride out the storm, only to return to the quarantine station. When the ship finally arrived at Nagasaki, the Japanese almost sent it back to the Philippines, before settling for a thorough disinfecting. Only then was she permitted to resume her interrupted honeymoon.

Some historians dismiss Mrs. Barnett as a wealthy socialite who meddled in Corps affairs, but it pays to remember her background and how it shaped her. A childhood with an improvident and absent father, a sickly mother, the dependence on the kindness of relatives, a bookish yet adventurous bent, a fierce loyalty, an ability to move beyond tragedy and losses, and a taste for progressive and proto-feminist politics. Definitely not a delicate flower, she was as at ease joining her husband on training exercises in China as she was hosting elegant Washington events.

While Barnett was preparing this memoir, his wife started her own account, which she titled "Command Performance." It was never completed and is very fragmentary, but serves as the source for much of the above.

Suggested Reading

Martin, Ralph G. *The Woman He Loved.* New York: Simon and Schuster, 1974.

Chapter XIV

The Peking Legation Guard

The next morning after we arrived in Peking, my wife went to the dining room and kitchen and looked over the whole establishment. It was the only time during our stay that she was obliged to visit the kitchen. The cook was near perfection, and Chung, a Chinese boy, our butler, was a constant joy.

When having a dinner party, all it was necessary for my wife to do was to put name cards at the different places, and she could always be sure that the table would be perfectly arranged, with perfect decorations, and proper wines, cigars, etc. would be served at the proper time and in the proper manner. A delightful custom of great assistance to housekeeping was that an agent called and took orders for everything needed in the household in the way of provisions, wines, liquors, and cigars. These were placed in the store room and you were given an inventory and a key, while the agent retained a duplicate key and a duplicate inventory. At the end of each month he took inventory again and you paid for what had been removed from the storeroom.

American money at that time was at a great premium. We used to get about two dollars and sixty cents Chinese money for one dollar in American money, so during my stay in China I felt really rich. At the end of the month I would exchange my money for Chinese money and we paid all our servants with it and it seemed almost as if we were getting them for nothing. However, we paid the cook twenty dollars, one boy fifteen dollars and a second boy twelve dollars, and the coolies about eight dollars each—all this in Mexican money at the rate above stated. The Number One boy gets a "squeeze" on everything that comes into the house, and even with that, he buys so carefully that one could not, with the closest dealing, buy the same articles for less, and after all, if one should buy them, the "squeeze" system is run so carefully that in the end you would pay it anyway. The "squeeze" business is thoroughly established in China, and it seems hopeless for anyone to try to break it up.

The day after their arrival the children were thrilled by the sight of camels on the streets, many acting as coal carriers. The children wanted to ride one, so Mrs. Barnett told the Number One boy, Chung, to go out and get a camel for the children. He soon returned and said, "Missy, twelve piecy camel have got," and sure enough, Chung had brought in twelve camels and their drivers, and the children spent the day screaming with delight and having their pictures taken on these queer animals, and all for a mere pittance.

Before my family arrived I had secured a fine Australian mare for my wife and ponies for the children, and we rode nearly every day. In fact, almost everyone in Peking rode, as it was one of the chief amusements. The roads were good almost all winter, as the air was so dry that there was no ice on them, and there was almost no snow and never any slush.

Paper chases were very popular. At their end the ladies would give tea parties and they were very enjoyable. During our rides we visited many Chinese temples, not only in the city but outside the wall; in fact there was never a day that we would not ride to some place of real interest, and even in not going to any place in particular, the street sights were a never ending source of amusement and joy.

As soon as the Chinese merchants hear of a new arrival they bring their wares to your house and besiege you in their attempts to sell their wares. They will bring anything that you may even look at and leave it for days or weeks, thinking that you will eventually buy it and in this they are wise. They are born tradesmen, and like nothing better than to bargain, even over a small purchase. The dealers all knew their own articles, and never mixed them, no matter how many consignments were in the house at the same time. I am sure that in my house at one time, I have had as many as a thousand sable or ermine skins, desiring to pick out a few that would exactly match; and there was never any trouble about getting the skins mixed up, as the traders could, by some mark or other, instantly identify any certain article.

Although it was not necessary to visit shops, we often did it for amusement, to see the way things were manufactured, and also we were always interested in seeing the street sights en route to the shops. The shops are often located in the most unexpected places. One will go through a small door almost unnoticeable. Inside will be a yard filled with shops containing the most priceless articles, such as furs, jades, silks, and jewels of all kinds.

In certain parts of Peking there are fairs almost every day. These fairs are worthy of a visit many times, because, besides the wares of tradesmen attractively displayed, are to be seen Chinese jugglers and acrobats and other exhibits. One fair frequently visited by us was called the Liulichang. The children went very frequently and were much delighted with what they saw. We bought several fine specimens of Pekingese dogs at this fair. More than likely

Marines in formation at the U.S. Legation in Peking. Barnett commanded the Legation Guard 1908–1910 and arranged for photographs of the expanded Guard and the Legation (Library of Congress).

they were stolen from the palaces. At one of the fairs the venders had a good pearl now and then, and my wife, one by one, picked up enough of these pearls for a really handsome necklace at a price very small in comparison to what we would pay here for the same stones. It is almost impossible not to buy things in Peking. The Chinese are wonderful salesmen and marvelous judges of human nature, and know how to approach their customers to assure sales.

In going to and from the fairs, it is not an uncommon sight to pass an immense crowd of people gathered around a public story teller or reader, and although we could not understand what he said, we knew it was funny because, in many cases, the people were uproarious in their laughter. This is quite different from Japan, where the people take themselves so seriously that it is almost an unknown sight to see a Japanese laughing in the street.

One summer my wife went to Japan and left the children with me. She had hardly gotten away before I had khaki boy suits made for the girls; they were little things then, and during the whole time my wife was away the girls rode all over Peking and the surrounding country with me in their khaki suits, and to the disgust of my wife she found them in these same khaki suits when she returned.

During the time we were in Peking, our fleet made a cruise around the world, and one day we got a telegram from Mrs. Henry Mustin, my wife's sister, who was the wife of a naval commander and who was in Yokohama, stating she was on her way around the world following the fleet and would like to visit us in Peking and bring a friend with her. We replied that we would be delighted to have them come, and a short time afterwards, she and her friend, a very attractive young widow, arrived. They got there in the evening and the next day there happened to be a race in Peking, one of the important social functions in that city. Nobody had seen the two new arrivals, and the next day when they went out to the races they created quite a sensation. They were both very beautiful and well dressed. I am sure they never had a better time in their lives. The young widow was supposed to be very rich, and by the time she left, her fortune had, according to rumor, risen to some ten millions of dollars. Needless to say, she was much sought, especially by the so-called eligible men. She withstood their importunities and afterwards came home and married an American naval officer.

While we were in Peking, it was the custom of the families residing there in the legation quarter to lease a temple in the western hills about fifteen miles from the city for the spring and fall, and to camp out there about a month each season. The temple contained an enormous compound with several small compounds inside of it. These temples were provided with kitchens, stables and necessary quarters for living purposes. Taking Marine mess equipment, cots, mosquito nets and other necessities, we enjoyed life there al fresco. Frequently we went on rides to other temples and greatly enjoyed life in general.

Our temple had a very handsome carved teak table and a wooden Buddha which now adorn our Washington home. These we purchased from the priest. We got up a riding party while occupying this temple and about fifteen of us went west to visit a temple far back in the mountains. With us were a group of natives and pack mules to carry our camp equipment and provisions. When we arrived at the Ho river, a rapid running shallow stream, the women were afraid to ride across on horseback and had to be carried across on the backs of natives, much to the amusement of all concerned, and members of the party snapped a number of amusing pictures of the novel scene.

More and more trees loomed up as we neared the mountains. Finally we came to a very heavily wooded country with very deep ravines, and in going up one of them, we came to a small native village and just beyond it a fine group of temples all in fine repair. The buildings, especially the roofs, were works of art, wonderful old trees were within the temple enclosures, and also mountain streams coursed their way between the temples. The whole place showed good care and attention.

Buddhist priests were everywhere. They had three services a day; the last one being at eleven at night, and we were informed that not a single service had been omitted in six hundred years. The priests gave us a special compound with living quarters, and they also furnished us with delicious food as well. They ate no meat, but their vegetables cooked in oil were ample for anyone. We had hot water for our baths, and were given splendid care in every way. We spent much time going through the different temples.

The first night we were there we attended a remarkable service in which about one hundred priests officiated. It was conducted in a huge hall, the roof being supported on magnificent teak pillars, very large and very high. In this hall was an immense statue of Buddha. The altar of the temple was magnificently dressed and the priests were in elaborate regalia. There was no instrumental music other than drum beats, but sonorous chanting by male voices wonderfully trained. At one part of the service it resembled that of the Roman Catholic Church and one part was much like the administration of Holy Communion. The lights were very dim and the weird chanting and incense in the air and the quaint priests dressed in yellow oriental robes presented a scene I shall never forget.

We returned by another route, well satisfied with our journey. We passed on the way a temple which had a pagoda, originally one of the architectural beauties of China, but during the Boxer troubles of 1900 it was rumored to have been used as a signal tower by the Boxers. After the capture of Peking it was partially destroyed by British troops. This seemed to be wanton destruction and a practice that should not be indulged in by civilized troops.

The Emperor and the Empress Dowager were still alive while we were in Peking, but during our stay, they died. We made official visits to them, inside the Forbidden City and also at their summer palace. Wonderfully fine and dignified men comprised the emperor's court. They all wore sable coats and dignity was the order of the day. At this time the emperor was practically confined to a temple on an island within the Forbidden City and the Empress Dowager was the real ruler.

The last luncheon given by the Empress Dowager was at the summer palace. She sat in the place of honor and lower down at her left sat the emperor. It was she who received the foreign ministers and who replied to them through her interpreter. She was a remarkably strong character. From what I saw of her, I can unhesitatingly say that she absolutely lacked fear. Especially was this true of matters in which she felt her own interests or those of China at stake.

During the address I stood within ten paces of her and looked steadily at her and I am sure that not even an eye lash moved in that time. After the dean of the corps had finished his address, she turned her head very slowly to the interpreter as an indication that he might now begin her reply with which he had been furnished in advance. The reception over, we went into another hall for luncheon.

The day before the luncheon, my Number One boy had requested a day's leave, which I granted him. When I sat down at the Imperial luncheon I found I was being served by my Number One boy and the same thing was true of the other members of the diplomatic colony present. They were all being served by their Number One boys.

The next morning, after the inimitable Chung had served me my breakfast, I asked him if he had enjoyed his day at the summer palace; he replied that he not only enjoyed it, but had received fifteen taels for his services. A tael being about $1.40 Mexican money. He then took from his sleeve a small package, nicely wrapped, and handed it to me. I asked him what it contained and he said, "Look see and you will savez plenty." I found that it contained several small menu holders from Her Majesty's table, and I asked him how he happened to have them. He replied that as he knew Master liked souvenirs, he had taken them. I said, "You rascal, do you know what would happen if I told on you?" I, at the same time drew my finger across my throat, thus indicating that he would lose his head. He said, "Yes, Master, I savez plenty; I also savez plenty that Master no tell." The menu holders were of no particular value but certainly were good souvenirs of a delightful occasion, especially as that was the last official luncheon given by the Empress Dowager. Later on when my wife used these menu holders at a ladies' luncheon at home, one of the guests walked off with one of them—she also was fond of souvenirs.

As I said, the Emperor and the Empress Dowager died during our stay in Peking. Their funerals were the most unique affairs I have ever witnessed. It is still a mooted question whether the Emperor or the Empress Dowager died first, as the dates were kept secret. Personally, I think the emperor was the first to die. The manner of his death remains unknown, at least to the western world. The bodies were placed in very wonderful Chinese coffins and placed in a temple inside the Forbidden City, where they were kept about a year before burial. During this time, members of the diplomatic corps accompanied by the officers and attachés of their staffs, visited the Forbidden City several times and paid homage to the coffins.

Like all other official Chinese funerals, a very great deal was made of the funerals of the Emperor and the Empress Dowager. The Chinese custom of making articles in miniature of papier-mâché, representing things used by the dead, was followed out in great detail in honor of the emperor and empress. In the case of the Empress, miniatures of every house in which she had lived were made, and a miniature ship one hundred feet long, was made of a ship on which she had once sailed. Her sedan chairs, carriages with horses and riders and postilions, were reproduced in life size; replicas were also made of every detail of the harness, saddles, etc. The carriage was so accurately reproduced that inside was a reproduction of the clock and mirror, cigarette case, and even the upholstery was reproduced as accurately as though it were the real thing. There were reproductions of every gift received by Her Majesty from the royal family throughout her whole life.

The papier-mâché gifts received by the royal family at this time included many imitation rolls of silk, articles of adornment and bric-a-brac. These articles were burned daily at five p.m. in a public square with a great deal of ceremony. Unless this custom had been observed, there would have been no place to store them, as there were so many of them.

From all parts of China came silken banners, usually about ten feet long and two feet wide, which were covered with Chinese characters in gold leaf. Different officials had sent the banners as funeral mementos from the provinces. The banners were hung in a large room and they completely covered the walls. The poor people brought gifts of fruits and cakes by the thousands. They were piled on tables in pyramid style and made a wonderful picture. After exhibiting these gifts for a time, they were distributed to the poor. While these ceremonies were taking place, the family, attired in white cotton cloth, was in constant attendance on the corpse.

Great preparations were made for the state funeral and finally the day for it arrived. Special pavilions were erected for the diplomatic corps and their families, including the officers of the military guards stationed in Peking. The funeral procession was almost endless in length. First came a great number of societies bearing enormous banners describing who and what they were.

The catafalque on which the body rested was a truly gorgeous affair, draped with silken embroidery all in imperial yellow. This catafalque was borne by one hundred and twenty-eight men and followed by others carrying the miniature papier-mâché articles that had not been burned.

Then followed more men carrying enormous dragons made of papier-mâché and fairies riding on the backs of monster birds, dragged along on wheels. These birds were life size and of marvelous coloring and artistic work. Chinese bands marched here and there in the procession. Before the entire procession came the military escort, Chinese troops, cavalry, infantry, and artillery.

This was the last mortal appearance of the great Empress Dowager, Tsi-an, really one of the most remarkable women the world has produced. I personally hold her more responsible for the Boxer uprising than any other person. In her heart, to my mind, she was always absolutely anti-foreign and unscrupulous, but possessed of a very strong character. She kept the emperor virtually a prisoner while she ruled China with an iron hand. His modern ideas did not suit her, and when she heard of innovations he had planned, she quietly summoned the troops of Chihli to Peking, and then confined the emperor and ruled in his stead the remainder of her life, and his, too, for that matter.

During my stay in Peking, it was the custom for the Marine Guard to take a hike each summer. It kept them in good physical condition and also gave them a chance to see as much of China as possible. I usually accompanied them on horseback and camped with them at night.

My wife went with me on one of these hiking parties. We left Peking about five o'clock one morning headed for the Great Wall of China at Nan Pass, where the wall comes nearest to Peking. A Peking cart and a Marine camping outfit had gone ahead of us to the spot where we had planned to camp that night. This was at Tsung Shan Baths, twenty-three miles north of Peking.

When we arrived there that afternoon, we selected one of the temples with an enormous enclosure around the baths for our resting place. Our cart had not arrived by luncheon time, so I went scouting into a little neighboring village to see what I could secure in the way of food. Only the tea seemed appetizing, but as we were hungry, I asked my wife if she could eat boiled eggs. She said, "Yes." As I did not know the Chinese word for egg, I put my thumb and forefinger together somewhat in the shape of an egg and flapped my arms and crowed. The natives cleverly understood and brought some fresh eggs which we boiled and had some tea with them.

Tsung Shan was the favorite recreation place of the Ming emperors. They believed in the virtues of the hot baths, two in number, fed by hot springs, with a very strong sulfur flavor. The baths were quite sumptuous, of white marble, ten or twelve feet deep and eighteen by twenty feet wide, and were surrounded by a white marble balustrade, and a marble walk. The first bath was so hot that eggs were soft boiled in it in about fifteen minutes. The second bath was also hot, but we could endure it by getting into it very slowly and it was most refreshing.

Finally our cart arrived and the officers and men selected various temples for their camping places, mess hall, etc. and there we spent two very delightful days. It had myriads of lotus ponds and wonderful marble bridges, but was dilapidated.

We left Tsung Shan Baths for Nan Pass, my wife and I riding ahead of the general party after leaving word where the cart was to meet us that night. It was very hot, and about ten o'clock in the morning we rode into a shallow stream to water our horses. My horse finished first, and I rode on ahead. Suddenly I heard my wife scream and turning around I saw her horse had rolled in the water, upsetting her and getting her very muddy and wet. When she reached the bank, she took off her riding skirt, washed it out and hung it over the rump of my horse to dry. In a short time all was dry and she was able to put her skirt on again. Needless to say she was furious because I laughed at her, but anyone was entitled to a good laugh for the incident was so ridiculous.

That night we camped at Nan Pass, and the next morning we went up to the Great Wall. The men made camp just inside the gate which leads out to Mongolia and my wife and I pitched our tent on top of the wall and enjoyed our stay in this novel spot. Every school boy has heard of the Great Wall of China, which is truly one of the wonders of the world. The Marines with us felt the novelty of the situation, and many of them used their cameras to good advantage taking pictures to be sent home to the states.

At another time I went from Peking to the Nan Pass by rail because I wished to take my children and their governess with me. On going through the gate we had to lean forward as far as possible and push our way through on account of very strong winds drawing through the gate from the plains of Manchuria.

While at the Great Wall the first time, they were building a railroad from Peking to Kalgan [Zhangjiakou], Mongolia, a distance of about one hundred and sixty miles. This, I believe, was the first Chinese railroad designed and built entirely by Chinese engineers. Just at this particular time they were tunneling through the mountain under the gateway of the Great Wall at Nan Pass. The railway up through Nan Pass was a fine piece of engineering and remarkably well carried out. The country is very mountainous and required a great deal of tunnel work.

The head engineer, Jeme Tien Yow, who was a graduate of Yale, when I introduced myself to him, said in perfect English, "Colonel, I am glad to see you; will you have a drink?" When I said "yes," he held up his hand clasping his two middle fingers and extending the fore and little fingers, saying "Will you have about two fingers?," thus showing that he remembered an old American way of measuring a good stiff drink.

I also saw a great deal of Liang Dunyan, Minister of Foreign Affairs, and took dinner with him and his family several times. His son frequently took our children out in his dog cart, and they were great chums. Once, the children, while playing at the Liang Dunyan home, greatly enjoyed a game of climbing over the roofs of the different houses in his compound. They induced the governess to go up on the roof and then, without her knowledge, got down, took the ladder away, and left her up on the roof.

I was in Peking during the visit of Ex-Vice President Charles Fairbanks, and when I learned that he was not going to stop at the American Legation, we invited him and his wife to stay at our house. I had known him very slightly, but I thought it most improper for such a man to go to a hotel in a foreign country where American representatives were living. They accepted our invitation and we had a delightful three weeks with them. The vice president, or rather, the ex-vice president, was extensively entertained by the Chinese because of his official position, and one party was especially charming, that of a trip by rail from Peking to Urga [Ulan Bator]. We were invited, but because of the pressure of official business I could not go, but my wife went and greatly enjoyed herself.

The party visited Tientsin, and there a luncheon was given for them by the viceroy of the province. In connection with that luncheon a laughable incident occurred. The Chinese court was in mourning on account of the death of the Emperor and Empress Dowager, The Viceroy felt that it would be inappropriate to have a man of Vice President Fairbank's standing without a band, and yet it was not Chinese etiquette to have music during a period of mourning. So the band appeared, simply went through the motions of playing, but without sound, thus, according to the Viceroy's viewpoint, rendering full honor to the distinguished guest, but without breaking an honored Chinese custom.

In the matter of official entertainment there is a great difference between the practices of the Chinese and those of the Japanese. In Japan, for centuries the military class had been the highest while in China for an equal period, it was the lowest. At a luncheon given at Hang Chau, across the river from Hankou, about a thousand miles up the Yangtze river, in honor of the American admiral of the Asiatic squadron, two thousand Chinese soldiers were turned out in command of a brigadier general to do honor to the admiral, but not one of the officers was invited to the luncheon; they merely waited outside to be able to present arms again to the admiral when he reappeared after luncheon. In Japan the military officers would have had the place of honor next to the admiral. I cannot but think of this when asked, as I very often am, for my opinion of the yellow peril, so-called. Until this policy is abandoned, there cannot be much accomplished in the military line in China. Yet, well trained and well led, I think the Chinese would make excellent soldiers, as they have many of the qualities which count greatly in the makeup of good soldiers. They are strong, hearty, uncomplaining, and can live on what an American or European would consider almost starvation.

During my stay in Peking, regulations were in force requiring officers to take a test ride of ninety miles per month. This ride had to be completed in three days and within a certain number of hours each day. Once while starting out on this ride with my wife, an Italian naval officer asked if he might join us. I said, "Delighted," and we went out the east gate of the Chinese city and turned northward, and at first intended to come in at the north gate of the Tartar city, but the horses went so well, and the day was so fine that we continued our ride clear around the city. Altogether the ride was thirty-one miles long. We thought nothing of it, as we were used to long rides, but the Italian officer was not seen for a week, and he never asked to join us again for a ride.

There was a wonderful Chinese juggler in Peking whom we called "Lung Tung," because all during his performances he talked a great deal and about all he said was "Lung Tung, iga Lung Tung." He was one of the best jugglers I have ever seen. He performed every evening at the hotel, and was always in demand at children's parties held at private homes. All his tricks were enacted in the center of the room surrounded by spectators with no paraphernalia other than that which he carried on his person.

Once my wife broke some jewelry and our Number One boy brought in a native jeweler; one of the largest men I have ever seen. My wife called him "Tiffany" at once. He wanted to know why, and she explained that Tiffany in New York was one of the biggest jewelers in the world, that he was the biggest jeweler in Peking beyond doubt. The native was charmed with the story and immediately had cards made on which were printed the words, "Tiffany, Chinese Jeweler." He adopted this as a firm name, and he became a rich man because of the popularity of his wares, and his unique title, and the magic of this name to foreign visitors.

Another good friend of mine in Peking was an American, Charles D. Jameson, an engineer who had done wonderful rescue work during the Boxer rebellion. Shortly after I arrived in Peking, Mr. Jameson asked me if I wanted to see a wonderful mandarin coat of sable. I said, "yes," and he brought it to me. It had come from a high class mandarin who had to go into mourning with the court for three years because of the death of the Emperor and Empress Dowager, and he wanted to sell it. After months of dickering, I bought it for a ridiculously small sum. I think it was the best purchase I made in China and it greatly delighted my wife.

I had learned something of furs during my Alaskan tour and was frequently called upon by friends to judge specimens, and when my wife wanted an ermine coat and ruff, I picked out, from thousands submitted to us, enough skins of absolutely perfect quality and pure white, and had a mandarin coat made of them with a muff to match. These garments have added materially to the comfort and pleasure of my wife since that time.

The winters are cold in Peking but very dry, and one of the chief pleasures of winter is skating, indulged in by foreigners all winter long. They have some excellent skating rinks in Peking and good care is taken of them. Every night after the skating is finished, the ice is swept and sprinkled and in the morning it is absolutely perfect again. Many of the legation guards had skating rinks, and we at the American Legation had a very good one indeed. I never saw any amusement more enjoyed by the officers and enlisted men than was our skating rink. All winter long we had skating parties every night and frequently masquerade carnivals.

Each year in Peking, we of the American Legation Guard got up a competitive rifle match between all the legations guards in Peking. I am happy to say that during the three years I was there, the American legation guard won every match. The matches were held on the international rifle range just outside of Peking. I remember in particular an answer I got from the commander of the French guard the first time I asked him to take part in the International Shoot. He replied that he had read over our proposed rules and saw that the ranges were put down in yards and as their sights were ranged in meters, it would be impossible for them to take part. I sent him a table showing him how to convert meters into yards and vice versa, and also gave a copy of this to the commanding officers of the other legation guards and we all had a laugh on the Frenchman. The fact of the matter was, he did not want to shoot with us and this was the excuse he gave. We all told him that in case of war we wondered if an enemy would always stop so many meters away.

There were many legation guard dinners while I was there, and they were all very enjoyable. The most amusing one of all was a dinner given by Colonel Lavr Kornilov—afterwards famous in the Russian Revolution—at the Russian guard officers' mess. This dinner was given in honor of the Japanese Military Attaché, Major General Kazutsugu Inouye. This being the first time the Japanese and Russians had met socially in Peking since the Russo-Japanese War, they made a great occasion of it. All the military officers in Peking were invited. Before dinner, in the living room of their quarters, they had a table prepared in the ordinary Russian way "zakuska," which consisted of caviar sandwiches, olives, radishes, and even a couple of hot dishes, and vodka also was served. It seemed as though this zakuska was almost enough for a dinner itself.

Finally we went into the dining room and sat down to dinner, and in the hall, outside, were about forty Cossacks, singing wild Cossack songs throughout the dinner. At the proper time during the dinner, Colonel Kornilov arose and said that he had a very pleasant duty to perform in proposing the health of their guest of honor, Major General Inouye. We all arose to drink this toast, and had just seated ourselves again when the folding doors opened and in rushed these forty Cossacks and grabbed General Inouye, who was a short stout man, and tossed him to the ceiling and back several times, catching him in their hands. We all laughed a great deal at this and the General took it in good humor.

A little later Colonel Kornilov again arose and proposed the health of the next senior officer present, which happened to be myself, and the same performance was gone through. I certainly thought every time I came down I was going to fall to the floor, but never did. Just as the dinner was over, the Commanding Officer of the British Legation Guard, Colonel J.H. Anderson, who had been unable to attend the dinner owing to a previous engagement, came in. He had not seen any of the fun, and no man was ever more surprised than he when these Cossacks grabbed him and tossed him to the ceiling. After dinner we all adjourned to the living room and there many of the Russian officers and enlisted men gave exhibitions of Russian dances.

Peking was a very great place for parties and dancing. There was something taking place nearly every afternoon or evening at one of the Legations. I remember one very funny incident at a ball given at the British Legation, where for the first time I saw the high class Chinese girls dance. A young Chinese Princess was there, dressed in the regulation Chinese costume, short jacket and trousers, and at the same dance was an officer of the British Legation Guard, a Scotch Highlander, who was in full regalia. I have never seen a more amusing sight on the floor than this little Chinese Princess with her coat and trousers, dancing with the Scotch Highlander with his kilts.

Finally the time drew near for me to leave Peking and the day before my family was to leave, we gave a reception in order to see all of our friends in the legation quarters, and to say goodbye to them. Everybody came. During the reception, Colonel Anderson of the British Guard rapped for attention, and he took from his pocket a small square silver box and a roll of parchment, and announced that the officers of the legation guards and the military and naval attachés in Peking had had a meeting at which they had decided to confer upon Mrs. George Barnett their order of "United Flags," and that he had in the box number one of the order, as it was gotten up especially for Mrs. Barnett. This order consisted of a decoration in the shape of a cart wheel, made of cloisonné, and between the spokes of the wheel were enameled flags of the different countries represented, and attached to this decoration was a ribbon to go around the neck. He then opened the parchment and read from it the inscription which stated that, "We, the Military and Naval Attachés and Officers of the Legation Guards in Peking, hereby confer upon Mrs. George Barnett, the wife of Colonel Barnett, commandant of the American Legation Guard, our order of the United Flags in memory of her never having failed to observe the policy of the open door, of her house, in China." This is one of my wife's most cherished possessions. The parchment contained the signatures and seal of each of the officers who had gotten it up.

The next day when my family left, practically everyone in Peking came to see them off, and the compartment occupied by them was practically filled with beautiful flowers. It is needless to say that my wife and the children were all very sad as they were leaving a place where they had enjoyed every moment of their stay, and many good friends. It has been our good fortune in Washington to meet many of them again, particularly General Louis Collardet of the French Army, and His Excellency Baron de Cartier, Ambassador of Belgium, also the present Chinese Minister to the United States.

Editor's Comments on Chapter XIV

From its founding, the Marine Corps enjoyed a special relationship with the State Department, to the extent that at many points they functioned as the "State Department's soldiers." Marines were conveniently at hand when an ambassador needed escorting or when an embassy was endangered, though these were ad-hoc deployments, not permanent postings. When the foreign legations in Peking were threatened by the Boxer Rebellion in 1900, Marines from nearby ships rushed to help defend them. Marines also played a role in the relief of the ensuing siege. They then returned to their regular postings.

In view of the unsettled situation in China, the State Department decided to establish its first ever permanent legation guard there. An army detachment was already on site, but the ambassador requested Marines. They had performed well and could be reinforced without fuss or delay from nearby ships. This was formalized in 1905 by an executive order, which established the first Marine Legation Guard. In 1913, a similar guard was authorized in Nicaragua with a mission that extended well beyond diplomatic security. These long-term efforts in China and Nicaragua failed as exercises in nation building, but were the origins for the later Marine Security Guard program.

Since this new mission was in development, the Legation Guard in Peking was an important post. John Russell succeeded Barnett and was followed by Dion Williams. Thomas Holcomb was on detached duty there during Barnett's tenure, learning Chinese. Despite the sometimes uncertain security, it was a desirable posting. Living was inexpensive, with a household of several servants the norm for officers. The Imperial Court and foreign embassies provided a social scene that few other postings could match. Furs and other luxury items were readily available. Mrs. Barnett amassed a sizable collection of jade, enough to host and outfit a jade themed party when she returned to Washington. The Chinese Revolution would not begin until 1911 and Barnett's years in China were relatively quiet.

After the devastation wrought by the Boxers, the Legation Quarter was totally rebuilt, with an eye on defense. The American compound expanded to include a barracks and parade ground. Stout walls and fortified gates were erected to protect the Quarter. A buffer zone, known as the Glacis, was cleared around it. The Quarter evolved into a miniature city within a city, with its own Grand Hotel. Chinese could not live in the Quarter and were only allowed in as servants, tradesmen or invited guests.

The Yale educated railroad engineer Barnett encountered, Jeme Tien Yow (Zhān Tiānyòu), is often called "The Father of China's Railroads." Jeme was one of a group of students sent to study in the United States and received his civil engineering degree from Yale the same year Barnett graduated from Annapolis. The Empress Dowager commissioned him to build a line from Peking to Kalgan (Zhangjiakou) and the Great Wall, which was completed in 1909.

Liang Dunyan also studied at Yale. He rose to minister of foreign affairs (1908–1910) and was minister of transportation in the new republic (1914–1916). His final office was as minister of foreign affairs in the brief second reign of Emperor Puyi. It was his misfortune to achieve such offices as the central government was disintegrating and China was descending into chaos.

Henry Mustin and his wife Corrine appear briefly in Barnett's narrative, but both deserve better. Corrine DeForest Montague was nearly sixteen years younger than her sister, so that Lelia played a significant role in helping to raise her. During Barnett's "Gordon setter" period, he was taken ill and Lelia and her sister visited him regularly. While Lelia nursed Barnett upstairs, Corrine was being charmed by Navy Lieutenant Henry Mustin downstairs. Despite a thirteen year age difference, the relationship developed and they were married in October 1907, with Barnett serving as best man. Corrine followed her husband when he sailed with the Great White Fleet and visited the Barnetts in Peking. After her husband's death, Corrine married George D. Murray, another navy officer. Between her marriages, the Barnetts were a great help to the young widow and her children.

Henry Croskey Mustin (1874–1923) was a major figure in the development of naval aviation. He established the navy's first permanent air station at Pensacola in January 1914 and served as its first commanding officer. The first operational missions of naval aircraft were flown under his command during the Vera Cruz landings in 1914. On November 5, 1915, he successfully flew an AB-2 flying boat off the stern of the USS *North Carolina* in Pensacola Bay, making the first catapult launch from a ship underway. Unsatisfied with the results, he pushed for the development of ships designed to launch aircraft. He even helped design the Naval Aviator Insignia and is one of several officers who can justly be referred to as "The Father of Naval Aviation."

Suggested Reading

Biggs, Chester M. *The United States Marines in North China, 1894–1942.* Jefferson, NC: McFarland, 2003.
Chang, Jung. *Empress Dowager Cixi: The Concubine Who Launched Modern China.* New York: Alfred A. Knopf, 2013.
Clark, George B. *Treading Softly: U.S. Marines in China, 1819–1949.* Westport, CN: Praeger, 2001.
Daugherty, Leo J. *The Marine Corps and the State Department: Enduring Partners in United States Foreign Policy, 1798–2007.* Jefferson, NC: McFarland, 2009.
Ewing, Charle, and Bessie Ewing. *Death Throes of a Dynasty: Letters and Diaries of Charles and Bessie Ewing, Missionaries to China.* Kent, OH: Kent State University Press, 1990.
La Motte, Ellen N. *Peking Dust.* New York: The Century Co., 1919.
Leibovitz, Liel, Matthew Miller, and Matthew I. Miller. *Fortunate Sons: The 120 Chinese Boys Who Came to America, Went to School, and Revolutionized an Ancient Civilization.* New York: W. W. Norton, 2011.
Morton, John Fass. *Mustin: A Naval Family of the Twentieth Century.* Annapolis, MD: Naval Institute Press, 2003.
Moser, Michael J., and Yeone Wei-chin Moser. *Foreigners within the Gates: The Legations at Peking.* New York: Oxford University Press, 1993.

Chapter XV

Philadelphia, the Advanced Base Force and Culebra

After returning from Peking, I was ordered to duty in command of the Marine Barracks at Philadelphia, Pennsylvania.

Shortly after my arrival in this country, I had the sad duty of attending the funeral of my sister Laura. My sister and I had been unusually close to each other. While I had been away from home practically since I was a boy, when she was about fifteen years old, she came east to attend school in Baltimore and I saw her frequently there. After she finished school in Baltimore, she went to the Boston Conservatory of Music, where she graduated. For a number of years thereafter, she lived with me, keeping house for me. She never had been very strong. She died much younger than I had expected and when I returned from China, it was sad news for me when I arrived in San Francisco to learn that she was desperately ill in Washington. I hurried to Washington and fortunately got there a few days before she died. I do not believe that anybody in this world, excepting my mother, ever thought more of me than she did, and I know of no one in the world who would have been half as proud of seeing me appointed major general commandant of the Marine Corps, as she would have been.

Shortly after reporting in command of the Marine Barracks at Philadelphia, I was promoted to the rank of colonel, so that during the whole four years that I was in command of that barracks, I held that rank.

During this tour of duty there was established at Philadelphia the Advanced Base School of the Marine Corps, where we taught many of the subjects considered necessary for officers and men of an advanced base force to know. This included instruction in infantry, artillery, signals, submarine mining, wireless, ordinary telegraphy, search lights, etc.

During this tour of duty I went on four expeditions to the West Indies.

None of these amounted to much, but like all similar affairs, one never knew whether they were going to amount to anything or not.

In January, 1914, I was ordered to the Island of Culebra, in the West Indies, in command of two regiments of Marines, and an advanced base outfit to try out the instructions we had been giving in the Advanced Base School in Philadelphia. We sailed from Philadelphia on the USS *Hancock* and the USS *Prairie*, and in due time arrived at Culebra and were given the problem in hand, which had been made out by the admiral of the North Atlantic Fleet and his staff.

The problem was that we were to land the Marines, our advanced base guns, mines, etc., and have six days in which to plant our mines, mount our guns for the defense of the entrance, dig rifle pits, trenches, etc., on the island to prevent a landing from any direction, and at the end of six days we were to be attacked by certain designated forces of the Atlantic Fleet.

Among other things we planted five 5 inch guns at the entrance of the harbor on an elevation of about 240 feet, and it was no small task getting these guns ashore from the transport on to the beach and then dragging them up this precipitous height, through a tropical jungle. Everybody worked practically night and day, as much as it was possible for men to do. About three o'clock in the morning, following the sixth day, we were attacked by a landing party from the fleet.

Umpires had been appointed to observe the attack and see that certain rules were carried out and decide which was the winner. Rear Admiral (at that time captain) William S. Sims was the chief umpire. He was on shore, living in one of our camps, and when word came that the attack had been started, the whole camp was routed out and he, with the others, started towards the point of attack.

There had been some talk a few days before about officers of the fleet being on shore spying out our defenses, and we did not want anybody connected with the fleet to know where they were. The night that Admiral Sims started toward where the attack was to be, he met a Marine and asked him if he knew where the attack was. The Marine, thinking that the admiral was one of the officers from the fleet, and remembering what had been said about the spies from the fleet being on shore, took the admiral for a spy and instead of leading him towards the attack, led him around in a different direction entirely away from the place of attack. The admiral soon found that this Marine was leading him away from the attack and changed his course and arrived shortly after the rest of us did and witnessed most of the attack.

After the different umpires had met and conferred with each other, they decided that the Marines won, which was very gratifying to all of us. As a result of these maneuvers very complimentary reports were made to the Navy Department by the chief umpire and Admiral Badger, commander in chief of the North Atlantic Fleet, copies of which are incorporated below:

"17. During his observations, extending over about 24 hours, during which time the Chief Observer personally inspected all the advance base positions west of Great Harbor, except that at the point "C," he was very greatly impressed with many evidences of the very high degree of efficiency on the part of the men and officers comprising the detachment. They appeared to be in splendid physical condition. Their morale was very high. They entered into their work not only with interest but with admirable enthusiasm. Their plans for the defense of the island seemed most excellent; positions were well chosen, and the improvised defenses for the same, notwithstanding the great physical exertion involved, were carefully made to the last detail possible within the time they had been at work upon them.

"18. Attention is invited to the very complete outfit of the Advance Base Detachment and to the great variety of military work required of officers and men. Rifle pits and bomb proof shelters have been dug, 3" and 5" guns have been landed in transports, dragged up steep declivities and installed ready for firing. Methods for both direct and indirect fire have been perfected for both fixed and field artillery. Mine fields have been laid, and an aviation camp has been established. The problem of supply to the numerous outlying camps has been well worked out in a waterless country almost devoid of supplies. A very complete system of communications, including 4 miles of telephone system, a radio plant, a night and day heliograph system, and a flag semaphore system have been established. All parts of this work seem to have been done in an extraordinarily efficient manner.

"20. In conclusion, and in addition to such commendation as has been expressed above in its appropriate place, I beg to state that observing and reporting upon these operations has been not only very agreeable as a personal experience, but has proved peculiarly valuable as an inspiring example of efficiency.

"An examination of the installations made on shore, the astonishing amount of work required to create the defenses in the rocky soil (with, incidentally, inefficient tools for such work) makes it apparent that such results could have been accomplished only by a harmonious combination of thorough planning and admirable administration, actually by the driving force of an enthusiastic devotion to duty extending throughout the entire command. It is a most gratifying example of the great military value of a high degree of esprit de corps and cheerful devotion to duty in overcoming discouraging obstacles and difficulties.

I really think that this report had considerable to do with my eventually being selected as major general commandant of the Marine Corps. There had been a vacancy in this position for some time and the secretary of the navy was undecided as to which officer to recommend, and I think that this letter together with a telegraphic report made by Admiral Badger had considerable to do with his decision. I have no real knowledge on this subject. I have heard it so stated and believe this, because almost immediately after the admiral's telegraphic report, I received notice of my appointment.

During the time we were in Culebra, a traveling theatrical troupe appeared on the island thinking that they could pick up a good deal of money from the Marines on the island and the sailormen from the fleet who came ashore. Unfortunately everybody was too busy to take much interest in theatricals, and the troupe went broke. There were three men and two women in the party, and I do not know what they would have done if it had not been for the food we gave them from our mess.

When it came time for us to go away, I learned that this troupe was absolutely broke, so I asked the captain of the *Prairie* if he would take them as far as San Juan, Puerto Rico, which he consented to do. One man of the troupe named Raymond, one of the best sleight of hand performers I had ever seen, did not deserve to go broke, but there he was down and out. I saw this and asked him if he had any money, and he replied that he did not have a cent, so I loaned him fifty dollars.

When I told Major Louis Magill of this he kissed the ends of his fingers and said "goodbye fifty." Raymond promised to return the money to me the first moment he could do so. Some of the other officers quoted the old expression, "a fool and his money are soon parted." But that man needed that fifty dollars far more than I did, and I was willing to help him. The result proved that I was correct, because about two years later I got a draft from Raymond from Buenos Aires, Argentina, and a letter filled with thanks for what I had done for him. In this letter he said that the fifty dollars I loaned him looked greater to him than five thousand dollars had looked to him many times in his life. I was very glad to get this money, not only for its sake alone, but because it confirmed my judgment in this particular man and in human nature.

Editor's Comments on Chapter XV

In 1910, Barnett was on the short list for the office of commandant. He was a colonel, the highest permanent rank available in the Corps at that time. That the less senior Barnett was considered is a tribute to his reputation and that of the rising USNA graduates in the Corps.

Barnett references the Advanced Base School only in passing, but it was a turning point in Marine history. Barnett was an early supporter of the use of Marines to seize and hold advanced bases for the navy. The Old Guard was insistent on retaining shipboard duties that were no longer relevant and saw new missions as a threat. Other officers had developed their careers as colonial infantry and saw that as the future of the Corps. As early as the 1890s, it was Barnett and his Annapolis classmates who aimed at an amphibious future.

The Advanced Base School was where the Corps started developing the doctrine, tactics and equipment necessary for amphibious warfare. Though the Advanced Base Brigade would not be used as originally intended until the concept had undergone significant development, its beginnings are important for several reasons:

- It pioneered regular amphibious operations. Operations like the 1914 landings at Vera Cruz and the ongoing Culebra exercises gave the Marines opportunities to explore the many difficulties inherent in landing troops in combat situations. As war with Japan looked increasingly likely, the Marines trained to hold or seize islands.
- It demonstrated the need for specialized equipment, especially landing craft.
- Since Advanced Base brigades were created on both coasts, it required permanent formations and justified new bases. Until this time, the Corps had formed mainly ad-hoc battalions and operated out of crowded urban navy yards.
- It transformed the Marines from a light infantry force to a combined arms force that would closely integrate infantry, artillery and even aviation.
- It quieted the powerful voices who had advocated for the abolition of the Corps by demonstrating that it had a vital role to play in a modern navy.
- The Advanced Base School required that the Corps develop a rigorous and wide ranging training regime that could be scaled up.
- Without the new training regime, permanent formations and bases, the Marines would have been ill prepared to participate in World War I.

Suggested Reading

Bartlett, Merrill L. *Assault from the Sea: Essays on the History of Amphibious Warfare*. Annapolis, MD: Naval Institute Press, 1983.

Bartlett, Merrill L. "Ben Hebard Fuller and the Genesis of a Modern United States Marine Corps, 1891–1934." *Journal of Military History* 69, 1 (2005): 73–91.

Clifford, Kenneth J., *Progress and Purpose: A Developmental History of the United States Marine Corps, 1900–1970,*. Washington, D.C. History and Museums Division, United States Marine Corps, 1973.

Cosmas, Graham A., and Jack Shulimson. "Continuity and Consensus: The Evolution of the Marine Advance Base Force, 1900–1922." In *Proceedings of the Citadel Conference on War and Diplomacy*. Eds. David H. White and John W. Gordon. Charleston, SC: Citadel. 1977.

Cosmas, Graham A., and Jack Shulimson. "The Culebra Maneuver and the Formation of the U.S. Marine Corps's Advance Base Force, 1913–14." In *Changing Interpretations and New Sources in Naval History.* Ed. Robert W. Love, Jr. New York: Garland 1980.
Daugherty, Leo J. *Pioneers of Amphibious Warfare, 1898–1945: Profiles of Fourteen American Military Strategists.* Jefferson, NC: McFarland, 2009.
Smith, Holland M. *The Development of Amphibious Tactics in the U.S. Navy.* Washington, D.C.: History and Museums Division, Headquarters, U.S. Marine Corps, 1992.
Shulimson, Jack. *The Marine Corps' Search for a Mission, 1880–1898.* Modern War Studies. Lawrence: University Press of Kansas, 1993.

CHAPTER XVI

Appointment as Commandant

My headquarters were in a small square brick building. I had one room, my adjutant had one room, there was one room used as the mess room, and across the hall from my room my two aides lived. A telephone was in the hall just outside my door. This telephone was connected with the *Prairie* outfit, so we got our wireless messages by telephone from the USS *Prairie*.

About three o'clock one morning I heard the phone ring, but it had been ringing so much of late, and I had gotten up several times before to answer it. I decided this time that I would not get up but let it ring until one of my aides heard it. Presently after the telephone had rung several times, I heard one of the aides take down the receiver and say "Well, what is it?" About a second later he dropped the receiver, and came running into my room yelling like a wild Indian, telling me I had been appointed major general commandant of the Marine Corps. It was not very long until everybody in camp was up and heard this news.

My adjutant Major Louis Magill, called up the two camp commanders, lieutenant colonels Charles Long and John Lejeune,

A beaming Colonel Barnett, just before his promotion to commandant in 1914 (Library of Congress).

XVI—Appointment as Commandant

and told them the news. Colonel Long's tent was quite a distance from the telephone in his camp. When the orderly answered, Major Magill asked him if Colonel Long was there and the orderly replied that as it was raining, he would take the message for Colonel Long. Major Magill said "No," that he wanted to speak to Colonel Long. The orderly shortly came back to the telephone and said that Colonel Long wanted him to take the message. Major Magill then replied that the major general commandant wanted to speak to Colonel Long. Colonel Long again sent the orderly back and asked that he be given the message. Major Magill telephoned back to the orderly to tell Colonel Long that the major general commandant was not in the habit of receiving such answers and he wanted him to answer the telephone at once. Then Long caught on and he came to the phone.

At day break Colonel Lejeune and staff appeared on horseback and shortly afterwards Colonel Long and his officers appeared from the other camp by boat. We had a great celebration. I sent to the ship and got all the champagne they had in the wine mess and we had a real party. I forgot to mention that in the middle of the night when we got the news, it was very hot and rainy, but it made no difference to us; we all took our lanterns and in our pajamas had a regular parade through the camp.

Major Magill, who was a great friend of mine, caught me by the collar of my pajamas and gave me a kick and said "just for once in my life I am going to have the satisfaction of saying that I kicked a Major General."

That day, later on, I received several wireless messages of congratulations. It is strange that the first one I received was from the commanding officer of the Legation Guard, Managua, Nicaragua, whose wireless had picked up the original message from the secretary of the navy notifying me of my appointment.

The next message I got was from Admiral Frank Beatty, commanding one of the divisions of the North Atlantic Fleet. His wireless operator had picked up a message from my wife to me simply saying, "Congratulations." The admiral, knowing that I was hoping for this appointment, concluded that I had been appointed and sent me a wireless congratulating me.

After we finished our maneuvers and re-embarked all of our material and men, we sailed for Pensacola, Florida, where I left the ship and proceeded to Washington. When I came on deck to leave the ship in the harbor of Pensacola, I was very deeply impressed to find that the side boys consisted of officers of my own command. As the Marine Guard presented arms, the band played an appropriate march, and these side boys saluted. I thought I was about as much touched as it was possible to be. When I went over the side, I found that the cutter was manned by officers of my own command, which also touched me very deeply and I shall never forget it.

This act of officers acting as side boys and manning the cutter told me that those with whom I had been serving held me high enough in their regard to be of personal service to me. I have always found during my long service that one can have duty well performed, in fact better performed, by having a happy peaceful command. I never believed that in order to get better efficiency one must be a martinet; in fact, I have found it quite the opposite.

I believe in strict discipline, but I abhor nagging. I believe in quick, firm decisions. I believe in reprimanding officers and men when necessary but never have believed in reprimanding an officer or a man in a way to hurt his feelings and pride. The object of a reprimand should be to correct faults, so as to get better service in the future. This cannot be done if a sore spot is left; I have always believed that better duty is done when there is confidence and loyalty than through fear. I think that much of the trouble in the service over disobedience of orders comes from wrong orders having been given; in fact almost every case of disobedience of orders comes from the fact that the order disobeyed should never have been given.

Early in my career I remember the definition an old officer gave me of discipline. He said that true discipline consisted in never giving an order that was likely to be disobeyed. While this cannot be taken absolutely literally, it is almost literally true; at least so I have found it in my service.

Officers and enlisted men are inclined to obey orders and those that are disobeyed are ninety-nine times out of a hundred, orders that should not have been given, or that were given in a way that was unnecessarily harsh, or in a way to create anything except the spirit of cooperation, and without cooperation there is no success. Success can best be accomplished by team work. These remarks may seem out of place at this time but they were brought to mind as I thought back to the time when these officers acted as side boys and others acted as the crew that pulled me ashore.

At Pensacola, I met my brother-in-law, Commander Mustin, who was then in command of the USS *Mississippi* on aviation duty. I left that night for Washington accompanied by Colonel Lejeune and Colonel Wendell Neville, who had been ordered to Washington for examination for promotion. In due time I reported in Washington for duty and appointed Colonel Lejeune as my assistant.

Naturally, one's life in any business or service is spent in looking forward to the possible day of being at the head of his profession. Therefore it was with sincere satisfaction that I took the oath of office as major general commandant of the Marine Corps.

I decided at once that there were several things that I always thought should be done and that now was the time for me to try them out. I had always been of the opinion that there was altogether too much secrecy at Headquarters, and that the officers in general, particularly the older officers of the Corps, should know, as far as practicable, of what was going on at Headquarters.

Since that time I have carried out this idea as far as practicable, and I find that it has created much better satisfaction throughout the Corps. Several times while I was on duty in Philadelphia as a colonel, I received telegraphic orders to sail in command of an expeditionary outfit with no notice whatever until the telegraphic orders arrived. I have always thought that this was unnecessary, and now I know it, because I know that practically no expeditionary duty crops up on the moment, and therefore it is entirely feasible to give the senior officers some warning ahead of time; that they could at least be told that if certain contingencies arose, they would be detailed for this duty and therefore should be ready to leave almost at a moment's notice.

Later, I was appointed an ex officio member of the General Board of the Navy, largely I think at the request of Admiral Dewey, the president of the board. I was gratified by this appointment because I considered it highly proper that the Marine Corps should be represented on a board where practically all naval matters are thoroughly considered and because the Corps is an integral part of the navy and very often had questions considered by the Board. I enjoyed my duty as a member of that very important Board, and I always felt that if Marine Corps matters presented did not at all times meet the approval of the Board, I at least had had my day in court, and had been able to present the case from the Marine viewpoint. It was an extreme pleasure to be a fellow member with the splendid officers who formed the Board and who at all times treated the Marine Corps and me with courtesy and consideration.

Editor's Comments on Chapter XVI

It was certainly not a coincidence that Barnett was appointed commandant after the successful conclusion of the 1914 Culebra exercises, but the success of the Advanced Base Force Brigade was far from the only factor. Politics and personalities were as important in the selection process as military accomplishments. Littleton Waller was the senior colonel and marshaled his supporters. Both Democratic senators from his home state of Virginia made personal appeals to President Wilson on his behalf. Thirty-one Democratic senators signed a petition supporting him. Lincoln Karmany was also senior to Barnett and had Biddle's support, but a messy divorce disqualified him. Lejeune, seven years junior to Barnett, was clearly a remarkable officer and worthy of consideration. In the end, Secretary of the Navy Josephus Daniels felt that he could not justify promoting Lejeune over Barnett and the anti–Imperialist Wilson could not stomach Waller's reputation as "The Butcher of Samar." Though Barnett's appointment was a great personal accomplishment, it also marked the arrival of the Fabulous Fifty at the pinnacle of power.

The notion is sometimes advanced that Barnett unworthily obtained the commandancy through political or social means, even though all candidates freely used whatever political muscle they could muster. While Barnett had friends in high places, many of them were Republicans and thus without influence on Wilson. Mrs. Barnett's social connections would have been a liability rather than an asset in dealing with the teetotaling, anti-elite Daniels. Politics mainly entered into it in that Waller's past was politically unacceptable to Wilson and Daniels.

Barnett's record was exemplary, if somewhat short on powder burns. He was a proponent of the Advanced Base Force, which the navy had been demanding the Marines develop for fourteen years without much result. He had the right mixture of political, social and naval connections to get things done in Washington. He would lead the Marines where they needed to go to survive. If he was more an administrator than a great combat leader, he was the right man to lead the Corps at this crucial juncture.

That politics had any influence at all might seem inappropriate today, but it was commonplace at the time. In 1910, Waller was widely expected to be appointed as commandant. At the last moment, Pennsylvania's Congressional delegation made it clear to President Taft that their ongoing legislative support depended upon the selection of William Biddle. Biddle was senior, but more importantly, he was a Pennsylvanian. On that basis, the lethargic Biddle became commandant and the energetic Waller was sidetracked.

Except for USNA graduates, all Marine Corps officers of the time were presidential appointments. Applications were necessarily accompanied by letters of recommendation from prominent people. The process was so overtly political that a joke had it that USMC stood for "Useless Sons Made Comfortable." No training, education or military background was required for a commission, but connections were essential. Waller, for example, came from a prominent Virginia family. Hoping for a military career, he applied to the cavalry, which turned him down as too short. With his family background, his height was no barrier to a commission in the Marines.

Even placement of Annapolis graduates was subject to such influence. During John Lejeune's cadet cruise, he watched forty-three of his shipmates die during the Apia cyclone of 1889. Convinced that the naval life was not for him, he applied for the Marine Corps upon graduation. As he was sixth in his class, the navy refused his request, since only lower ranked graduates were allowed to join the Marines. Lejeune appealed the decision to the top of the chain of command. He was turned down and cautioned to not raise the issue again. He involved his senators and a deal was soon arranged for him to join the Marines.

Commandants did not have final say on personnel matters and were often frustrated when trying to discipline wayward officers or assign postings. If the officers involved had enough political muscle they could, and did, have the commandant over-ruled by his civilian masters. For example, in 1909, Colonel Charles Lauchheimer exchanged words with Commandant Elliott over a legal case. Lauchheimer was Adjutant and Inspector, one of the top staff positions at Marine Headquarters. After much bureaucratic infighting, and despite the involvement of Congressman Weeks, Lauchheimer found himself assigned to the Philippines. He stayed in exile for a year, before the political pressure on Taft became too strong to resist and he was restored to his office.

When direct commissions were reinstituted in 1898, Smedley Butler, the son and grandson of congressmen, had no trouble obtaining a commission, despite being only sixteen. A brave, inventive and resourceful officer, he had an outsized career because his father served on the House Committee on Naval Affairs. When he failed the physical exam for promotion to captain at age eighteen, Butler sought and received his father's assistance in obtaining a waiver. When Haiti was where the action was, he insisted on being assigned there. In his very complimentary *Maverick Marine*, Hans Schmidt documents Butler using his father's political influence on numerous occasions.

Direct lobbying of Congress by officers was inevitable, common and strictly forbidden. As newsman Benjamin Standish Baker wrote "when it comes to being in constant and effective touch with members of Congress, and thus securing desired legislation and favors, the Marine Corps is the easy leader." Such lobbying was rarely overt. Lauchheimer and Barnett kept in close contact with their classmates, senators Weeks and Weller. During World War I, Lejeune had two senator's sons on his staff. He requested the son of Secretary Daniels, but Butler had already recruited him for his staff. This served to further cement the Daniels/Butler relationship.

The Marines needed such political pull just to survive. In 1908, President Roosevelt signed Executive Order 969, which redefined Marine duties while excluding shipboard service. His plan was to merge the Corps into the army, in part because their oversized political influence offended him. Commandant Elliott and his staff went into action and a budget rider sponsored by Congressman Butler over-ruled Roosevelt.

The Marines and the navy formed a tightly knit community, though family relationships and social ties weren't always apparent. Barnett's sister Laura was married to Dr. Emory Reisinger, son of a navy captain. Emory's brother Harold C. Reisinger (USNA 1900) was a Marine staff officer and later reached brigadier general. Harold was married to Daisy Badger Elliott, the daughter of Marine Commandant George F. Elliott and the niece of Admiral Charles Badger. It was true that each new officer might one day become a relative.

It was equally true that each new officer might become an adversary. The Corps was a badly fractured operation, subject to fratricidal infighting. It was those promoting a naval mission versus those who wanted to continue as colonial infantry. It was the Annapolis graduates versus those directly commissioned. It was staff officers versus line officers. There was a generational split, with the early Annapolis graduates versus those who followed them a decade later. It was even the "wets" versus the "drys." These factions overlapped and were complicated by a natural ambition for limited commands and advancement. Overall, there were two main groups. Barnett stood in the first rank of the professionally trained, pro-navy, pro-amphibious one. The seat of the pants, anti-navy, colonial infantry group extolled Waller as their exemplar and claimed Butler as their rising star. Every controversy during this era exhibited some element of this major split.

It can only be conjecture what course events might have taken if Waller had been appointed in 1910 or 1914. He was not a supporter of the Advanced Base concept and did not have Barnett's close connections with the navy. It is likely that he would have resisted the navy's demands, which would have strengthened the voices calling for the Corps' abolition. The Advanced Base brigades were an important rationale for an expanded Corps and the acquisition of Quantico. It is unlikely that Commandant Waller would have been able to force the AEF to accept Marines for service in France and seen to their transport. Though some felt (and still feel) that Waller deserved the commandancy, it was fortunate for the Corps that he never achieved it.

Suggested Reading

Millett, Allan Reed, and Jack Shulimson.. *Commandants of the Marine Corps*. Annapolis, MD: Naval Institute Press, 2004.

Schmidt, Hans. *Maverick Marine: General Smedley D. Butler and the Contradictions of American Military History*. Lexington: University Press of Kentucky, 1987.

Wiegand, Wayne A. "The Lauchheimer Controversy: A Case of Group Political Pressure During the Taft Administration." *Military Affairs* 40, 2 (April 1976): 54.

Chapter XVII

The Great War

When I took command of the Marine Corps, it consisted of about 343 officers and 10,000 men. Since that time changes have been made as follows:
August 29, 1916: 597 officers, 14,981 men (permanent)
March 26, 1917: 693 officers, 17,400 men (permanent)
May 22, 1917: 1,197 officers, 30,000 men (temporary)
July 1, 1918: 3,017 officers, 75,500 men (temporary)
July 11, 1919: 1,093 officers, 27,400 men (permanent)

When I saw that we were soon to enter the war, I went to Secretary of the Navy Josephus Daniels and told him that in all wars we had had, Marines had served with the army, and that as far as we were concerned, I felt that it would be very largely fighting on land. I invited his attention to the fact that the law gave the president in time of war the authority to, by executive order, transfer the whole or any part of the Marine Corps to the army; and that in all previous wars, he had availed himself of that privilege. I told the secretary that I considered it absolutely essential that such an executive order be procured, and that unless Marines were to serve with the army, we could not secure good recruits, and that it would kill the Marine Corps. The secretary obtained the executive order, and the order stated that in so far as related to the Marines serving in France, I was constituted an officer of the War Department, so that I could communicate with Secretary of War Newton D. Baker.

We had used the slogan "First to Fight" on our posters, and I did not want that slogan made ridiculous, so felt it essential that some Marines must be gotten over with the first AEF outfit sailing for France. I received assurances that one regiment of Marines would be included in the first outfit to sail from New York under naval convoy. The names of the ships to carry them and their date of sailing were kept secret, but I knew about these matters.

The Fifth Regiment of Marines was ready to sail and I waited for word as to what ship was to take them, but I did not wait too long without making other tentative arrangements. The day before the ships were to sail, I received a letter written personally by the secretary of war, about as follows:

> My dear General:
>
> I am very sorry to have to tell you that it will be utterly impossible for the War Department to furnish transportation for a Marine regiment with the first outfit sailing, but will do my best to furnish transportation as soon as possible

I at once personally wrote about as follows:

> My dear Mr. Secretary:
>
> Your letter of this date just received, telling me you cannot furnish transportation for the Marines on the ships taking the first forces of the AEF to France. Please give yourself no further trouble in this matter, as transportation for the Marines has been arranged for on board the naval escort ships.
> Very respectfully,
> George Barnett.

After the war I was asked to write an account of my greatest thrill during the war and I replied that I had no <u>particular</u> thrill. In reply, I was urged to write something as most other general officers were doing so. I therefore described getting the Marines over with the first outfit as told above and wound up by saying that not for a million dollars would I have foregone the circumstances which made it possible to write as I did to the secretary of the War Department. Our slogan was not made ridiculous and the work done by the Marines in France fully justified me in wanting to have them at least among those present.

The secretary of the navy and the Chief of Operations, William Benson, had stated to the Committee on Naval Affairs at the time the different increases were being granted, that in their opinion, 30,000 Marines were sufficient for naval purposes. I agreed with this statement, but in view of what I have said above, I thought it necessary to get into the game with the army. I later asked that the Corps be increased to 75,000 men with the necessary officers.

I told the secretary of the navy and the General Board that I promised them to at all times be ready to supply as many Marines as might be required for the naval service, even if every Marine had to be brought back from France. I said this because the only reason for the existence of the Marine Corps is naval, and I did not intend to have the navy ever call for extra Marines and be unable to supply them, no matter how I would have hated not having them serve with the army at that time.

I told the Committee that I did not see how they could go before their constituents if they voted to close any soldier factory during war, and that at Parris Island I had what might be called a good factory for turning out well trained soldiers. The next day, the Chairman of the Naval Committee of the House, Mr. Lemuel Padgett, told me that it would be impossible to get that through the Committee unless I could get word that General Pershing could use Marines in France. I therefore wrote a telegram to General Pershing, for the signature of the secretary of the navy , and called at the secretary's office and told him that while I knew he and Admiral Benson had recommended a limit of 30,000 men for the Marine Corps for naval purposes, I asked him to listen to me a few moments, as I believed I could convince him that that was the wrong stand to take. I told him that we were in a serious war, and that, in my opinion, with the comparatively small number of trained troops we had in our camps, it was necessary for every branch of the service to turn out as many men ready for fighting as possible. At Parris Island, South Carolina, Mare Island, California, and Quantico, Virginia, we had accommoda-

Admiral Victor Blue, Commandant George Barnett, Captain A. Fechteler, unknown aide, and Admiral Bradley A. Fisk with Secretary of the Navy Josephus Daniels (seated) in 1917. Daniels preferred that his military aides work in civilian clothes (Library of Congress).

tions where, in my opinion, during the year, we could properly train up to 75,000, and that nobody was justified in putting any limit on the number of men for any branch of the service as long as they could be properly trained. I convinced the secretary of the navy that I was right. He took the telegram and went with me to the acting secretary of war, who said he would forward the telegram to General Pershing in France.

After waiting several days, about a week in fact, and no answer having been received from General Pershing, I went to see the secretary of the navy again, and invited his attention to the fact that seven or eight days before he had asked the secretary of war to send the telegram and that no answer had been received. I told him what I had heard, that an answer had been received in the War Department, but that he, the secretary of the navy, had not been given a copy of it. He again went with me to the assistant secretary of war's office, as he was still acting secretary of war, and stated to the assistant secretary that eight days before he had asked to have a certain cablegram sent to General Pershing but as yet he had received no answer. The assistant secretary of war informed the secretary of the navy that he would repeat the telegram and have an answer for him the next day about four o'clock. This seemed rather strange to me that he could guarantee an answer by four o'clock the next day, when eight days had already elapsed without an answer. I had heard that the answer received in the War Department was unsatisfactory, from my point of view. This I do not know, but I believe it to be true if any answer was received. Personally I do not believe the original telegram was ever sent. I think they intended to forget it.

A couple of days after the sending of the first telegram a member of Congress had made a speech on the floor of the House of Representatives, accusing officers of the army of being so jealous of the Marines that they would not allow any more to go to France. If the answer to the telegram was received and was unsatisfactory, it was my belief that it was not given to the secretary of the navy because of the fact that they did not wish to give out the unfavorable answer in view of this speech that had been made. That would have convinced people at large that there was some truth in the jealousy spoken of by the congressman.

I do not wish to intimate that there was any jealousy on the other side at all, and I wish to say, that General Pershing gave the Marines absolutely fair and square treatment at all times. It was up to him as Commanding General to use the troops under his command in any way he saw fit, and without a doubt he at all times used them to the best advantage to accomplish the results desired.

To illustrate more clearly what I mean, shortly after the 5th Regiment of Marines went to France, they were placed on military police duty, which was very much to the disgust of many Marines in the United States and of those in France, and I was asked repeatedly what I was going to do about it. My reply was that I was going to do nothing about it at all as it was none of my business; that it was my business to get as many Marine fighting men as possible to France, and have them report to General Pershing, and after that it rested entirely with him as to where and how he should use them. A short time after this, I got an exceedingly nice letter from General Pershing stating that he had no doubt that friends of the Marines at home felt aggrieved about the Marines being put on police duty when they wanted to go to the front line, but that there was only one regiment of Marines there so far, and therefore, they were the most suitable for the necessary police duty. As soon as another regiment of Marines got over, he said he contemplated brigading them, and this he did as soon as the Sixth Regiment arrived. It was unnecessary for General Pershing to write this to me but I very greatly appreciated his having done so, as it told me what I already knew, that he would in a great big way do what he thought best under all circumstances.

As I said above, the assistant secretary of war had promised an answer to the cablegram the next afternoon at four o'clock, so the secretary of the navy told me to be at his office at four o'clock the next day, and I was there. The assistant secretary of war came in in about fifteen minutes and asked me many questions, among others, whether the Marines used the same rifle and ammunition as the army, and fortunately I could say that they did. He asked me whether they used the same drill book, and fortunately again I could answer in the affirmative. He asked me if it would require two lines of supplies in order to supply the Marines with the necessary clothing, food, etc. and this I told him was unnecessary because the Marines we had over there were wearing army uniforms; that they were part of the army, attached to the army by order of the president of the United States as authorized by law, and that they were as much a part of the army while serving in France, as any outfit of infantry, artillery, cavalry or any other organization.

As I said above, fortunately I was able to answer in the affirmative with reference to the drill book and rifle. I had for thirty years been a strong advocate, and had used every influence possible, to have the same drill book adopted by the navy and Marine Corps as that used by the army, as I could see no possible sense in having separate drill books for different branches of the service. Fortunately only a comparatively short time before the war came, this idea was put across; and similarly with the rifle. I had always argued that it was absurd for the different branches of the service to have different rifles, as was the case only a few years before, when the army, navy, and Marine

Corps all had different rifles, and therefore combined operations would have been impossible.

After the assistant secretary of war had received affirmative answers to all of these questions, he drew from his pocket a cablegram which stated that the army could use more Marines in France. Again I say that it was a surprise to me that an answer to a cablegram could have been gotten in about twenty-four hours, when for eight days no answer to the first one had come. This led me to believe what I had heard, that the original answer or what purported to be an answer, was, and had been, in the War Department for a number of days. It likewise led me to believe that the answer to the second cablegram came from the War Department itself, because the chief of staff had told me personally that he did not want any more Marines; that the army had enough soldiers of their own. Personally I have never believed that either telegram was ever sent to General Pershing, but I have no knowledge to bear this out.

In this connection I wish to state that it was a requisite that any Marine who even contemplated going to the fighting line in France must be a qualified "marksman" or better; further than that he had to go through the training course at Parris Island and then through the Advanced course at Quantico. This course at Quantico was conducted by both American and foreign officers, who had been at the front in France and brought back as instructors. The training at Quantico was as near like the actual fighting in France as human ingenuity could make it. To illustrate this I wish to give a brief summary of the training the Marines received at Quantico.

In the first place, all the men had to go through an additional course on the range, not only firing the army and navy course, but improvised firing, especially at night, when by flash lights, the targets were exposed for only a few seconds at a time. They had numerous marches both by day and night, frequently starting at about eight or nine o'clock in the evening and going all through the woods regardless of the weather. This not only to harden them but to teach them to find their way at night.

Each battalion, before going over, had to construct trenches, dugouts, hospital stations, etc. and in fact to do all the work that it was necessary to do at the front, as far as their instructors could teach them. They constructed what would represent the allied trenches on one side and the German trenches on the other side, with all the necessary wire entanglements, connecting trenches, and everything as nearly as possible like what they would see in France, and with an excellent reproduction of No Man's Land. Each battalion had to attack the German trenches from their own side, crossing No Man's Land under war conditions, and the whole affair was as near like war as could be made without killing men. The so-called German trenches had numerous machine gun nests, each nest fitted with automobile horns electrically connected so that until shot up and communication broken by rifle fire, that trench could not be taken. These horns kept up an incessant scream until they were shot up by the attacking forces.

After finishing up these machine gun nests and knocking out the silhouettes which were just above the parapet of the German trenches, the men had to rush the trenches. Just as they got to the parapet, by an ingenious arrangement, silhouettes representing men bobbed up on the parapet, by the contrivance of springs. These had to be bayoneted, and then the men would jump into the trenches in order to do mopping up, and as they struck the bottom of the trenches, numerous so-called Germans by other arrangement of ingenious springs, would jump out and these would likewise have to be bayoneted.

As a final arrangement, each battalion before going over was given an opportunity to shell the German trenches with artillery to show the effect of artillery fire; and as I stated above, a Marine could not hope to go abroad and go into the firing line unless he was a qualified "marksman" or better.

Later on I crossed on a transport with 11,000 army troops and I do not think that I am exaggerating when saying that almost all of these so-called soldiers had never fired an army rifle. I realize the fact that it was necessary and wise to send these men over, because the moral effect of landing about 300,000 Americans a month on the shores of France had a very demoralizing effect on the morale of the German army. Nevertheless I am proud of the fact that the Marines who went over were, in my opinion, as well qualified as comparatively green troops could be to go to the front line at once. In fact, at least one of the replacement battalions of Marines did go almost directly from the port of debarkation to the front line trenches; and while in France I heard constantly expressions of surprise that during the first battle they were in at Belleau Wood, during the heat of battle, they were frequently seen to stop firing and alter their sights so as to as nearly as possible make every shot count.

I have no doubt whatever that the marksmanship of the Marines counted a very great deal towards their success at the battle of Belleau Wood, in the Chateau-Thierry Sector. That battle, although small as battles went in that war, was most important, because it taught our own people that our men would fight to the finish if necessary. This is shown by the fact that out of 8,000 Marines and about 500 officers who went into that fight, 5,199 men and 126 officers were casualties. It not only taught the Germans this, but gave the French confidence which they sorely needed at that time. I do not say this about the Marines, but about the whole AEF. If I place unusual stress on anything with reference to the Marines, it is simply because I am a Marine, and I imagine an army officer would do the same in reference to the army.

Up to September, 1918, all Marines were volunteers, and while we all believe and know that the draft was a necessity (and in fact I am a great believer in the draft) we were proud of the fact that our men were all volunteers up to this time. In September, we got orders to stop volunteer enlistments and take drafted men, but as I stated, practically all of our men were volunteers, as the Corps was about full when this order was received.

I know I am not boasting when I say that I think no service in the world ever had a finer personnel than the Marine Corps. We had an unusually large percentage of young college men. I think this was largely because of the fact that the battle of Belleau Wood and reports of it published in this country appealed to the young college men just at a time when they were graduated in June, 1918, and an unusual percentage of them chose the Marine Corps.

When the Sixth Regiment arrived in France, the Fifth and Sixth Regiments were brigaded and formed the Fourth Brigade of the Second Division, AEF. The commanding officer of the Fifth Regiment was Colonel Charles A. Doyen, U.S. Marine Corps. He was later promoted to the rank of brigadier general and placed in command of the Fourth Brigade, and served in that capacity until a few days before they were moved to the northwest of Paris, just preceding the Second Division's fighting in the Chateau-Thierry Sector.

Unfortunately General Doyen was surveyed for ill health and sent home. He was relieved by Brigadier General James G. Harbord, U.S. Army. No finer man ever wore the American uniform, and I think that I can safely say that no man in any branch of the service stands higher with the Marines than this army officer who commanded them at the battle of Belleau Wood and at Soissons.

At a very large dinner given at the Palace Hotel in San Francisco, in honor of General James Harbord, USA about 1922, the General was called upon to make a few remarks about his war service. After reciting that he had been Chief of Staff to General Pershing, he stated that about April or May, 1918, he had requested to be ordered to duty in command of troops. General Pershing told him that while he hated to lose his services on his staff, he recognized the wisdom of the request, and he then went on and said that he had just received word of the illness of Gen. Doyen, U.S.M.C., and so he was able to order him to command of the best brigade in the AEF—the Fourth Brigade of Marines. I have learned that General Pershing had come to that conclusion on account of an inspection he and certain foreign generals had lately made of the troops in a certain training area, where in his opinion, he had found the Marine Brigade quite up to the mark in all respects.

General Harbord then turned to me and said, "I want to salute my former commanding officer, General Barnett, who was commandant of the Marine Corps when I had the honor and pleasure of commanding a Marine brigade." He then said that never had he been happier nor prouder than when General Neville, U.S.M.C., had pinned on his collar the Marine Corps emblem, for as he said, that act conveyed to him in a delightful way the fact that he, an army officer, was accepted and so honored by the Marines who had done such fine work while under his command. At least two thirds of the people at the dinner were army officers and their wives, and yet General Harbord said as stated above about the Marine Brigade.

After General Harbord was promoted to major general, the Fourth Brigade was commanded by Brigadier General Wendell C. Neville, who had been colonel of the Sixth Regiment. General Neville commanded the Brigade practically all the time throughout the war after Soissons. He commanded it so successfully that he got practically all the decorations that anyone could get.

A short time after this Brigadier General John A. Lejeune went to France and was for a short time in command of the Fourth Brigade. Shortly after his arrival in France, however, he was promoted to major general and was placed in command of the Second Division.

At the time of the battle of Belleau Wood, some of our friends of the army in mentioning Marines stated that they were all right enough, but that when they went into a fight they had to be commanded by an army officer. In subsequent fighting, when the Second Division was commanded by the Marine officer, much more severe and much larger in scope, the remarks of these army friends were made much more ridiculous than they were at the time they made them.

Our army friends said that we were great advertisers. Our reply was that we were in the habit of advertising our wares in the hope of getting good recruits, but that advertising any branch of the service was like advertising anything else; one might advertise forever and spend enormous amounts of money, but could not put it across unless the article was good; that the proof of the pudding was in the eating of it, and that we were perfectly willing to stand on our advertising record because we had a good article. I often stated that our very best advertisers were Generals Pershing and Harbord.

I went to France under orders to go every place where the Marines had been, but unfortunately was taken seriously ill with influenza and double pneumonia, and so came home without seeing any of the battle fields where they had fought.

Editor's Comments on Chapter XVII

Josephus Daniels was a newspaper publisher and politician from North Carolina. A Southern Democrat, he rose to prominence after supporting the white *coup d'état* at Wilmington in 1898 and leading a successful movement to disenfranchise black voters in the state. His work in bringing the Bryan wing of the party to Wilson earned him the secretary of the navy post. Indeed, that was basically his only qualification for the position. He was a national leader of the Prohibition movement and famously banned alcohol from the officer's mess and official functions, though the phrase "cup of Joe" for coffee predates this action.

Daniels may not have been the best choice to ready the navy for the coming war. Daniels, Secretary of State William Jennings Bryan and President Wilson were all opposed to "preparedness," viewing it as provocative and inappropriate for a peace-loving nation. Bryan and Daniels were avowed pacifists and Bryan resigned to protest the drift toward war. Daniels was suspicious of entrenched authority and elites. Throughout his term in office he was more likely to listen to civilians and enlisted men than admirals or generals. Class and caste were abhorrent to him, except when race was involved.

Much that Daniels did was influenced by his very active and pro-preparedness assistant Franklin Delano Roosevelt, then a rising young politician. Whenever

Secretary of the Navy Daniels (without hat) and Barnett (right) decorating Marine heroes in 1919. Assistant Secretary of the Navy Franklin D. Roosevelt at far left (Library of Congress).

XVII—The Great War

Daniels was out of town, Roosevelt styled himself "Acting Secretary of the Navy" and often took significant actions. Officers understood that some requests were best delayed until Roosevelt could approve them. The Marine Corps was a special project of his, as was their occupation of Haiti. His cousin Theodore had used the position as a stepping stone to national elective office and Franklin would try to follow in his footsteps. By 1920, Roosevelt was the vice-presidential nominee of his party.

Being the first Annapolis graduate to head the Marines paid immediate dividends to Barnett and the Corps. He was able to re-open the Annapolis pipeline, so that a steady flow of academy graduates were commissioned as Marines. He embraced the Advanced Base concept, making it central to the Corps' training and doctrine. His appointment to the General Board reflected his close contacts and good relations with the navy.

One of Barnett's first priorities was the creation of a more robust headquarters staff. Lejeune was appointed assistant to the commandant, with responsibility for training, and a planning section was initiated. Over time, Barnett brought in Dion Williams, John Russell, "Pete" Ellis, Clifton Cates and Thomas Holcomb, giving the staff an intellectual heft it had lacked and mentoring the next generation of leaders. These reforms would be expanded under Lejeune.

Too many accounts of the Corps in World War I barely mention Barnett, as if Marine participation in the AEF was a given. It most certainly was not. He was the essential mover that prepared the Marines for service in France and saw that they got overseas. His actions, many undertaken during a period of official opposition to preparedness, were critical. In addition to convincing his civilian masters, he had to overcome resistance from both the navy and army.

To begin with, Barnett changed the drill, uniforms and equipment to make combined operations possible. This seems like a simple and sensible move, but no change in a military unit is easy. Moving to a new rifle required retraining every Marine. There were winners and losers in the marketplace, some of them long time suppliers to the Corps. That the move was long overdue speaks to the inertia that needed to be overcome.

He designated Parris Island as the central recruiting depot and expanded it. He acquired and established Quantico as an advanced training center, turning it from a swamp into a factory for combat ready infantry. Observers were sent to France to learn about the drastically changed conditions of modern warfare. The move from crowded urban navy yards to large rural bases was fueled by the new Advanced Base mission, but dovetailed nicely with preparing for war in Europe. When the time came, the Marines were ready to expand.

The executive order attaching the Marines to the army was more than a formality. It removed any legal barriers to incorporating Marine units into the AEF. That he was able to carry this forward in the face of opposition from the army speaks to his ability to convince his civilian masters of the need for such authorization.

The navy did not originally support Barnett regarding having the Marines serve in France. In 1917, they proposed an expansion of the Corps to 30,000 men, triple the size of the Corps when Barnett was appointed commandant in 1914. The navy had plenty for the Corps to do without worrying about the AEF. Brigade sized units were required in the Dominican Republic, Haiti and Cuba, with smaller formations in China, Nicaragua and guarding the Texas oil fields. The Advanced Base brigades on both coasts needed to be maintained, at least nominally. Marine guards were needed at an expanded number of ships and bases. Convincing navy brass and Secretary Daniels that the Corps should expand to 75,000 men required all of Barnett's considerable persuasive powers.

The army actively opposed having Marines in the AEF, but was finally unable to turn down combat ready units. Even at the last moment, as the AEF was preparing to embark, the army notified Barnett that Marines were welcome to join the AEF—at some indefinite time in the future. Through an oversight, no transport had been provided for the Marines. Barnett, a veteran infighter and expeditionary leader, was ready for this gambit and had already arranged for transportation.

As Barnett's account implies, the army did not want any Marines in the AEF. When a regiment arrived anyway, they made it clear they wanted no more. When the arrival of a second regiment forced the formation of a Marine brigade, Pershing arranged to have it commanded by a trusted army officer. When a second brigade arrived with Butler and Eli Cole, they were assigned rear echelon duties. Barnett and other Marines wanted a Marine Division, but the AEF had no time or desire for such a formation. Butler repeated loudly and often that Barnett had denied him a combat command, a charge often echoed by historians who should know better. It was only through strenuous efforts that Barnett was able to get one brigade into combat. Even the expanded Corps could not have supported the losses of a second combat brigade. It was the army that decided that a loose cannon like Butler belonged behind the lines when they easily could have found him a combat command.

Barnett had to walk a fine line with the army. The Marines made up a nice brigade and achieved an excellent record. Promoting the Marines as an elite force was part of Barnett's job, one that he excelled at. At the same time, it was important to not overplay his hand. By the Armistice, the army consisted of four million men, two million of them in France. The army was quite properly focusing more on quantity than quality and resented any distractions. The brigade did require a separate personnel replacement pipeline. The Corps did recruit many college graduates that the army desperately needed as officers. Many army officers resented the intrusion on what they saw as "their" war, considering the Marines glory hounds and interlopers. The intra-service rivalry was fierce. Barnett needed to make the most of the Corps' accomplishments without further damaging the relationship.

Expansion changed the Corps in other ways. A vastly larger Corps meant more lieutenants and captains, which also meant more colonels and generals. As the Marines had rarely used large permanent formations, they tended to be light in the upper ranks. The expansion addressed that, at least temporarily. The Marines enlisted Marinettes (Marine Corps Reserve—Female), many of whom served at headquarters. Based on his experience with combined arms in the Advanced Base School, Barnett pushed initiatives in aviation. Marines flew anti-submarine patrols in the Atlantic and bombers over the front lines.

Overall, Barnett's administration of the Corps during the era of official opposition to preparedness and then through the vast expansion of the Corps was aggressive and innovative. Anything less and the Corps might well have spent the war mainly in the Caribbean, with only 30,000 men—no Belleau Wood, no "First to Fight," no Marine aviation.

In October 1918, Barnett embarked on an inspection of Marine units deployed with the AEF. This highlighted the Marine Brigade's anomalous position—within an army chain of command, but being inspected by their commandant. On the troop ship over, the 59 year old Barnett fell ill with influenza which developed into pneumonia. Thousands of healthy young soldiers were killed by the combination and Barnett was severely affected. He was incapacitated until after the Armistice, when he returned home.

Throughout the war, Mrs. Barnett was active, taking as her mission to be "the mother of Marines." This went far beyond writing columns, hosting fundraisers and attending the various women's institutes that were training thousands for war service. She trained as a nurse's assistant and prepared and served meals with the Red Cross. Her son enlisted in the Marines and was later commissioned. Perhaps because of this, she opened her Virginia home to serve as an officer's club for nearby Quantico. Most strikingly, she served as a court of last resort, where young Marines could receive sympathy and the possibility of assistance when they fell afoul of regulations. She received hundreds of such requests and responded to them all. While

Mrs. Barnett, shown here serving food in 1917 at a Red Cross event, was very active during the war years. She lectured widely, trained as a nurse and toured the recently active battlefields. Few Washington wives had her personal impact (Library of Congress).

many Washington wives were active in the war effort, few had the personal impact of Mrs. Barnett.

When Barnett was ill in France, Mrs. Barnett was so concerned about his health that she obtained permission to personally nurse him. After he was safely on his way to recovery, she visited battlefields in his stead, brought flowers to cemeteries and accompanied the Marines (among them her son) into occupied Germany. She traveled not in state, but dressed in her capacity as a Red Cross nurse's assistant. Walking the still ruined battlefields with wounded veterans in a tour arranged by General Harbord, she observed the work of the Graves Registration Service, which was engaged in moving the dead from temporary graves to permanent cemeteries. In one case, she retrieved a Bible from an opened grave and returned it to the Marine's mother. Not the behavior of a Washington socialite and dilettante, but just what one would expect from "the mother of Marines."

SUGGESTED READING

Axelrod, Alan. *Miracle at Belleau Wood: The Birth of the Modern U.S. Marine Corps.* Guilford, CN: Lyons, 2007.

Bartlett, Merrill L. *Lejeune: A Marine's Life, 1867–1942.* Columbia: University of South Carolina Press, 1991.

Bartlett, Merrill L. "Mrs. George Barnett 'Mother of Marines.'" *Fortitude : Newsletter of the Marine Corps Historical Program* 9, 3 (1979): 8–9.

Hewitt, Linda L. *Women Marines in World War I.* Washington, D.C.: History and Museums Division, Headquarters, U.S. Marine Corps, 1974.

Johnson, Edward C., and Graham A. Cosmas. *Marine Corps Aviation: The Early Years, 1912–1940 /* Washington, D.C.: History and Museums Division, Headquarters, U.S. Marine Corps., 1977.

Kolata, Gina. *Flu : The Story Of The Great Influenza Pandemic.* New York: Touchstone, 2001.

Lejeune, John Archer. *The Reminiscences of a Marine.* Philadelphia: Dorrance and Co., 1930.

Shulimson, Jack. "First to Fight: Marine Corps Expansion, 1914–18." *Prologue: The Journal of the National Archives* 8, 1 (Spring 1976): 4–16

Chapter XVIII

Post-War Demobilization

When the Second Division returned to the United States, they had the pleasure and satisfaction of marching up Fifth Avenue in New York, in review. I was proud indeed to see such a wonderful body of men with the marvelous fighting record behind them and commanded by a Marine officer. I wish to say, however, that in that Division there was no distinction made as to whether a man was an artilleryman, infantryman, or Marine; they were all Second Division men and proud of that fact.

After this review in New York the Marine brigade was sent to Quantico for demobilization. Before being demobilized, they had the honor and pleasure of being reviewed as a brigade by the president of the United States. Again I was exceedingly proud to witness such a wonderful body of troops with their splendid fighting record behind them, but it made me sad to think that within the next few days they would be demobilized and the Marine Corps would lose their services. This had its redeeming feature also, because I knew that every man of that brigade, no matter where he went, would at heart be a Marine, and it has turned out so. I have seen hundreds of letters about different service matters since they were demobilized, and in almost every case they used the expression, "Once a Marine, always a Marine," and have assured me that in case of need they would again flock to the colors and be proud to join the Corps again.

The Eleventh and Thirteen Regiments were also fitted out and left Quantico for France. Unfortunately when they reached the other side they were not sent to the front, but were placed on Military Police duty. I know from personal observation that they were two as fine regiments as any country ever sent to war, but they were only on the other side a short time before the armistice was signed. I am sure, however, if it had been their luck to have gotten into the fighting, that they would have proven themselves real fighters like the 5th and 6th regiments and the 6th Machine Gun Battalion. They

The Marine Brigade being reviewed in front of the White House in August 1919 by President Wilson (center), with Barnett and Franklin Roosevelt at left in the reviewing box. Two months later, Secretary Daniels discussed dismissing Barnett as commandant with Lejeune (Library of Congress).

would have made a name of which the Marine Corps would have been justly proud. They returned as the 5th Brigade and were demobilized at Hampton Roads, Virginia and what I said about the demobilization of the 5th and 6th Regiments and the 6th Machine Gun Battalion, applies equally as well to the 11th and 13th Regiments.

Fortunately, throughout the war we were able to keep the fighting strength of the 4th Brigade practically up to the limit all the time. Once or twice we had a very close call. We are proud of the fact that the Commanding General of the AEF did not find it necessary to fill the gaps in the ranks with any but Marines.

Immediately after the armistice, we began demobilizing the Corps as rapidly as possible, and in fact we accomplished it much earlier than we thought possible; so much so, that out of the appropriation asked for that year, we returned to the Treasury $50,000,000. The Corps was speedily reduced by getting rid of war time men as fast as possible until finally it was reduced down to a strength of 15,000.

While I have mentioned particularly men in the Corps who served on the other side, I wish to commend the many thousands of excellent Marines who were unfortunate in not getting over. They did their duty in the same splendid way as the men in France did theirs, and they did it under harder conditions because every man of them wanted to get over and was heartsick because he did not get there. Men in Haiti and Santo Domingo, who were practically on a war footing the whole time, rendered services of which the country may well be proud. Men on ships of the fleet were ready for whatever might happen and they are deserving of full credit although they were not fortunate enough to get into actual fighting.

Whatever success the Marines met with during the war was largely due to the loyal support given by the officers and men, not only to their country, but to their Corps. The esprit de corps has never changed and I hope never will. Any service has a right to be proud of having the esprit de corps which is well known to exist in the Marine Corps. Esprit de corps may be defined in a loose way as justifiable pride, and after all, without pride or at least a reasonable amount of pride, no organization can amount to much. If a Marine thinks he is better than some other soldier, so much the better, for he will try to live up to that tradition. It has been the doctrine of the Marines ever since I have known anything about them, to do what they have to do to the best of their ability, in the shortest time, and to do it with the tools at hand, instead of finding fault with the tools furnished. Any branch of the service that follows this principal cannot go far wrong, and will, in my opinion, make excellent soldiers under all conditions.

After demobilization the Marine Corps was reduced to 17,400 men, which was entirely insufficient to perform the many duties required of it. During the next session of Congress it became necessary for me, as commandant, to present to Congress my views as to the number of officers and men I thought necessary to perform the duties required of the Corps in peace time.

After very many conferences, it was finally decided by the Congress that the Marine Corps should consist of 1,093 officers and 27,400 men, and arrangements were promptly made for recruiting the Corps up to this strength, and numerous recruiting offices were established throughout the country. The strength gradually grew, but it did not get up to the required number of enlisted men, before Congress passed an appropriation act only authorizing pay for 20,000 men. The final report in reference to the retention of temporary officers in the Marine Corps was not made until some time in January, 1921.

After demobilization, my ordinary duties as commandant of the Marine

Corps were carried out, and as these duties were more or less routine, I do not consider it worthwhile to define them.

Editor's Comments on Chapter XVIII

While the Second Division paraded through New York, only the Marine Brigade got the honor of a presidential review. It was a victory lap for Barnett, with Wilson, Daniels and Roosevelt on hand to review the triumphant Marines.

With the end of the war, the shrinking of the corps brought as many decisions as its temporary growth had. It was not simply a matter of fewer officers, but of which officers, at what rank and in what order. Seniority still governed promotions and there was an immense difference between the top first lieutenant, who would soon be a captain, and the bottom one, who might have to wait a decade or more for promotion. As Barnett noted, many fine officers were required elsewhere during the war. Future commandants Ben Fuller and John Russell spent World War I primarily in Haiti and the Dominican Republic respectively, both of which were simmering combat zones. Would retention and seniority be guided by heroic service in the AEF or by the Corps' need for officers to develop offensive amphibious capabilities?

To a great extent, World War I was a junior officer's war, with lieutenants and captains winning distinction in combat. Many valiant sergeants earned battlefield commissions. Thus many of the officers evaluated were either pre-war noncommissioned officers or war time volunteers, with little of the training or education that would be needed to prepare the Corps for the next war.

Barnett established a board headed by Colonel Russell, a proponent of offensive amphibious warfare, to select which officers to retain and at what rank. The members of the board were selected because they had not served in France and would have a broader and more impartial view of fitness. Russell was aware that the board was selecting the next generation of Marine leaders and wanted to build a strong officer corps, not just reward combat experience. He also commented to the board that the officers retained would be entertained in their homes and might marry their daughters. While true, that comment would haunt him, as it seemed to place social standing over hard won laurels.

The board's report and Russell's comment brought quick reaction. Daniels had made it a rule to reward wartime heroism, opposed educated elites and had little enthusiasm for preparing for the next war. General and Congressman Butler were both outraged. Factions, quiescent during the war, resurfaced and old battles were refought. Both sides were right about one thing—the future of the Corps was at stake. Congress acted to put the board recommendations on hold, which only delayed the final reckoning.

Suggested Reading

Nalty, Bernard C., and Ralph F.Moody. *A Brief History of U.S. Marine Corps Officer Procurement 1775–1969.* Marine Corps Historical Reference Pamphlet; Washington, D.C.: Historical Division, Headquarters, U.S. Marine Corps, 1970.

Williams, Robert H. "Those Controversial Boards." *Marine Corps Gazette*, November 1982.

Chapter XIX

Dismissal of Commandant Barnett

On May 3, 1920, I left Washington under orders on an inspection trip. My orders were to inspect the Marine Corps posts on the west coast. Brigadier General Charles McCawley, Quartermaster General of the Marine Corps, accompanied me, as did also my family.

En route to San Diego, we stopped at the Grand Canyon in Arizona, and then went to Los Angeles, and from there to San Diego, where I inspected the new advance base post being built there. At San Diego I saw that great progress had been made since my last visit when I went there to select a site for this base. I received many courtesies, both officially and personally, while in San Diego and Los Angeles. In fact, wherever I went on the west coast I found that every possible arrangement, both personally and officially, had been made for my entertainment. These arrangements were largely made through the recruiting officers at the different places, and I realized it was because of the fact that I was commandant of the Marine Corps, an organization which had done such wonderful work during the war, that these preparations were made, rather than for me personally. Although during this trip, I met a great many relatives and friends of ex–Marines who said that I had helped them out in many ways while I was at headquarters.

I returned to the east via Victoria and Vancouver, on the Canadian Pacific, and reached Washington on June 8th or 9th. From that time until the 18th of June, 1920, things went on about as usual.

At 1:30 p.m. Friday, June 18th, I received a letter from the secretary of the navy, Josephus Daniels, informing me that he contemplated making a change in the position of commandant of the Marine Corps, and that the change would be made "one day next week most suitable to you."

This naturally came as a great surprise to me, because I had seen the secretary almost daily and no word had ever been spoken with reference to this contemplated change; and besides there never was a time during my service as commandant of the Marine Corps when the secretary expressed anything but satisfaction in regard to my performance of duty. In fact, his report on fitness in my case was all that any officer could wish; and to me he seemed to have gone out of his way to express satisfaction at the manner of performance of my duty, and he had recommended to the Board of Awards that I be awarded the Distinguished Service Medal on account of the way I had performed my arduous duties in a position of very great responsibility.

In this letter to me the secretary directed that I report to him, in writing, that afternoon, whether or not I wished to avail myself of my right, according to the law, to retire as a major general, or remain on the active list as a brigadier general, and if I preferred the latter, to inform him what duty I desired. This in reality only gave me three hours to make up my mind, as office hours were over at 4:30 p.m. I therefore had only three hours to decide my whole future life on the active list. I remarked to my wife that if I were a bachelor, it would not take me five minutes to decide. She replied, "I am with you as far as making this decision is concerned, and you may consider that you are a bachelor." I decided at once, and so informed the secretary of the navy, that I would remain on the active list and was ready for any duty to which I might be assigned. In obedience to his orders, I further stated that I preferred to be ordered to duty in command of the Marine Corps post at Quantico, Virginia, and further, as I had had no leave since 1918, that I be granted my accumulated leave which amounted to four months. I was informed by him, in writing, that Quantico had been promised, and that I could have two months leave.

I would not have been surprised at this treatment if there had been any official reason for it, for, to the best of my knowledge and belief, I had performed my duties satisfactorily, with no complaint of any kind by the secretary. In fact, I had received nothing but praise in his reports on fitness. I saw the secretary the next day and he appeared to be very much surprised that I was anything but pleased—that I had not expected it. He said that under similar circumstances, if his resignation was called for by the president, he would thank the president for past courtesies and say that he acquiesced in it with pleasure. I remarked that even a servant was entitled to thirty days notice and that he only gave me three hours. I told him that I did not feel that way; that I felt that I had been treated unjustly, after long years of faithful service. He then remarked, "Then that very materially lessens the sorrow of our parting." I said, "Good day, sir," and left his office.

In this connection it might be well to mention an occurrence which happened when I was reappointed commandant of the Marine Corps on February 25, 1918, after having served one tour of duty of four years in that position. The day that my time was up the secretary of the navy sent for me, and because of the importance of what took place every word of his remarks is absolutely engraved on my memory. He said, "General Barnett, the President has decided to reappoint you commandant of the Marine Corps, but desires you to sign your resignation in blank, the same as the chiefs of bureaus of the Navy Department, who have been reappointed, have done." I flushed at this and replied that I was unwilling to sign a resignation in blank and saw no reason for it, because my commission read for "four years or at the discretion of the President." I said that I was greatly pleased that the president should wish to reappoint me for another four years, because that showed me that he was satisfied with the administration of my office during my first term. I said that I would like to see the president about the matter of signing my resignation in blank, and the secretary said, "I will see the President about it." The next day the secretary sent for me and said, "About the matter that I spoke to you of yesterday, never mind; let it stand as it is." He then gave me my commission as major general commandant for four years, or at the "discretion of the President."

Naturally, I expected to serve out my four years in case my performance of duty was satisfactory to the secretary and to the president, and it has been shown that such was the case by the reports on fitness signed by the secretary, which were all "Excellent," and in several cases he went far beyond "Excellent" by adding complimentary remarks,

Since I have been relieved as commandant of the Marine Corps, I have felt that personally the secretary had all the time been resenting the fact that I refused to sign the resignation in blank. Personally, I do not at all believe that the president ever wanted me to sign any resignation in blank, because I cannot conceive why the president would require an appointed officer to sign a resignation in blank, when he, the president, by the terms of the commission, has the right to relieve that officer at any time. With an officer of the service it is not at all like a civilian appointed to office. The president, as commander in chief, can relieve an officer at any time, so why sign a resignation in blank.

In fact I have heard that the president did not make any such request. Whether or not the chiefs of bureaus who were at about the same time reappointed, signed their resignations in blank, I do not know. I know only what the secretary said. I sincerely hope that there was no truth in that, just as I believe it to have been in my case.

I spent two months leave at home in Virginia, and afterwards awaited orders to duty. I have heard since I was relieved, that the secretary of the navy told the president that I wanted to be relieved and that the president, who was a very ill man, gave his consent. I cannot give the name of my informant, but if such report was given the president, it was absolutely false.

~

Remarks made by General Barnett to the officers assembled at the time he was relieved as commandant of the Marine Corps. Washington June 30, 1920.

Gentlemen:-

We are assembled here today to hear read my orders from the secretary of the navy, relieving me as commandant of the Marine Corps, and the orders to General Lejeune appointing him in my place. To me, this is a solemn occasion because of the fact that it takes me from a position I have occupied for the past six and a half years, and separates me from those here at Headquarters who have done their utmost to assist me in every possible way in the performance of the arduous duties pertaining to the office. During my term as Commandant we have passed through the World War in which the Marines took such prominent part and added so much to the glory of the Corps. Before leaving my position I wish to extend to all those of the Corps, both officers and men, who not only did their utmost for the welfare of their government and Corps, but who have willingly and loyally aided me at all times, my sincere and heartfelt thanks; to the exceedingly small number of those who have not seen fit to fully co-operate with Headquarters, I wish to call attention to the fact that only by loyal co-operation and team work can best results be accomplished, and I hope that they will return as speedily as possible to the old-fashioned Marine Corps way of considering only what is the greatest good for the greatest number, and will not let personal differences militate against the welfare of the service.

Six years and a half ago the Marine Corps consisted of 10,000 men and 543 officers; today we have an authorized strength of 27,400 men and 1,093 officers. Six years ago we had no warrant officers; today we have one hundred warrant officers and forty-two pay clerks, and fifty additional warrant officers authorized by the present bill. We had no general officers except the Commandant; we now have twelve general officers. Many other things have been gotten for the Corps, and they have been gotten by co-operation, and not by dissention.

The work of the men who were fortunate enough to get into the fighting in France has been recognized by the world as magnificent, but we should remember that all of those who did not get over were quite as anxious to go and no doubt would have distinguished themselves equally satisfactorily. Their services were as essential on this side as were the services of those on the fighting line, and the whole credit is due to the Corps as an integral fighting machine. In saying good-bye I wish to express to those officers and men, who have loyally supported my administration, my heartfelt thanks and wish them continued success.

It is needless for me to say that this change has come to me as a shock and a surprise. I had hoped to complete my term in my present position; but

Commandant Lejeune (seated) and General Smedley Butler in the commandant's office in 1925 (Library of Congress).

this being denied me, I leave you with this earnest advice; get together, pull together, and give the best there is in you willingly and loyally to the service. If you at any time differ as to ways and means, let your opinions be known officially so that those with whom the responsibility rests may make the proper decisions. I love the Corps so much that I shall remain on the active list performing any duty assigned me to the best of my ability

I say good-bye to you with the steadfast conviction that, in the future, as in the past, the Marine Corps will carry on.

Editor's Comments on Chapter XIX

In 1910, Biddle was appointed commandant with the understanding that it was for a four year term, a limit subsequently enacted into law. Previously, commandants served until retirement age. Daniels came into office opposed to anything that smacked of elitism and was specifically opposed to having officers serve more than one term in any position. Despite this, Daniels himself served eight years as secretary of the navy.

Biddle retired in 1914, reportedly unwilling to work further with Daniels, so reappointment was never an issue. Barnett was appointed for a four year term in 1914 and was re-appointed for a second four year term in 1918. As only the second commandant to be appointed for a fixed term and the first re-appointed, Barnett had every reason to expect that he would serve out that term. That was rather the point of a fixed term for the position. Yet, in June 1920, Barnett was abruptly informed that his services were no longer needed.

Many Corps histories do not make even a passing mention of the dismissal. Lejeune and Butler both fail to mention it in their memoirs. Daniels remembered it as a matter of a defiant commandant who refused to honor his promise. There is a good reason for this amnesia. It is a story of politics, personal animosity and factions. No participant was ennobled by their role in it. The necessarily covert nature of much of the plot makes unraveling details difficult, but Bartlett's "Ouster of a Commandant," Schmidt's *Maverick Marine,* and Ballendorf and Bartlett's *Pete Ellis* provide good outlines.

The official press releases portrayed the dismissal as a simple promotion for Lejeune, the just reward for his service in Europe. This was met with incredulity by many. Barnett had recently been awarded the Navy Distinguished Service Medal, the highest non-valorous award possible, with the approval of Daniels. Congressman Butler was on record praising Barnett for his administration of the Corps and Daniels had written several glowing fitness reports. Representative Britten (R–IL), a member of the House Naval Affairs Committee, called the action "a national disgrace" and Daniels' explanation "the rankest camouflage," promising an investigation. He also publicly doubted that Wilson was fully conversant with the facts of the matter, laying the dismissal squarely on Daniels. Senator King (D–UT) anticipated that the Senate would investigate the matter if the House didn't.

That this was not a standard or orderly transition is evident. The rumors, which Barnett refused to believe, but which everyone heard. General Butler in Washington on a pretext, instead of at his command on Puget Sound. The Butlers closeting with Daniels for weeks right under Barnett's nose. The plans finalized while Barnett was touring west coast bases, a tour approved by Daniels to get Barnett out of Washington. The ultimatum, delivered by messenger on Friday afternoon. The immediate deadline, so Daniels could use the weekend to defuse any political fallout. The refusal of earned leave, though Barnett had taken no leave since the start of the war. The eviction of Barnett and his family from the commandant's quarters on short notice. The shocked reaction from members of the House and Senate Naval Affairs Committees. Daniels and the Butlers fully expected that this treatment would convince Barnett to accept retirement as a major general and go quietly. The opportunity to heap coals on Barnett was a welcome bonus. What had happened to create such animosity? Why was it so important to dismiss Barnett at this juncture?

The Russell Retention Board—More than anything else, the retention board controversy was the immediate cause of Barnett's demise. It inflamed the parties that would act against him. It highlighted their main themes of heroism versus social standing and education. It provided a sense of urgency, victimhood and righteousness that would justify any action they might undertake. If they had not acted when they did, Barnett could have controlled the new board or delayed its work until Daniels was out of office.

After Barnett's dismissal, a new board headed by AEF veteran Wendell Neville, but run by Butler, reshaped the officer corps. Ordered by Lejeune within days of Barnett's removal, the board's actions weren't confirmed until the very last day of the Wilson administration. While this board rewarded bravery in combat, they also created an officer corps that had little connection to the navy or interest in amphibious operations. If the Russell board had inappropriately applied peace time standards, the Neville board overcompensated by ignoring normal fitness criteria. The dead wood that the Neville board put into the officer corps would drag it down until John Russell became commandant a decade later and instituted advancement by selection and retirement for those not advanced.

The "Barnett Amendment"—In crafting the 1918 naval appropriation (HR 10854), a number of Senate amendments concerning the Marine Corps were considered. An uncontroversial one created two major general slots, one permanent and one for the duration of the war. This was devised by Barnett specifically to allow Lejeune sufficient rank to command a division, as was being planned. The other slot went to Waller, the senior brigadier. The House concurred in this amendment. A second (Senate amendment 37) would make the commandant a lieutenant general for the duration. All navy bureau chiefs were being advanced in rank and/or pay in the bill and the Corps was now larger than the pre-war navy. The Senate saw it as a matter of equity to temporarily advance the commandant too. After all, Barnett now headed a Corps of 75,000. A third (Senate amendment 47) would temporarily promote the three Marine bureau heads to major general. This proposal would have given them equal rank with their more numerous navy counterparts. It is clear that Barnett supported increased rank for his subordinates. Some of his opponents claimed he lobbied for his own promotion, a charge which was vigorously denied by his supporters.

The House rejected both 37 and 47 after an acrimonious debate. Throughout, the two proposals were conflated, causing much confusion. Congressman Butler (R–PA) referred to Barnett as "a swivel-chair warrior" as the general and his wife sat in the gallery. Kearns (R–OH) started to propose the court martial of Barnett. Meeker (R–MO) sprang to Barnett's defense, as did Talbott (D–MD), Britten (R–IL) and Oliver (D–AL). Daniels was quoted as opposing the proposals, while Congressman Butler was quoted on how essential Barnett and the headquarters staff were to the Corps' success. The importance of supporting the brave troops overseas was employed by both sides. The staff promotions were an insult to the fighting Marines. Demeaning Barnett, who was beloved by the troops, was an insult to those same Marines. With the defeat of the proposals and lacking support from the Wilson administration, the matter seemed closed.

It was not. In conference, the Senate insisted on amendment 37, but with softened language that authorized, but did not require, the president to temporarily promote Barnett. As Daniels was opposed to the move, the amendment would have had no effect and was a face-saving surrender by the Senate. Despite this, it again set off a firestorm in the House. Mondell (R–WY) railed against the "swivel-chair warriors who are lingering here safely behind the lines." It got hot enough that Padgett (D–TN), who opposed the provision, asked his colleagues to "not asperse his [Barnett's] character. Do not impugn the integrity and the patriotism of a man who is as brave and chivalrous as any man who was ever in the military service of the United States." The House insisted on killing the innocuous provision, thus delaying the passage of the overall bill. Neither Daniels nor Congressman Butler was amused by what they called "the Barnett amendment."

Prohibition—Daniels was one of the leaders of the great moral crusade to save the soul of the nation that was Prohibition. He was a featured speaker at the rally held to celebrate its taking effect. In addition to banning alcohol from the officer's mess, he (following Wilson's lead) also forbade it at any official function. As the Barnetts lived in the commandant's residence at the Marine Barracks, this covered much of their entertaining. Mrs. Barnett enquired if this included cooking alcohol and Daniels agreed that it did not. Mrs. Barnett then hosted a meal where every course was saturated in alcohol, from sherry soup to brandied peaches. During dessert, one senator reportedly said "Madame, I really can't eat another drop." While this is a humorous anecdote, Daniels was unlikely to have enjoyed the joke.

Personal Differences—Secretary Daniels, who originally selected Barnett, was the key figure in his undoing. The "Barnett amendment" and retention board flaps certainly reduced Barnett in Daniels' eyes. Barnett favored a highly educated officer corps, while Daniels stood with the "masses, not classes." Daniels pushed the Marines and navy into vocational education and opposed military spending as a rule, while Barnett was a professional in charge of preparing for the next war. Mrs. Daniels was said to be jealous of Mrs. Barnett's prominent social position. Daniels enjoyed referring to Barnett as "The-Man-Afraid-of-His-Wife," which was more likely projection on Daniels' part, as he was a target of Mrs. Barnett's barbed wit. Barnett and many of his supporters were Republicans, while Daniels was a Democratic politician. Daniels was heavily influenced by the Butlers, father and son. Barnett was one of many high ranking officers who found Daniels difficult to work with.

General Smedley Butler and Congressman Thomas Butler—The Butlers were unhappy with Barnett for many reasons. They had supported Waller when Barnett was appointed and now could avenge the insult to Waller. General Butler considered himself the representative of the rough and ready fighting Marines as opposed to the high brow professionals like Barnett. His behavior towards Barnett was unprofessional, as Butler loudly referred to him as a "god damned old fogey" or "weak old woman." He also blamed Barnett for not getting him a combat command in Europe, though Butler had pulled strings to be assigned to Haiti and his "bush war" record did not impress the army. The Butlers were also offended by the "Barnett amendment" and the retention board flap, though those probably only confirmed their earlier views. Finally, General Butler was openly ambitious, wanting to succeed Lejeune at Quantico and then as commandant.

Timing—In June 1920, the Wilson administration was in its last days and the Democratic Party's chances were bleak in the coming elections. The country had rejected Wilson and the Democrats in the 1918 midterm elections and would soon give Harding a landslide victory. For Daniels and the Butlers, this was their last chance to accelerate Barnett's retirement and undo the Russell board. Lejeune could be appointed at once and possibly approved by the Senate before the election. While there was little political support for removing Barnett, a recess appointment of the deserving Lejeune would be easy to make permanent.

Daniels discussed Barnett's dismissal with Lejeune in September 1919 and planned to act then. Wilson suffered a severe stroke shortly after that and was in seclusion for the remainder of his term, which short circuited the plans. The extent of Wilson's disability was a closely guarded secret and remained so until after his death in 1924. Only very serious matters were brought before him, with cabinet

Barnett as depicted by James Montgomery Flagg, who produced many iconic posters during World War I. The image must have pleased Barnett, as he used it in the 1921 reunion booklet for the Class of 1881 (editor's personal collection).

members handling everything else. It was only in May 1920, as the retention board issue flared and the end of the Wilson administration neared, that Daniels again raised the matter with Lejeune.

Daniels did indeed meet with the partially paralyzed Wilson before dismissing Barnett, presenting the matter as nothing more than Barnett had promised to do. Admiral Cary Grayson, Wilson's personal physician and close friend of the Barnetts, witnessed the discussion. He later passed the details on to Barnett, who discretely refuses to name him. Whatever Wilson agreed to, it bore little resemblance to the process Daniels had in mind.

Just what role did Lejeune play? He was aware of the plot as it developed without being part of it. The plotters wanted to appoint Lejeune as commandant to legitimize Barnett's removal, but that does not mean they would not proceed without him and they made that clear to him. Lejeune could justly claim that "his hands were tied," as Daniels had ordered him to silence.

How about Roosevelt? It is unlikely that the assistant secretary had a hand in Barnett's dismissal. Roosevelt was a very busy man at that time. In July 1920, the Democratic convention would select him as their vice-presidential candidate on the ill fated James Cox ticket. He was already busy planning the next stage of his ascent. In the immediate aftermath, Mrs. Barnett wrote to Roosevelt without her husband's knowledge, asking for his assistance. It was not forthcoming, but the letter is an indication that Roosevelt was a potential ally, not an known enemy. Even after her husband's death, Mrs. Barnett would assail Daniels, Butler and Lejeune, but not the Roosevelts, with whom she retained a cordial relationship.

Clifton Cates, then Barnett's aide and later commandant, witnessed Barnett's handover of the office to Lejeune. He makes it clear Barnett did not hold Lejeune responsible, but was disappointed in him.

> It was a very unofficial thing, it looked like. General Lejeune came in. I showed him into the office and he started to sit down. General Barnett said, "John, stand up there just a minute. We've been good friends all our lives—close friends. Why didn't you let me know what was going on?" General Lejeune replied, "George, my hands were tied." General Barnett said, "Don't you know that if I had been in your place, I would have come to you and told you exactly what was happening?" And General Lejeune said, "George, my hands were tied." General Barnett said, "All right. I stand relieved, you're the Commandant."

From this exchange, it is clear that Barnett did not see his dismissal coming. He was hurt and bewildered by the unprecedented events. Outside Marine headquarters, hiding in a car, Smedley Butler was waiting to watch and celebrate as Barnett exited the building.

There is no doubt that this very public repudiation was a blow to Barnett, one that might have crushed a lesser man. Still, he rather upset plans by accepting the rank of brigadier instead of retiring with two stars. Barnett requested the command at Quantico and refused to accept anything less. As the officer who had established the base, the posting made military sense. The command had been Lejeune's and was open, but it had been promised to Smedley Butler, so Barnett's request was rejected. A slot as major general was open and should have automatically gone to Barnett as senior brigadier. Lejeune even recommended this, but Daniels would not allow it and the position remained vacant. Clearly, the plotters were not interested in accommodating or placating Barnett. They wanted him gone.

Daniels and the Butlers were certain that they had triumphed over Barnett, but Barnett would play the weak hand he had been dealt for all it was worth. He knew that Daniels was a lame duck and that removing a sitting commandant in the middle of a term of office was unprecedented. The Barnetts rallied their friends and fought back. Lejeune was not confirmed by the outgoing Senate, leaving him in limbo as acting commandant for the rest of the Wilson administration. Lejeune had the good sense to create a new posting for Barnett in San Francisco, which took him out of town without publicly demeaning him.

After Harding's victory, Barnett gained some vindication. While there was talk of restoring Barnett, Daniels and the Butlers had calculated correctly. In a deal brokered by Secretary of War Weeks, Barnett was promoted to major general, but left in San Francisco. At the same time, Lejeune was confirmed as commandant and Butler promoted to permanent brigadier general and given Quantico.

Despite this success, Butler would never be commandant. Lejeune served two full terms (1920–1929) as commandant and was succeeded by AEF veteran Wendell Neville (1929–1930). When Neville died in office, Ben Fuller (1930–1935) continued the string of USNA graduates to hold the position. Twice Butler was the senior officer, but was passed over. He retired in 1931. The death of his influential father in 1928, President Hoover's strong dislike of him and possibly his role in Barnett's sacking kept him from his ultimate goal.

Throughout this process, Barnett's behavior cannot escape examination. Like many senior officers, he never developed a warm personal relationship with Secretary Daniels. During his six years as commandant, he had not healed the splits in the Corps. The "Barnett amendment" was a serious overreach and should have been squelched by him. The Russell board was a disaster which empowered his opponents to remake the Corps in their image.

Mrs. Barnett may not have helped matters. Despite her hardscrabble childhood, Daniels and others saw her as the exemplar of everything they hated. Too rich, too powerful, too outspoken, too socially connected, too politically adept. Not what they valued in a woman. Her biting wit always made news, but didn't always win friends. Not one to walk away from a fight, she pulled no punches in defending her husband, but lacked ammunition against the lame duck Democrats.

Still, one should be careful not to blame the Barnetts and absolve the conspirators. Barnett's dismissal did not resolve any of the problems the Corps faced. The factions did not disappear and would resurface whenever the commandant's post was vacant. The outspoken Smedley Butler continued his erratic career, performing exceptionally well in China and at Quantico, while also earning distinction as the first general officer to be placed under arrest since the Civil War. The move to an amphibious navy-based mission remained contentious. Barnett's main failing in the affair was to insufficiently acquiesce in his dismissal and disgrace. Sometimes minimized as a socially and politically connected officer, he was undone by a conspiracy that was equal parts personal and political and had little to do with his service record.

Suggested Reading

Ballendorf, Dirk Anthony, and Merrill L Bartlett. *Pete Ellis: An Amphibious Warfare Prophet, 1880-1923*. Annapolis, MD: Naval Institute Press, 1997.

Bartlett, Merrill L. *Lejeune: A Marine's Life, 1867-1942*. Columbia: University of South Carolina Press, 1991.

Bartlett, Merrill L. "Ouster of a Commandant." *U.S. Naval Institute Proceedings* 106, 11 (November 1980): 60-65.

Cates, Clifton B. *Reminiscences of Clifton Bledsoe Cates: Oral History, 1967*. Interview by Benis M. Frank, 1967.

Frank, Benis M. "The Relief of General Barnett." *Records of the Columbia Historical Society* (1971-72): 679-693.

Lejeune, John Archer. *The Reminiscences of a Marine,*. Philadelphia: Dorrance and Co., 1930.

Schmidt, Hans. *Maverick Marine: General Smedley D. Butler and the Contradictions of American Military History*. Lexington: University Press of Kentucky, 1987.

Chapter XX

The Haitian Affair

About the 24th of August, 1920, while on leave, I received a telegram from the major general commandant of the Marine Corps, asking me to report anything that I knew with reference to a report from Colonel Russell, Commanding Officer of the Marines in Haiti, as to an investigation ordered there by me under date of September 27, 1919. I replied, and stated that, as, I remembered, sometime in September, 1919, two general court martial cases of privates in the Marine Corps named Walter Johnson and John McQuilken came before me, and after reading these cases, especially the statement of counsel for the accused in the case of Johnson, I was of the opinion that an investigation was demanded and the guilty parties brought to trial.

I also stated that a few days later, sometime early in October, 1919, I had re-read the cases and was so impressed with the importance of the matter that I wrote a personal letter to Colonel Russell in Haiti urging an immediate investigation and correction of the serious faults. I also stated that I had received a reply from Colonel Russell in which he stated that he fully understood my letter and had taken immediate steps to correct any faults existing, and he furnished me with a copy of a proclamation which he had issued in accordance with the contents of my letter.

I forwarded this proclamation and Colonel Russell's letter to Headquarters with my reply. A few days later I received a telegram from the secretary of the navy to proceed to Washington to consult the files at Headquarters, and make a more complete report with reference to the Haitian matter. I went to Headquarters the same day, and went to see the secretary. I took with me a copy of my official letter of September 27th; also a copy of my personal letter of October 2nd and another letter written by General Haines, or General Long, about the same matter in Haiti. I showed these letters to the secretary, and, in my presence, the secretary read them from start to finish and we discussed them fully. I told him all I knew about the case, and he told me to make a report of the matter, in writing, from the official records.

The next day I handed him this report which contained as appendages these three letters just mentioned. The secretary took this report which was about ten pages in length, and the next day sent for me, and handed me back the report, and said to me, "This is all right as far as it goes; but I wish a complete report on Haiti from the occupation by the Marines in 1915 up to June 30, 1920." "I want everything put in, good or bad, commendatory or otherwise, and as to these three letters which are appendages to this report, put them in the body of your final report so that whoever reads it will not have to look back and see what the appendages referred to are."

I went to work, and with the assistance of Major Edwin McClellan and the historical section, this report was gotten out in about two weeks, as I remember it now, under date of October 18th. I took this report to the secretary and handed it to him about one o'clock in the afternoon. He said, "This is too long to read now—I will take it home with me tonight and read it." He told me to be at his office the next day about one o'clock.

I was there the next day and the secretary told me that the report was all right and I could carry out my orders which I had received some time before, to proceed to San Francisco, California, for duty. The next day I started for San Francisco, got as far as Chicago, and was ordered back for consultation with reference to Haitian affairs.

In the meantime the report I had handed in to the secretary of the navy had been given out by the Navy Department and the newspapers were making a great deal of stir about the wording of my letter wherein I used the term "indiscriminate killing." After I returned, the secretary asked me about the use of this term—if I had meant that the whole Marine Corps was killing indiscriminately in Haiti, and I told him, by no means, that I was writing with reference to the facts brought out in the court martial of Privates Johnson and McQuilken, and that in my opinion indiscriminate killing meant killing without judgment or killing unlawfully. I stated that I had used that term because the counsel for the accused, who was a commissioned officer, had stated that Private Johnson was no more guilty than others had been, and that he himself had been present at numerous unlawful killings.

When the statement in reference to my letter was published in the morning press, the same papers contained a statement from the secretary of the navy that he had never seen my letter until that morning when it was published from my report. When I reported to the secretary that day on my return from Chicago, I said to him: "Mr. Secretary, I have noted a statement of yours in the morning paper to the effect that you never saw my letter to

Colonel Russell until it was published in the morning papers." He replied, "I never saw it until this morning." I said, "Mr. Secretary, excuse me, sir, you did see it, several times. You saw it the first time you spoke to me about the Haitian affairs several months ago. I handed it to you. I sat down at your desk and you read it from start to finish and we then discussed it very fully."

He again said, "I never saw it until it was published." I said again, "Excuse me, sir, you saw it a second time under the following circumstances; when I was ordered by you to make a report on Haitian affairs, I made a report about ten pages long covering the cases of Privates Johnson and McQuilken. That original letter to Colonel Russell, a second letter, a personal one, but put into the files of the department together with a letter written by either General Haines or General Long, were attached to that report as appendages. You took that report home with you and the next day you sent for me and said that you wanted a more complete report of all the operations in Haiti from start to finish. You further remarked that you wanted the appendages included in the body of the letter so whoever read the report would not have to look back to see what the appendages were. As I said before, the much discussed letter was one of these appendages."

"When my final report was made, these letters were included in the body of my report which I handed to you and which report the next day you pronounced satisfactory. So that is another time that you had the letter in your possession for twenty-four hours or more."

The secretary could not have pronounced the report satisfactory unless he had read the letter, or should not have so pronounced it.

I said further to the secretary at that same meeting; "Mr. Secretary, the second time I handed you that letter, fortunately General Haines was present and saw me hand you the letter and remembers it just as well as I do."

The secretary then said, "Of course, if you and General Haines say that I had that report, I must have had it, but I don't remember it."

I said, "Mr. Secretary, in the morning papers you did not say you did not remember having seen it; you said positively that you had never seen it."

I feel now, as I felt then, that no intelligent man could have had that letter in his possession on two separate occasions as the secretary did, without fully knowing its contents, and especially so as no intelligent judgment could be passed on any of its proceedings without having read the whole correspondence, and again I state most positively that when I first handed the secretary that letter, he not only read it carefully but discussed it from whereas to Amen.

As I intimated above my only object in writing anything about this affair is so that my friends may know the exact facts of importance in reference to the affair, especially so as I have heard that some people even imagine that I was relieved as major general commandant on account of the Haitian Affair, when in fact; I was relieved long before and for no cause whatsoever other than the personal desire of the secretary of the navy .

Editor's Comments on Chapter XX

The Marines occupied Haiti in 1915. The occupation was under the command of a navy admiral, with considerable input from the State Department and Franklin Roosevelt. In practice, the brigade commander had great latitude and the Marines effectively replaced the government. As with the AEF, Barnett's role was to provide the needed manpower and he had no power to oversee operations.

It was Barnett's job to review court martial records, so that Headquarters was aware of any issues. The records in the Johnson and McQuilkin cases raised red flags. Though Barnett was not in his chain of command, he wrote to Russell, first confidentially and then privately. The potential blot on Marine honor troubled him greatly and he wanted reassurance that Russell was dealing with the matter.

During the election of 1920, Harding raised the issue of Haiti, attacking Wilson and Roosevelt for the occupation, which had already dragged on for five years. Reports of Marine atrocities added fuel to the fire, especially among Black voters, then mainly Republican voters. Daniels ordered Barnett to prepare a report, including the confidential and private letters. Daniels then released the report to the press, where it caused a brief sensation in the months before the election. Daniels erred badly in releasing the report, which he probably didn't read, and then blamed Barnett for the resulting furor. Barnett wanted it known that these were confidential communications and that it was the incompetent and deceitful Daniels who was responsible for their publication. This was especially important to him in light of his recent dismissal.

That the letters were used to attack the Corps troubled Barnett deeply. He was insistent that the efforts of the Marines in Haiti be recognized and appreciated. The entire matter seems to have affected him as much as his dismissal, since his dismissal was mainly a personal affront, while this affected the honor of the Corps.

A quickly convened navy inquiry unsurprisingly found no fault with the occupation, a finding echoed in a report by commandant Lejeune. After Harding's election, a Senate committee heard evidence of atrocities, but dismissed them and approved the continued occupation, which would not end until 1934. Barnett's testimony to the committee is reflected in this chapter and includes the letters he cites.

Suggested Reading

McCrocklin, James H. *Garde d'Haiti, 1915-1934; Twenty Years of Organization and Training by the United States Marine Corps.* Annapolis, MD: United States Naval Institute, 1956.

United States. Congress. Senate. Selected Committee on Haiti and Santo Domingo. *Inquiry into Occupation and Administration of Haiti and Santo Domingo.* Washington, D.C.: 1921.

Schmidt, Hans. *The United States Occupation of Haiti, 1915–1934.* New Brunswick, NJ, Rutgers University Press, 1971.

Chapter XXI

Major General Barnett

When the new administration took office in Washington on March 4, 1921, my case was very quickly taken up by the new secretary the navy, the Honorable Edwin Denby. At ten o'clock in the morning of March fifth, I received notice from Washington that I had been nominated to the rank of permanent major general in the Marine Corps. In ordinary cases a nomination is referred to the committee concerned, and after a report from that committee is made to the Senate, two executive sessions must pass before that nomination can be confirmed. This nomination was not referred to the naval committee, but was confirmed by the Senate immediately. I think this was intended as a vindication in my case by friends in the Senate. I, at least, took it to be such and all my friends have so considered it.

There had been a vacancy in the rank of permanent major general since July 1, 1920, so the former secretary, by his action in not filling that vacancy, deprived me, or some other officer, of additional rank and pay during all that time. I cannot imagine that Mr. Daniels was very much pleased when he read my appointment and confirmation for he must have seen that it was a repudiation of his refusal to so appoint me, although he had said he would do so, if it could be done legally. The Judge Advocate General informed him that it would be legal, but he had changed his mind and would not carry out his promise.

My new commission as permanent major general in the Marine Corps is dated March 5, 1921, thus as far as commissions go, completing my record as having held every position in the Marine Corps from second lieutenant to major general commandant and permanent major general. I did not retire, according to law, until December 9, 1923 and completed my full tour of service in my present grade.

On April 11, 1921, I received a telegram, in reply to one from me to the commandant of the Marine Corps, granting me leave of absence for one month, plus travel time, and I started that evening for Washington, D.C. En route I received telegraphic notice of the death of my mother at Minneapolis, Minnesota, so I branched off before I reached Chicago and proceeded to Boscobel, Wisconsin, where my mother was to be buried. There I attended her funeral. I met all of the old friends of my youth who were still alive; after which I proceeded to Washington, D.C., reaching there too late for the marriage of my step-daughter, Lelia S. Gordon to Mr. Robert Dickey, Jr., of Dayton, Ohio.

After reaching Washington, I learned that our class reunion was to take place May 30th—June 1st, in Washington and Annapolis, so I applied for an extension of leave to cover that period, which leave being granted, I had the pleasure of meeting forty of my old academy classmates, and I had a most enjoyable time. Among the number were Ex-Senator Weeks, then secretary of war, Senator Weller of Maryland, Admiral Baron Uriu of the Imperial Japanese Navy, who came from Japan for the reunion, Admiral Henry B. Wilson, commander in chief of the North Atlantic Fleet, Doctor Frank E. Bunts, a noted surgeon of Cleveland, Ohio, and many others I had not seen since graduating forty years ago.

We had a delightful trip to Mt. Vernon on the president's yacht, the *Mayflower*. The President and Mrs. Harding received us at the White House, and the president and his secretary, Mr. George Christian, attended our class dinner at the Hotel Lafayette. The president made a wonderful speech. We all went to Annapolis on June 1st to attend the wedding of Miss Fay Doyen and Ensign Felix Johnson, the bride being the daughter of our late classmate, General Charles A. Doyen, U.S.M.C.

During our class reunion, Secretary of the Navy Honorable Edwin Denby gave a dinner in honor of Admiral Uriu. During that dinner Uriu made a speech during which he suggested that a year from that time we hold our class reunion in Tokyo and that if we would do so he would see to it that during our visit we should be the guests of the Japanese nation.

The secretary of the navy made a speech also during which he stated that he thought Admiral Uriu's idea a very excellent one and if he were secretary of the navy at that time he would furnish a navy transport to take the members of the class and their wives to Japan and back and that he would accompany us. This was received with great applause and the whole proposition then seemed too good to be true.

The president of the class, Senator Weller of Maryland and the class secretary Charles Stewart of Washington went to work getting this information to the different members of the class all over the world and getting replies on how many would like to go. Their work was so satisfactory that the trip actually took place.

We were due to sail from Norfolk on the USS *Henderson* on May 28, 1922. The day before our departure, the U.S. Senate passed a resolution to the effect that such a trip was unwise and ought not to take place. Nearly everybody but the secretary of the navy was up in the air fearing the trip would be stopped at the last moment. I telephoned Senator Weller immediately and found that he had already received word from the secretary of the navy that he, the secretary, had the assurance of the president that this trip would be made. The secretary and the president both believed that such a trip would be bound to have beneficial results towards promoting friendship between the two nations. We left on schedule.

We stopped at Port-au-Prince, Haiti, where we were entertained by the president of Haiti and by U.S. High Commissioner General Russell. We then proceeded to the Canal Zone, where we spent two days. A great many of the party had never seen the Canal and had the opportunity under very favorable circumstances. In Panama, the whole party was entertained by the president of Panama.

From Panama we proceeded to San Diego, California, where we were beautifully entertained by the city and officially visited the numerous naval and Marine Corps activities in and near San Diego. One incident happened during a Chamber of Commerce luncheon which may be worth mentioning. Everyone in the Marine Corps knows of General Pendleton's love of San Diego. He thinks the sun really rises and sets there and that time spent any place else is utterly wasted. During the luncheon I sat next to him and finally I was called for a speech. Then I rose and said that I was very sorry indeed I had been called upon and that if I said anything I naturally wanted to express my real thoughts, but that I hated to say anything derogatory of one of their prominent citizens, but I could not help it. I said that when I knew I was going to make this trip, I ordered General Pendleton to proceed to San Francisco, California, and relieve me in command of the department during the four months I would be away. I said that I had known General Pendleton for forty-six years and had always known him to be a good fellow and up to the present time I had always considered him a good soldier. I was sorry to say that in this I was wrong. The first duty of a good soldier is to obey an official order without question, but when General Pendleton received my order, he wrote me a letter in effect as follows: "Sir, I have received your orders to proceed to S.F. and relieve you during your absence in China and Japan with the secretary of the navy . I wish to protest against this order on the ground that it is not my turn for foreign duty."

From San Diego we proceeded to Honolulu where we were most delightfully entertained by Governor Wallace and Mrs. Catharine Farrington and by General Charles and Mrs. Laura Summerall. We had the pleasure there of witnessing a review of all the departmental troops. Many of the party had been in Honolulu years ago and they found their many friends there as charming as ever. It would almost take a book to describe the many courtesies extended then and on our return trip. I am sure that all felt as I have always felt on visiting Honolulu that it was well called the "Paradise of the Pacific."

From Honolulu we proceeded direct to Yokohama, Japan. When we arrived there we were met by quite a large delegation from Tokyo among whom were several members of the Cabinet, Admiral Baron Uriu, Mr. Shidehara, at that time Japanese ambassador to Washington and Mr. Hanihara, the present ambassador. A special government train was waiting for us docked just alongside the ship. We left on this train for Tokyo where the party was received by many high officials and a large concourse of people. Quarters had been reserved for us in the new Imperial Hotel which was not finished, but enough so we could live in it during our stay there. In this connection it is worthy of note that the hotel was one of the large buildings that escaped destruction by the earthquake of 1923.

Almost every moment of our time in Yokohama was taken up by entertainments of all kinds, sightseeing, luncheons, garden parties and dinners. I wish to state here that never in my whole life in the service, which has taken me all over the world, have I seen more beautiful entertainments than given us in Japan.

During our visit, unfortunately, Prince Higashifushimi Yorihito died and we officially attended his funeral.

Editor's Comments on Chapter XXI

Barnett could have retired in 1920 as a major general. In four decades of service, he had achieved the pinnacle of his profession and had a well deserved rest ahead of him. His health was not good and may have been permanently compromised by his war time illness. Wakefield Manor awaited his return and finances were not an issue. Why did he immediately accept a demotion and remain on active duty until he reached retirement age? Pride was certainly a factor. Politicians and disloyal subordinates would not force him out of the Corps that had been his life. If a desk job was all he could negotiate, he would make the best of it, just as he had at many worse postings. Littleton Waller similarly held on until retirement age, despite being shunted aside in favor of younger officers during World War I.

Young Clifton Cates almost resigned before Barnett convinced him to stay in the post-war Corps. In 1920 he was Commandant Barnett's aide-de-camp at Headquarters and he followed him in the same position to the Department of the Pacific. After Cates' term as commandant (1948–1951), he too spurned retirement and continued serving at his previous rank.

The fortieth reunion of the Class of 1881 was hosted by President Harding and was front page news. An invitation to repeat the reunion in Japan was a golden opportunity for some quiet diplomacy and it became an official visit, complete with Secretary of the Navy Denby. This took place just after the Washington Naval Conference, which set limits on the Japanese, British and American navies. Parties on both sides of the Pacific objected to the limitations, so an opportunity for public amity was welcome.

Chapter XXII

San Francisco, 1920–1923 and Retirement

When I received orders to command the Department of the Pacific with Headquarters at San Francisco, I at once telegraphed the Bohemian Club there to see if I could get a room at the Club, and fortunately I received a favorable reply. I lived there three years and found it a most delightful place to live. In my opinion it is in many ways the most interesting club I have ever seen, and I wish to register my very sincere appreciation of the many courtesies extended to me by the presidents, officers and members.

During my duty in San Francisco, I attempted to make myself a citizen of the city and took part in all official functions, and never have I seen official functions better conducted. They have the greatest civic pride I have ever seen and nothing seems too much trouble. Every distinguished visitor receives a welcome which will make him number San Francisco above other places.

On October 22nd, 1923, in accordance with my request, I was detached from my command of the Department of the Pacific in order to proceed to Washington, D.C. to report to the major general commandant Marine Corps for duty at headquarters. I so reported and was granted leave up to the time of my retirement, December 9, 1923, at which date I was retired for age in accord with the law.

Editor's Comments on Chapter XXII

Barnett enjoyed his time in San Francisco. His wife joined him and they cruised to Hawaii, where he had many friends. He then returned to Washington to prepare his report on the mess in Haiti. His permanent promotion to major general came through, so that he was able to attend his fortieth class reunion with two stars.

All told, it was a busy couple of years, though militarily, the Department of

XXII—San Francisco, 1920–1923 and Retirement

Barnett in retirement at Wakefield Manor in 1926. Top row: Mrs. Barnett, holding Basil Gordon Dickey, Corrine Montague Mustin, Lelia Gordon Dickey, Lelia Sinclair Montague in chair, George Barnett holding Robert Dickey. Middle row: Anne Gordon Suydam, holding Henry Suydam. Bottom row: Lloyd M. Mustin, Henry A. Mustin (courtesy Lelia Sinclair Baldassari).

the Pacific was not an active command. Aside for his immediate staff, Barnett commanded no unit. If Barnett had been given Quantico, he might have further developed the Advanced Base Force or otherwise contributed. He was exiled to San Francisco so that he could have no further influence.

After retirement, he started work on his memoirs. In the original typescript, the names of many people he knew well are misspelled. This indicates that he dictated the text and someone unfamiliar with the correct spellings typed it out. Some have opined that Mrs. Barnett must have been involved in the composition, but there is no foundation for that. Her style was much more blunt and she was not known as a typist. Barnett was a well educated man and the memoir is consistent with his other writings. Some of the anecdotes had appeared elsewhere virtually word for word. These were stories he had told many times and carefully polished.

With his retirement, Barnett nearly disappears from history and the public record. He worked with the American Red Cross, serving as chairman of the district chapter. Riding remained a particular pleasure and he indulged in sharp semiofficial uniforms. His health was not robust and he was hospitalized in 1923 and 1924 with further heart and lung problems. In the end, it was pneumonia that killed him in 1930, at age seventy.

Mrs. Barnett did not have an office to retire from. She remained active socially and politically. In 1922, she was mentioned as a possible candidate for Congress. In 1924, she was an alternate delegate to the Republican national convention. As women delegates had been admonished to "mind their knitting," she very visibly finished a sweater during the sessions. Like her husband, she was active with the Red Cross, especially when it focused on providing assistance to military personnel.

After Barnett's death, his wife guarded his reputation. She never forgave or forgot the conspirators who so summarily dismissed her husband from the commandancy. Daniels, who would help elect Roosevelt in 1932, remained an enemy, as did Smedley Butler. Lejeune was a lesser target, though not immune from her attentions. She threatened lawsuits to prevent publication of comments she thought libelous, though such efforts had little legal basis. Her efforts to get Barnett's unfinished autobiography published were likewise futile. She died in 1959.

Epilogue

Despite his transformational impact, Barnett is nearly absent from general Marine Corps histories. Most of his service took place in the seemingly uneventful years between the Civil War and World War I. Even Littleton Waller has trouble emerging from those shadows. The Great War created many Marine heroes, but Barnett was not one of them. Indeed, many accounts of the Marines in World War I barely mention him. The mission of this edited version of his memoirs is to establish Barnett in his rightful place as the most important Marine of his generation.

Barnett joined a Corps that was in serious danger of extinction. Powerful voices, both civilian and navy, demanded that the Marines either undergo a complete reinvention or be eliminated. For decades, the Corps resisted the needed reforms. When they had no choice in the matter, they turned to Barnett to head the Advanced Base School. In short order, he had to oversee the creation of an entirely new type of military force, handicapped by limited resources and annual deployments. Failure would have had severe consequences, quite possibly including the elimination of the Corps. His success there and with the Advanced Base Brigade at Culebra in 1914 provided a new and secure future for the Corps.

The contrast between Barnett and his predecessors demonstrates that he was the first modern commandant. Having established a new mission for the Corps, Barnett proceeded at full speed to implement it. Lejeune, Ellis and others were set free to develop the doctrine necessary to carry out the new mission. Marine Headquarters became a hub of activity, with the next generation of leaders being mentored and empowered. Bases at Quantico and on the West Coast were created from the ground up, with new and wide ranging training regimes. Marine aviation was promoted. In just a few years, the Corps pivoted from its Age of Sail roots and reinvented itself. Barnett was the key figure in that reinvention.

With World War I on the horizon, Barnett positioned the Corps to fight in France. He did this in the face of the Wilson administration's official antipreparedness stance and with a secretary of the navy who was an avowed pacifist. When war arrived, Barnett had to overcome official resistance from the navy, who envisioned a much smaller role for the Corps. Finally, he had to overcome serious resistance from the army, which went to great lengths to keep the Marines out of the AEF. During his Commandancy, there were multiple times when a wrong step or insufficient assertiveness would have relegated the Marines to the sidelines. The AEF would have managed fine without Marines, but sitting out the war would have severely damaged the Corps. Barnett's performance saved the reputation of the Corps as "First to Fight" and prevented the hollowing out that would have happened as quality recruits enlisted for service in France.

Though seemingly defeated and dismissed in 1920, Barnett must be seen as the long term victor. His amphibious vision for the Corps endured. Lejeune and his successors built on the foundation Barnett established and created a force like no other in the world. Like him, future Marines would be soldiers and sailors too.

Index

Numbers in **_bold italics_** indicate pages with photographs.

Advanced Base mission 157–158
Advanced Base School 1, 134–136, 138, 191
African-Americans 16–17, 27, 39, 43
USS *Alaska* 46
alcohol 38–39, 57, 93, 173; *see also* Prohibition
Amazonas see USS *New Orleans*
Anahootz 60–61, 70
Anderson, J.H. 130
Annapolis *see* United States Naval Academy
Apia Cyclone of 1889 76, 80
appointment as commandant 140–141, 143–144
Argentina 45, 101
Arica 48

Badger, Charles 136–137, 145
Baker, Benjamin Standish 145
Baker, Kitty (Katherine) 69
Baker, Newton D. 147–148, 150–152
Baker, Orris 68
Ball, Caroline Linton 68
Ball, Mottrom D. 68–69
Ball, Richard 99
Ball, Sallie Lewis 68
Barber, Joel A. (Navy officer) 11–12, 15
Barber, Joel Allen (congressman) 15
Barden, Delia 69
Barnett, Charles H. 13, **_14_**
Barnett, Elizabeth (Callis) 11–13, 184
Barnett, James 10–13
Barnett, Laura Ethel 13, **_14_**, 134, 145
Barnett, Mrs. Lelia (Gordon Montague) 110–117, 159–160, 167, 173, 175–176–176, 188–190

Barnett, Martha (Mattie) 13, **_14_**
Barnett Amendment 172–174, 176
Beatty, Frank 141
Belknap, George 46
Benjamin, Park 35
Benson, William 148–149
Berryman, Otway 43, 56, 78
Bevington, Martin 40
Biddle, William 143–144, 171
Bleecher, John van B. 92–93
Blow, George P. 37–38
Blue, Victor 149
Bohemian Club 188
Boscobel, Wisconsin 10–13, 184
Brady, Cyrus 35
Britten, Frederick 171, 173
Brownson, Willard H. 25
Bryan, Charles Page 101
Bryan, Samuel 46–47
Bryan, William Jennings 156
Bunts, Frank E. 184
Burleson, Albert S. 111
Butaritari, Gilbert Islands 72–74
Butler, Smedley Darling 2, 57, 145, 158, 164, 170, 172–176, 190
Butler, Thomas Stalker 2, 145, 164, 171–174, 176
Butt, Archibald 109

Cairo 98
Callao, Peru 42, 48
Callis, Elizabeth *see* Barnett, Elizabeth (Callis)
Callis, John Benton 12–13
Cape Verde Islands 39–40

193

Capehart, Edward E. 32
Carlos I of Portugal 94
Cartier de Marchienne, Baron Emile-Ernest de 131
Casey, Silas 90
Cates, Clifton 57, 157, 175, 186
Catlin, Albertus 56
USS *Charleston* 76
Chase, Richard M. 19
USS *Chicago* 98, 100–102
chimpanzee *see* Peter
cholera 111, 117
Christmas 23–24
Chung 118–119, 123
Cixi *see* Empress Dowager Cixi
Cochrane, Henry 57
Cole, Eli K. 56, 158
Collardet, Louis 131
Collier, George W. 54–55
Columbia Exposition of 1893 88–91
USS *Constellation* 25
Coquimbo, Chile 47–48
Courcelle, A.V.S. 28
courtship of Mrs. Gordon 110
Cowles, Byron K. 68–69
Cowles, Lucy 69
Cristóbal Colón 95–96
crossing the line 44
Culebra 1, 135–137, 140–141, 191
Cusack-Smith, Thomas 83
USS *Dale* 19–20, 35

dancing 38, 47–48, 89, 116, 130; native 61–62, 80
Daniels, Josephus 1–2, 143–145, 147–151, 156, 158, 164, 166–168, 171–176, 178–181, 183, 190, 192
Dashiell, Robert 46
Denby, Edwin 183–185, 187
Denver, Andrew 19
Dewey, George 143
Dickey, Basil Gordon 189
Dickey, Lelia Gordon *see* Gordon, Lelia Sinclair
Dickey, Robert Jr. 184
discipline 142
Dominican Republic 163
Donnelly, Michael J 11, 16–18
Doyen, Charles A. 31, 55–57, 154
Doyen, Fay 184

Eldredge, Houston 27
Elliott, Daisy Badger 145
Elliott, George 56, 117, 144–145

Ellis, Earl "Pete" 57, 157, 191
Emmett, William L. R. 31, 39
Emmons, George Thorton 65, 70–71, 90–91
Empress Dowager Cixi 122–125
Enouye, Yenosuki 32, 106
entrance examination 18–19, 32–34
USS *Essex* 36–49
Evans, Robley

Fairbanks, Charles 127
Fanua 84
Farrington, Catharine 185
Farrington, Wallace 185
Fay, Claude 18
Fay, Mary Helen 18
Fay, William G. 18
Fay, William W. 18
Fechteler, Augustus 149
fishing 20, 66–67, 85–86
Fisk, Bradley A. 149
Fleet Marine Officer 104–108
Folger, William Mayhew 97
Forshew, Robert P. 32
Fourth Marine Brigade 151, 153–155, 158–159, 161–162, 1626
Fredonia 48
Fuller, Ben Hebard 56–57, 164, 176
Funchal 37–39
funerals 62–64, 123–124

Gardiner, Anthony W. 43
Garfield, James A. 29–31
Gartley, William H. 32, 48–49
General Board of the Navy 143, 148
Gilman, Howard 58
Gordon, Anne Hamilton 111–116, 120–121, 126–127, 189
Gordon, Basil 114, 116
Gordon, Basil, Jr. 111–113, 116, 120–121, 126–127, 159–160
Gordon, Catharine Douglas 116
Gordon, Lelia Sinclair 111–116, 120–12, 126–127, 184, 189
gouging 27
graduation 29–30
Grayson, Cary 175
Great Strike of 1877 16
Haines, Henry C. 56

Haiti 163, 178–181
Hamilton, Elisha 84
USS *Hancock* 135
Hanihara, Masanao 186

Harbord, James G. 154–155, 160
Harding, Warren G. 181, 185
Harding, William G 176, 184, 187
Hazelton, George C. 10–11
hazing 17, 22–23, 25, 34
USS *Henderson* 185
Hendrickson, W.W. 29
Heneberger, Lucien G. 75, 79
Heywood, Charles 53–54
Holcolm, Thomas 57, 131, 157
honesty 12
Honolulu, Hawai'i 72, 86, 185–186, 188
horseback riding 10, 31, 81–83, 86, 105, 108, 119, 126, 128, 187
Howison, Henry L. 27, 98
Hughes, Thomas 49
Huntington, Robert 56

Indian doctors *see* Shamans
influenza 159
Inouye, Kazutsugu 129
Iquique, Peru 48
USS *Iroquois* 72–86

Jaluit, Marshall Islands 72
Jameson, Charles D. 128
Jameson, Leander Starr 99, 102
Japan 105–106, 108, 111–112, 186
Jeme Tien Yow 126, 132
Johannesburg, South Africa 99–100
Johnson, Walter 178–181
Johnston, Marbury 94, 97
Juneau, Alaska 66–67

Kalākaua, King of Hawai'i 86
Karmany, Lincoln 55–56, 143
USS *Kentucky* 104–106
Killisnoo, Alaska 60, 66–67
King, William H. 171
Kinkead, John Henry 68, 70
Kipling, Rudyard 9, 12
Kornilov, Lavr 129–130

Lancaster, Wisconsin 9, 12
Lane, Franklin K. 111
Lauchheimer, Charles H. 28, 31, 53, 56, 144–145
Laupepa, Susuga Malietoa 83–84
Legation Guard *see* Peking
Lejeune, John A. 56, 77, 140–144, 155, 170–172, 174–176, 178, 181, 190–192
Liang Dunyan 126–127, 132
Libby, William 65–66, 70
Liberia 39–40, 43

Lima, Peru 48
Logan, Leavitt C. 26
Long, Charles 56, 140–141

MacDougall, William 107–108
Mackenzie, Morris R.S. 36, 40, 44
Magill, Louis 137, 140–141
Mahoney, James 31
Mare Island, California 54–55, 72
Marine aviation 136, 138, 158
Marine Corps Reserve—Female 158
Marine Security Guard program 131
McCawley, Charles 166
McClellan, Edwin 179
McCormick, Alexander H. 40
McGrew, John S. 86
McLean, Emily Beale 116
McNair, Frederick V. 30
McQuilken, John 178–181
medicine 67, 79–80
Meiji Emperor 105–106
USS *Mohican* 78
Monrovia 39–40
Montague, Alice 114
Montague, Corrine DeForest *see* Mustin, Corrine (Montague)
Montague, Lelia Sinclair *see* Barnett, Mrs. Lelia (Gordon Montague)
Montevideo, Uruguay 45
Moses, Franklin J. 54–56
Mt. St. Elias 65, 70
Murray, George D. 132
Mustin, Corrine (Montague) 114, 121, 132, 189
Mustin, Henry A. 189
Mustin, Henry Croskey 132, 142
Mustin, Lloyd 24, 35, 189

Nakaeia, King of Butaritari 72–74, 77
USS *Nantucket* 35
Nazro, Arthur 92, 94
Neville, Wendell 56, 142, 155, 172, 176
USS *New Orleans* 94–97, 102
Newman, Gwendell B. 68–69
Nixon, Martha (Barnett) *see* Barnett, Martha

Ōyama Iwao 106, 114

Padgett, Lemuel 149, 173
Paine, Sumner 75
palolo 85–86
Panama Canal 49, 185
Parker, Foxhall A. 29

Parris Island, South Carolina 149, 152, 157
Partridge, James R. 50
Peking, China 111, 118–132
Pendleton, Joseph 56, 185
USS *Pensacola* 49
Perkins, Constantine 56
Pershing, John J 149–151, 154, 158
Peter the chimpanzee 40–43
Philadelphia, Pennsylvania 36–37, 104, 134–135
Philippine Islands 104, 107–108, 117
USS *Pinta* 58–59, 65–66, 70
Pitcher, Lura 68–9
politics and the Marine Corps 13, 15, 143–145, 171–176
potlatch 60–62
USS *Prairie* 135, 137
Prohibition 156, 173
protégés 57
Punta Arenas 45

Quantico, Virginia 146, 149, 152–153, 157, 159, 161, 167, 174–176, 191

Radford, Cyrus S. 88–89
Ramsay, Francis M. 52, 57
Raymond (entertainer) 137
Red Cross 159–160, 189–190
Redgrave, DeWitt 44
Rees, John L. 20
Reisinger, Emory William 13, 145
Reisinger, Harold C. 145
Reisinger, Laura (Barnett) Reisinger *see* Barnett, Laura Ethel
Reisinger, Laura Natalie 13
Rhodes, Cecil 99–100
Rick, Mrs. Adolph (Francis) 72–73
Rio de Janeiro 101
Rittenhouse, Hawley O. 24
Robeson, Henry B. 28
Rodgers, C.R.P. 19, 28
Rommel, Charles 53
Roosevelt, Franklin Delano 156–157, 162, 175, 181
Roosevelt, Theodore 145
Russell, Benjamin R. 88
Russell, John H., Jr. 56, 131, 157, 164, 178, 180–181, 185
Russell, John H., Sr. 72
Russell, William W. 28–29
Russell retention board 164–165, 172, 174, 176
Ruth, Melancthon L. 36

St. Helena 100–101
Samoa 78–86
Sampson, William 96
San Diego, California 166, 185
USS *San Francisco* 92–94, 97, 102
San Francisco, California 176, 188–189
San Juan, Puerto Rico 96–97
Santa Cruz de Tenerife 39
USS *Santee* 19–20, 26
Santiago de Chile 47
Santo Domingo *see* Dominican Republic
Schley, Winfield Scott 95, 101
Schwatka, Frederick 65, 70
Second Division 154–155, 161, 164
senority 55–56, 164
Serata, Tusuka 32
Seton-Karr, Haywood W. 70
Sewall, Harold 83
Shallenberger, Oliver 32
shamans 63–65, 68
Shanghai 112–113
Shidehara, Kijūrō 186
Sims, William S. 135–136
Sinclair, Upton 114
Sitka Tribe of Alaska 58–68
South Africa 99–100
Spanish-American War 94–97
Spicer, William F 92
Stayton, William H. 27, 55–56
Stevenson, Robert Louis 73–74, 77, 80–82, 86–87
Stewart, Charles 184
Stirling, Yates 107
Stokes, Charles F. 76
Straits of Magellan 42, 45–46
Strohm, Matthew 20
Summerall, Charles 186
Summerall, Laura 186
Sutton, Francis 53, 56, 77
Suydam, Anne Gordon *see* Gordon Anne Hamilton

Taft, Howard 144–145
Thayer, Harriet 113
Thayer, Rufus H. 113
Thomas, Charles M. 28
Tierra del Fuego 45
Tiffany (Chinese jeweler) 128
Titimaea, Tupua Tamasese 84
Townsend, Lawrence 94
Townsend, Natalie 94
Treadwell, Thomas 88
Trudeau, Edward 116

United States Army, opposes Corps participation in AEF 1, 148, 150–152, 155, 158
United States Naval Academy 16–35, 51–52; Class of 1881 35, 184–187
Uriu Iwako 33, , 112, 114
Uriu Sotokichi 32, *33*, 108, 112, 114, 184, 186

Valparaiso, Chile 46–47
USS *Vandalia* 77
Very, Samuel 26

Waller, Littleton W.T. 57, 97, 143–146, 172, 186
Wallis, Duchess of Windsor 114
USS *Wateree* 48
wedding 117

Weeks, John Wingate *18*, 19, 23, 32, 34, 109, 145, 176, 184
Weller, Ovington E. 19, 145, 184–185
Williams, Charles 55
Williams, Dion 56, 131, 157
Williams, Gardner 99–100
Wilson, Henry B. 184
Wilson, Woodrow 143–144, 156, 168–169, 174–175
USS *Wisconsin* 104, 106–107
Wood, Albert N. 46–47
World's Columbian Exposition *see* Columbia Exposition of 1893
Wright, Sallie Lewis 68

Zanzibar 98

www.ingramcontent.com/pod-product-compliance
Ingram Content Group UK Ltd.
Pitfield, Milton Keynes, MK11 3LW, UK
UKHW042009140426
5217IPUK00015B/1062